Play and Practice!

**Communicative activities and games
for building English language skills**

Anthony Chamberlin

Kurt Stenberg

Editors:
Marcia Seidletz
Linda Schinke-Llano

National Textbook Company
NTC a division of *NTC Publishing Group* • Lincolnwood, Illinois USA

Preface

Teachers and English language students will be delighted by the variety of stimulating games and activities contained in this set of twenty blackline masters.

Each blackline master serves as a basis for a game or activity that has been carefully designed to reinforce one or more of the four basic language skills—listening, speaking, reading, and writing—and to build critical-thinking skills. The Teacher's Guide included with this collection provides detailed instructions for playing each game, as well as statements of the purpose of the activity and the language required to participate in it successfully.

Teachers will also appreciate the flexibility of these blackline masters; they can be adapted for use in any number of classroom lessons and take-home assignments. Students will find the activities entertaining, and will be motivated to practice and increase their English language skills as they play.

Published by National Textbook Company, a division of NTC Publishing Group.
© 1995, 1986 by NTC Publishing Group, 4255 West Touhy Avenue,
Lincolnwood (Chicago), Illinois 60646-1975 U.S.A.

4 5 6 7 8 9 ML 9 8 7 6 5 4 3 2 1

Contents

Teacher's Guide

In, On, Under I and II

Purpose: To practice listening comprehension, especially prepositions of place.

Language Required: Knowledge of prepositions of place and words for shapes (circles, squares, etc.).

Game: Give a copy of In, On, Under to each student. Either the teacher or a student instructs the class to do a number of things. For example:
Put a cross in the circle.
Write your name under the line.
Write 4 to the left of the circle.
Students can easily correct their own sheets from a key the teacher shows them. The teacher can also collect the sheets.

For Game II, instructions can be more difficult. For example:
Put an antenna on top of the house.
Draw a car to the right of the house.
Draw a door on the house.
Draw three trees in a row to the left of the house.

Guide Me Through Town I and II

Purpose: To practice following directions.

Language Required: Phrases for finding the way must be practiced before the game.

Game: When using Game I, the teacher gives directions, letting the students follow them on the map at the same time. It is important to agree upon a starting point. For example:
Start at point A.
Walk down the street. Turn left at the second corner and walk up to the bridge. Turn right along the river. When you get to the next bridge, cross it. Walk up the street to the traffic lights. Turn left and then right at the next crossing. Where are you now? You are at the corner marked H.

Game II can be used with more advanced students to practice the names of building and streets.

Number Bingo I and II

Purpose: To practice understanding numbers in English.

Language Required: Numbers from 1-50 and 51-100.

Game: Give each student a bingo playing board and a sheet of number cut-outs. Have students first cut out the number squares and then place them at random on their playing boards. Students may choose any four numbers they like between 1 and 10 to put in the top four squares, any four numbers between 11 and 20 in the four squares in the second row, etc. The teacher draws numbered squares out of a hat or bag and calls out the number. Any player with that number on his or her card takes off the number.
Give the first prize to the first player with a complete horizontal or vertical line taken off. Give the next prize to the first player to remove all of his or her numbers. The teacher should check that the card is correct—if the counters are arranged in order as they are called out, it is easy to do this.

Variation: A variation of this game is Letter Bingo that is played the same way, substituting letters for numbers. The first row of the board is for letters A-G, the second H-M, the third row N-T, and the fourth row U-Z.

Hide and Seek

Purpose: To practice names of objects in a house and prepositions.

Language Required: Names of objects and rooms in a house and at least the prepositions "in," "on," "under," and "behind." Question form "Are you . . . ?"

Game: One student "hides" in the picture. He or she chooses a hiding place and imagines that he or she is hidden there—behind the clock in the dining room, for example, or under the table in the kitchen. The other members of the class try to guess where he or she is hidden by asking questions that can be answered with "Yes" or "No." Examples:

Are you upstairs?
Are you in the dining room?
Are you behind the chair?
Are you under the table?

You may limit the number of questions to ten so that as many students as possible have turns.

Comment: The student should tell the teacher beforehand where he or she has hidden, in case help is needed during the game.

Where's the Fly?

Purpose: To practice prepositions of place and direction.

Language Required: A knowledge of relevant prepositions and the names of objects in a room.

Game: Give one picture to each student. The teacher is the guide and everybody in the class the fly. The teacher may say:

Come in under the bottom of the door. Fly up the wall, across the ceiling to the lamp, down onto the table, across the room to the dresser. Fly into the open drawer, see what is in it. Fly out of the drawer, around the vase, and in behind the picture on the wall. Where are you?

The students (flies) try to follow the directions. When they hear the question, they answer, for example: "I'm behind the picture on the wall." The game can be repeated several times. Start with short directions and make them gradually longer and more complicated.

When the students are fairly good at the game, they can play it in twos, alternating the roles of guide and fly. Limit the number of directions to five or seven.

Comment: If the game is played more than once, students can trace the different routes of the fly using a different colored pencil for each route.

What's in the Square?

Purpose: To practice oral fluency in simple questions and answers. To practice "There is" and "There are."

Language Required: The students should be well acquainted with at least one of the following constructions:

"What's number four?" — "It's a cat."
"Where's the cat?" — "It's in number four."
"What is there in number four?" — "There's a cat in number four."

Game: This game may be played with the whole class, in groups, or in pairs. If played with the whole class, the teacher may wish to draw the grid and the pictures on the blackboard. The teacher or player draws nine objects, one in each square. For example, a cat in number one, a knife in number two, a dog in number three, a guitar in number four, and so on. The idea is to try to remember where all the objects are. If you are playing it with the whole class, go to the back of the room, and tell the students to look at you so they all have their backs to the blackboard, and then ask them where everything is. Several patterns are possible.

1. What's number four? — It's a guitar.
2. Where's the guitar? — It's in number four.
3. What's in number four? — There's a guitar in number four.

With beginners, use only one pattern during the lesson.

The patterns can, of course, be used to practice the plural as well—in that case, draw two or more objects in each square. Then ask:

1. Where are the guitars? — They are in number four.
2. What's in number four? — There are two guitars.

When played in pairs, each student draws nine objects and gives the sheet to his or her partner who asks questions about it.

Newspaper Reporters

Purpose: To practice questions and answers in past tenses. Writing a story as a follow-up from the game.

Language Required: The students should be fairly advanced and have practiced some kind of story writing before.

Game: Have the students read one of the outline stories on the sheet, for example, "Fire at Grand Hotel." Four students from the class are chosen. One is Arthur Smith, one John Robinson, one Mary Stevens, and one June Andrews. The other class members are newspaper reporters who want to get the "background" to the story. They ask questions, and the students at the front use their imagination in answering. For example:

Arthur Smith, why were you out at 3 in the morning?

What did you see?

John Robinson, why were you asleep?

How did you feel when they woke you up, Mary Stevens?

Why were you staying at the hotel?

After the reporters have gathered their information, they write their stories.

Comments: This game can only be used with quite advanced students who are prepared to use their imaginations. The "characters" can make up their own backgrounds—provided it fits in with the outline given—and everything each of them says can be agreed with or denied by the others.

Crossword Competition I and II

Purpose: To practice the alphabet and the spelling of simple words.

Language Required: The game can be played as soon as the students have done some reading and a little writing in English.

Game: This game can be played in pairs. The players turn their backs to each other, and then take turns calling out a letter. They must both put into their crossword all the letters that are called out, both their own and their opponent's. The idea is to build as many words as possible. They are free to choose in which square to put the letter, but must not change the position of the letters once they have been written.

For example, one crossword competition might look like this after seven letters have been called out:

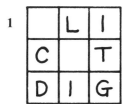 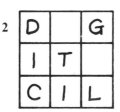

Number one will probably call out "A" to make the word "CAT."

Number two will probably then call out "O" to make "DOG."

Scoring: One point for each letter in each completed word. CAT = 3, IT = 2, and so on.

Crossword Competition II may be used with more advanced students or if the game is played in a group. If played with more than two, each person calls out one letter in turn. Players must, of course,

not look at each other's papers. When the crosswords are completed, score points as before, one point for each letter in each completed word.

Word Snakes I and II

Purpose: To practice spelling.

Language Required: The students must have a general vocabulary of at least three or four hundred words and be able to spell these words.

Game: This game is similar to making a crossword, but it is easier to adjust to different rules and levels of teaching. The students fill the snake with properly spelled words so that there are no empty squares and no letters outside the snake. The competition is to see how many can fill the snake with correctly spelled words within a limited time, for instance, three or four minutes. Played this way, the game can be used once or twice at an early stage. It is also possible to play the game in pairs or in groups of three or four, the pairs or groups competing with each other.

Give points for each correctly spelled word, one point for each letter, and take off points for spelling mistakes.

Alternatives: 1. Play the game as above, but allow only words from a certain subject—the weather, sports, house, garden, geography, or clothes.

2. Allow only nouns or adjectives or verbs.

3. Divide the class into groups of five or six students. The students fill in one word each, passing the snake around the group. Two or three students may have to write more than one word. The group that completes its snake first is the winner.

4. Play the game in pairs. The two students take turns filling in a word in the snake. The one who succeeds in finishing the snake is the winner. Each pair needs at least three snakes.

5. More difficult. Each word must start with the last letter of the previous word, thus, using this letter twice. If the snake is finished with the same letter as the first letter of the first word, give an extra point. Such a snake could look like this:

6. More difficult. The snake must contain a full sentence. Play in pairs, each player contributing alternate words. The first pair to finish correctly wins. Example:

Jumbled Words I and II

Purpose: To practice spelling.

Language Required: Nouns relevant to the subjects chosen.

Game: Students work individually or in teams to identify the words within a given time, say, one minute for each group of words. The winner is the one with the most words correct.

Jumbled Words I Answers

This is what I ate for breakfast: toast, butter, jam, cornflakes, milk, sugar.

In the classroom you can see: blackboard, chalk, door, books, teacher, students.

In a city, you can find: stores, movies, city hall, station, parking lot, library.

Jumbled Words II Answers

Some people in the newspapers are: police, senators, actresses, criminals, firemen, president.

In a hospital, you can find: medicine, patients, wheelchair, nurses, beds, doctors.

On the weekend, I: study, golf, watch TV, swim, read, visit friends.

Alternative: Let each team work out a list of jumbled words which the other teams can try to solve. Each group of words should have a common theme until the class is very skilled, when single, difficult words may be used. This is a good way to encourage students to learn the new words in a text.

Out-of-Order Sentences

Purpose: To practice and evaluate reading comprehension.

Language Required: The students should be quite used to reading.

Game: Give each student a copy of the list of jumbled sentences. They must rearrange the sentences to make a coherent narrative.

Story:

John wanted to call his friend Martin. He looked around for a phone booth. He found one on Baker Street. He went in and searched his pockets for a dime. He found one, put it in the slot, and dialed the number. Ring. Ring. No answer. He hung up and then tried again. Bad luck again. John went out of the booth, wondering what to do.

Alternatives: 1. Take a passage the students know well and change the order of the sentences. Arrange them in a list. Make stenciled copies of the list.
2. After some practice, the students can jumble sentences themselves and give them to each other to solve.

Making a Sentence

Purpose: To practice fluency.

Language Required: The students should be used to writing English.

Game: Students, individually or in groups, try to make a sentence in which each word starts with one letter of the given word, used in the correct order. For example:

H A T can become
Harry ate tomatos.
C A S E can become
Charles asks Susan everything.
R I N G S can become
Roberta is not going soon.

In, On, Under I

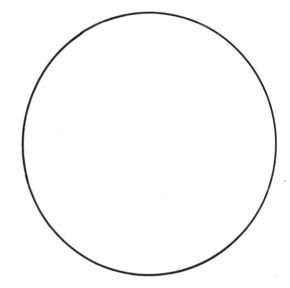

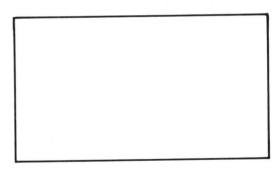

In, On, Under II

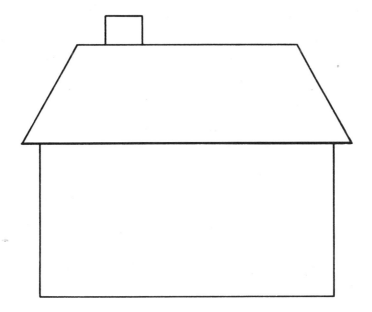

Name ______________________ Date ______________

Guide Me Through Town I

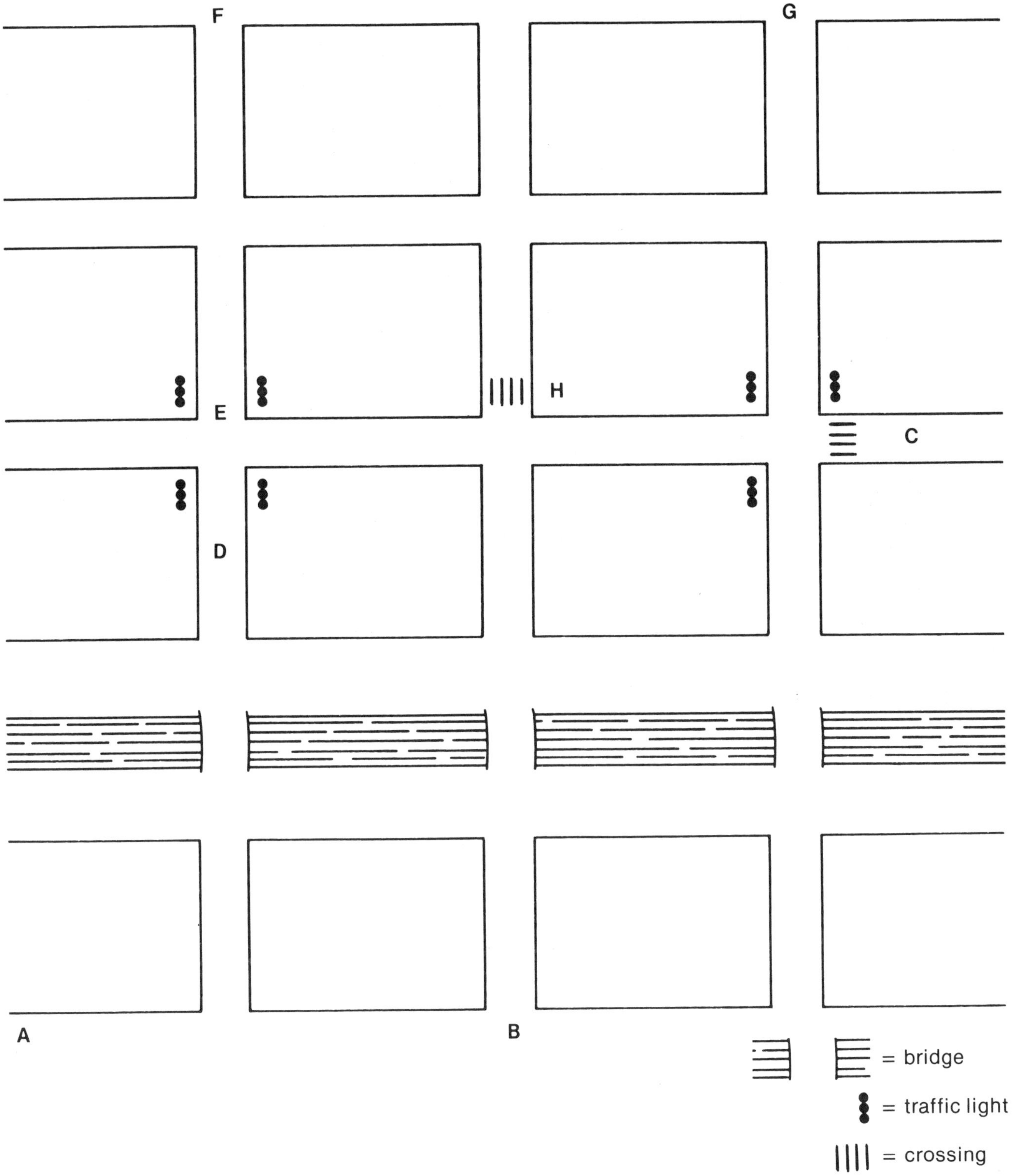
F
G
E
H
C
D
A
B
= bridge
= traffic light
= crossing

Guide Me Through Town II

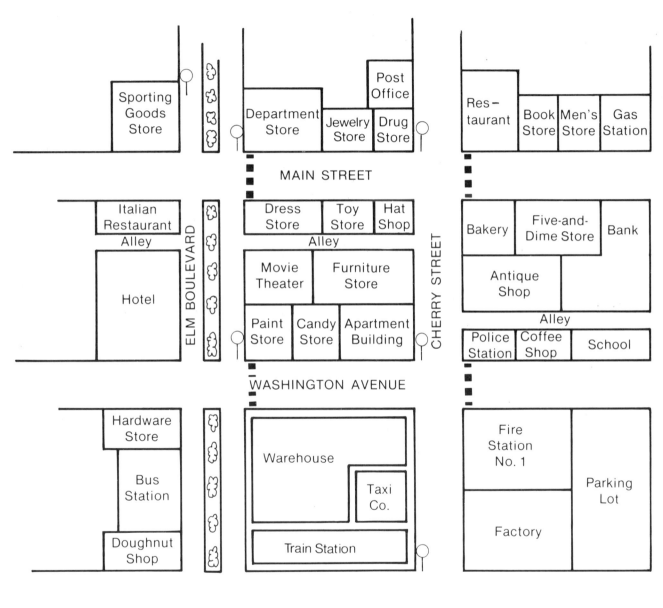

= Bus stop

= Railroad tracks

= Crosswalk

Number Bingo I

Playing Board

				1-10
				11-20
				21-30
				31-40
				41-50

Number Bingo I

Number Cut-outs

1	2	3	4	5
6	7	8	9	10
11	12	13	14	15
16	17	18	19	20
21	22	23	24	25
26	27	28	29	30
31	32	33	34	35
36	37	38	39	40
41	42	43	44	45
46	47	48	49	50

(Cut along the dotted line.)

Number Bingo II

Playing Board

				51-60
				61-70
				71-80
				81-90
				91-100

Number Bingo II

Number Cut-outs

51	52	53	54	55
56	57	58	59	60
61	62	63	64	65
66	67	68	69	70
71	72	73	74	75
76	77	78	79	80
81	82	83	84	85
86	87	88	89	90
91	92	93	94	95
96	97	98	99	100

(Cut along the dotted line.)

Hide and Seek

Where's the Fly?

What's in the Square?

1	2	3
4	5	6
7	8	9

Newspaper Reporters

Fire at Grand Hotel

Fire at Grand Hotel last night. Seen at 3 a.m. by Arthur Smith walking past. He woke John Robinson, porter. Phoned fire department. Together they woke hotel guests. Mary Stevens, on third floor, jumped out of window and broke leg. June Andrews, from same room, ran down stairs, was badly burned, now in hospital.

A Rescue

Rosemary Stevens, on vacation, ran into the sea yesterday and saved Peter Davidson from drowning. Peter Davidson was swimming when he started to shout for help. Only Rosemary ran to help him. Arthur Jones, also on the beach, said "I thought he was being funny."

An Accident

A car driven by Anthony Down hit Mary Smith as she was crossing the road. Her leg was broken. Mary Smith was on a pedestrian crossing. A jogger, Susan James, saw the accident. So did David South, who was looking out of a window.

A Car Thief

Margaret Davidson left her car outside her house on 52nd Street. She left her keys in the car. She saw Alfred Rose getting into the car. She ran out and managed to pull the key from the car. She shouted for help, and Gerald Turner phoned the police. Margaret Davidson stayed holding the door shut until the police came.

Crossword Competition I

Crossword Competition II

Word Snakes I

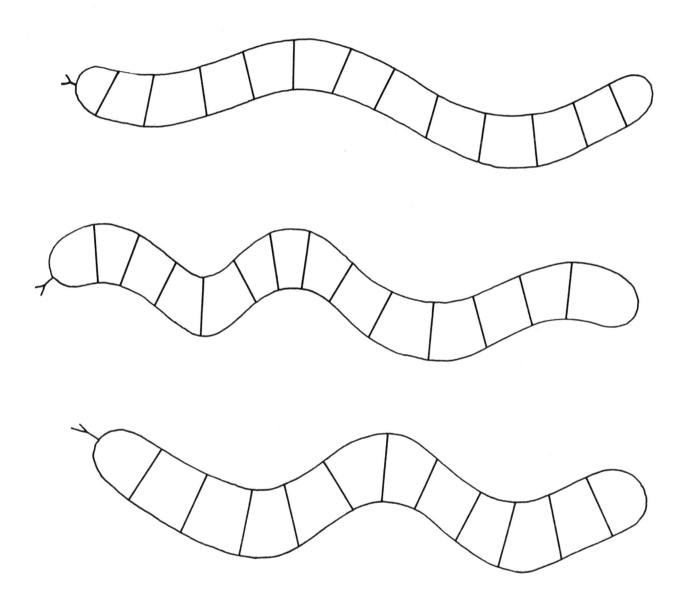

Word Snakes II

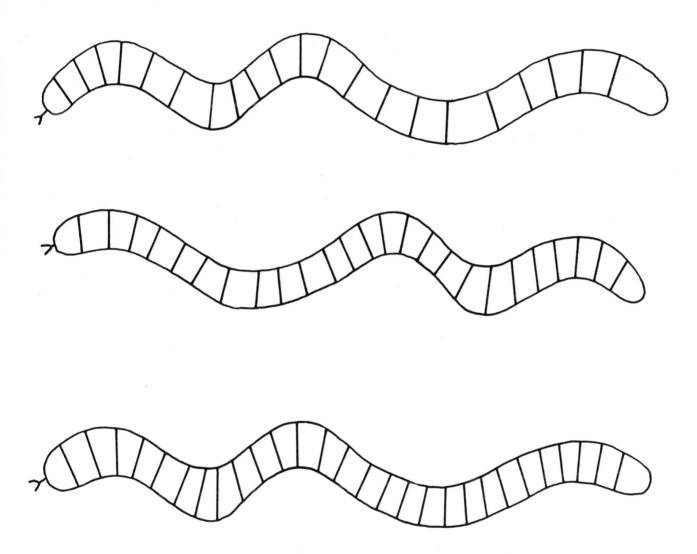

Jumbled Words I

This is what I ate for breakfast:

SOTAT _____   CRONSLAFEK _____

TRUBET _____   KLIM _____

AJM _____   GARUS _____

In the classroom you can see:

LOBBARCKAD _____   SOKOB _____

KLACH _____   ECRATHE _____

OROD _____   SDENSUTT _____

In a city, you can find:

TROSES _____   TOSATIN _____

SVIMOE _____   GNIRKAP OTL _____

YCTI LAHL _____   RABILYR _____

Jumbled Words II

Some people in the newspapers are:

ELIPCO _____   SETRONAS _____

SSACSTERE _____   CRALINIMS _____

NIMREEF _____   DRIPNEEST _____

In a hospital, you can find:

EDNIMICE _____   USRSEN _____

SAPENITT _____   SEBD _____

EELRAWHICH _____   STRODOC _____

On the weekend, I:

YSUDT _____   IWMS _____

FOGL _____   AERD _____

HWTAC VT _____   IISTV SDIFERN _____

Out-of-Order Sentences

Put the following sentences in order to make a story, then write the story on the blanks.

Bad luck again.
John went out of the booth, wondering what to do.
He went in and searched his pockets for a dime.
He found one on Baker Street.
Ring. Ring.
He hung up and then tried again.
No answer.
He looked around for a phone booth.
He found one, put it in the slot, and dialed the number.
John wanted to call his friend Martin.

_____

_____

_____

_____

_____

_____

_____

_____

_____

_____

_____

_____

_____

_____

Making a Sentence

From each word in capital letters, make a sentence in which each word starts with one letter of the word, used in the correct order.

Example: C A T *Carol ate turnips.*

1. D I G _____

_____

2. B O N D _____

_____

3. C H A I R _____

_____

4. F A I L _____

_____

5. E N E R G Y _____

_____

6. H O P E S _____

_____

7. W I N D M I L L _____

_____

8. R E P R E S E N T _____

_____

NTC ESL/EFL TEXTS AND MATERIAL
Primary and Elementary

Ready for English
Primary Learning System (four levels)
    Comprehensive Teacher's Manual; Teacher's Manuals;
      Placement and Exit Tests; Black-line Activity
      Masters; Story Cards; Vocabulary Cards; Alphabet
      Cards; Readers; Song Cassettes; Hand Puppet;
      Video; TESOL Professional Anthology

Hello, English
    Student Books 1-6
    Teacher's Editions 1-6
    Testing Kits, Levels 1-6
    Audiocassettes, Levels 1-6

Easy English Learning Activities Program
    Activities Book and Teacher's Guide
    Learning Cards and Teacher's Manual

Practical English Learning Activities Program
    Activities Book and Teacher's Guide
    Learning Cards and Teacher's Manual

English Experiences
    My Book Workbook and Teacher's Manual

English All Around Us
    Workbook and Teacher's Manual

Dictionaries and Activity Books
    Let's Learn English Picture Dictionary
    English Picture Dictionary
    Let's Learn English Coloring Book
    Let's Learn About America
    Basic English Vocabulary Builder Activity Book

Computer Software
    Basic Vocabulary Builder on Computer

Stepping into English
books/videos/filmstrips/audiocassettes/duplicating masters
    The City Mouse and the Country Mouse
    The Lion and the Mouse
    The Rabbit and the Turtle
    The Boy Who Cried Wolf
    Belling the Cat
    The Milkmaid and Her Pail
    Goldilocks and the Three Bears
    The Little Red Hen
    The Boy and the Donkey

SoundsAlive
    Alphabet Coloring Book
    Phonics Review Cards
    Alphabet Puzzle Book
    Workbook
    Teacher's Manual

Duplicating Masters and Black-line Masters
    Easy Vocabulary Games
    Vocabulary Games
    Advanced Vocabulary Games
    Beginning Activities for English Language Learners
    Intermediate Activities for English Language Learners
    Advanced Activities for English Language Learners
    Play and Practice!
    Basic Vocabulary Builder
    Practical Vocabulary Builder

TESOL Professional Anthology
    The Primary and Elementary Classroom

For further information or a current catalog, write:
National Textbook Company
a division of *NTC Publishing Group*
4255 West Touhy Avenue
Lincolnwood, Illinois 60646-1975 U.S.A.

PREPARING FOR THE

Pennsylvania PSSA Mathematics

GRADE 11

David J. Glatzer
Joyce Glatzer

AMSCO

AMSCO SCHOOL PUBLICATIONS, INC.

315 Hudson Street, New York, N.Y. 10013

David J. Glatzer is Supervisor of Mathematics (K–12) for the West Orange Public Schools, West Orange, New Jersey. He has served as President of the Association of Mathematics Teachers of New Jersey (AMTNJ), member of the Board of Directors of the National Council of Teachers of Mathematics (NCTM), and Northeast Director of the National Council of Supervisors of Mathematics (NCSM). He is a frequent speaker at professional conferences and has written numerous articles in professional journals including the *Arithmetic Teacher* and the *New Jersey Mathematics Teacher*. He has made contributions to NCTM yearbooks and to the NCTM *Algebra for Everyone* project. In 1993, he was the recipient of the Max Sobel Outstanding Mathematics Educator Award presented by the AMTNJ. In addition, he served as co-chair of the Mathematics Panel for New Jersey Core Course Proficiencies (New Jersey State Department of Education).

Joyce Glatzer is Supervisor of Mathematics (K–6) for West New York Public Schools, West New York, New Jersey. She has been a Mathematics Consultant and former Coordinator of Mathematics (K–9) for the Summit Public Schools, Summit, New Jersey. She has served as President of the Association of Mathematics Teachers of New Jersey (AMTNJ) and is an active member of the NCTM. She was the 1999 recipient of the Max Sobel Outstanding Mathematics Educator Award presented by the AMTNJ. She is a frequent speaker and workshop leader at professional conferences and staff development programs. She has written numerous articles in professional journals including the *New Jersey Mathematics Teacher* and the *Arithmetic Teacher*. In speaking and conducting workshops, her interests include problem solving, questioning techniques, communications, active learning with manipulatives, and use of calculators.

Reviewers

Elizabeth Barone
   Edward Bok Technical High School
   Philadelphia, PA

E. Lynn Brubaker
   Mathematics Department Head
   Mastbaum Area Vocational Technical School
   Philadelphia, PA

Daniel Krasnick
   Bok High School

Composition and design by Monotype Composition Company

Cover Design by Meghan J. Shupe

Some questions in the Sample Tests are reprinted courtesy of the New Jersey State Department of Education

Brief portions of this book were adapted from the following Amsco publications:

Amsco's Preparing for the Regents Examination Mathematics A

Amsco's Preparing for the Regents Examination Mathematics B

Florida: Preparing for FCAT Mathematics Grade 10

Please visit our Web site at: *www.amscopub.com*

When ordering this book, please specify: either **R 311 W** or PREPARING FOR THE PENNSYLVANIA PSSA MATHEMATICS GRADE 11.

ISBN 1-56765-577-7

CONTENTS

CHAPTER 3   Data Analysis, Probability, and Statistics   115

CHAPTER 4   Patterns, Functions, and Algebra   177

CHAPTER 5 Fundamentals of Calculus   238

Sample Tests

Index   295

GETTING STARTED

A. ABOUT THIS TEST

1. What is the PSSA?

The Pennsylvania System of School Assessment (PSSA) in Mathematics is a test given to students in the fifth, eighth, and eleventh grade. The PSSA Math is not a required graduation test. The test is aligned to the Pennsylvania Academic Standards. The PSSA Math has been developed to show whether or not you have a proficient level of performance in the subject area. The PSSA in Mathematics is not a minimum competency or basic skill test; it is a test of your ability to do higher-order thinking and to integrate topics in mathematics.

2. When do you take the PSSA?

The PSSA Math is given in the spring of each school year. Usually, the exams are given at the end of March into early April.

3. What math topics are included in the PSSA?

There are eleven academic standards tested on the PSSA Mathematics test.

1. **Numbers, Number Systems, and Number Relationships**
2. **Computation and Estimation**
3. **Measurement and Estimation**
4. **Mathematical Reasoning and Connections**
5. **Mathematical Problem Solving and Communication**
6. **Statistics and Data Analysis**
7. **Probability and Predictions**
8. **Algebra and Functions**
9. **Geometry**
10. **Trigonometry**
11. **Concepts of Calculus**

4. What kinds of math questions appear on the PSSA?

There are two kinds of math questions.

1. multiple-choice items
2. open-ended items

Although the multiple-choice questions on the test assess high levels of mathematical thinking, some abilities are difficult to assess with this format. Also, the format does not allow for multiple responses or for partial credit. To overcome these limitations, the test includes open-ended questions.

Open-ended questions require you to construct your own written or graphical responses and explain these responses. The responses can be scored for different levels of mathematical understanding as well as for partial credit. More about scoring and open-ended questions follows in Section C.

5. Do you need to memorize formulas?

No. A formula sheet is distributed to each student along with the test. This reference sheet contains any formulas you may need on the mathematics questions. Refer to page xiv for a sample of a formula sheet.

6. Are calculators allowed on the PSSA?

Yes. With the exception of the first five questions in Section One, you are allowed to use a calculator when you take the PSSA Mathematics test. A more detailed discussion of types of calculators allowed follows in Section B.

7. How is the PSSA scored?

Multiple-choice items are one point each and open-ended responses are four points each. Refer to page xiii for more information on the scoring of open-ended questions.

8. How can you find out more about the PSSA?

For additional information about the PSSA, ask your math teacher or guidance counselor.

B. ABOUT USING A CALCULATOR

With the exception of the first five questions in Section One, you will be allowed to use a calculator on the PSSA. The following information will help you make the most effective use of the calculator on the test.

1. On which questions should you use the calculator?

The calculator will not be needed for every question on the test. With respect to calculator use, questions will fall into three categories: calculator-active, calculator-neutral, or calculator-irrelevant.

Calculator-active questions contain data that can usefully be explored and manipulated using a calculator. These questions may deal with explorations of patterns, problem solving involving guess and check, problems involving calculations with real data, or problems involving messy computation.

Calculator-neutral questions could be completed using a calculator. They may be more efficiently answered, however, by using mental math skills or simple paper-and-pencil computation. For example, the average of -6, -7, -8, 5, 6, 7, 8, 2, 3, 0 can be more quickly found mentally by recognizing that the set contains three pairs of opposites that add up to zero. By the time you have put all the data into the calculator, you could have solved the problem mentally.

With calculator-irrelevant questions, a calculator is of no help because the solution involves no computation. For example, if you were asked to find the probability of selecting a red marble from a jar containing 2 red and 3 blue marbles, the calculator will not help you answer the question.

Determining which questions to answer with the calculator is an important skill for you to develop. Be sure that you do not waste your time on the test trying to use the calculator when it is not appropriate.

2. What calculator can you use?

The State Department of Education has indicated that you will be allowed to use a calculator that has at least the following functions:

  a. algebraic logic (follows order of operations)
  b. exponent key to do powers and roots of any degree
  c. at least one memory
  d. a reset button, or some other simple, straightforward way to clear all of the memory and programs

Graphing calculators are allowed on the test. However, calculators with QWERTY (i.e., typewriter) keyboards and those with beaming capabilities are not acceptable under the current guidelines.

3. What features of the calculator are you likely to need for the test?

In addition to the basic operation keys and number keys, be sure you can use these keys:

CE/C ON/AC	clear
M+ M− MR STO	memory
( )	parentheses
+/− (−)	sign change
%	percent
$\sqrt{\ }$	square root
x^2 y^x	powers
$x!$	factorial

4. What else should you consider when using the calculator on the test?

The most important thing is to be comfortable with the calculator you will be using on the test. Be sure you are familiar with the keypad and the functions available on the calculator.

If you are using a calculator on an open-ended question, remember that it is important to show the work by writing out what you put into the calculator and the answer given.

Think before pushing the buttons. If you try to use the calculator for every question, you will waste too much time.

Be sure to estimate answers and check calculator answers for reasonableness of response.

Remember:

Questions on the test will not be coded to tell you when to use your calculator. You must make the decision.

C. ABOUT OPEN-ENDED QUESTIONS

In addition to multiple-choice questions, the PSSA contains open-ended questions that require some writing. This section will deal with the variety of open-ended questions and offer suggestions for writing complete solutions.

1. What is an open-ended question?

An open-ended question is one in which a situation is presented, and you are asked to communicate a response. In most cases, the questions have two or more parts, and require both numerical responses and explanations, or mathematical arguments.

2. What might be asked in open-ended questions?

The following outline covers examples of what might be asked in these questions.

1. **A task with a request to show a procedure.**
    (possibly a combination of tasks).

Example: Find the area of the shaded region.
    Explain your procedure.

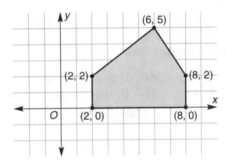

2. **A written explanation of why a result is valid or why an approach is incorrect.**

Example: The average test score in a class of 20 students was 80. The average test score in a class of 30 students was 70. Mich concluded that the average score for all 50 students was 75. He obtained the 75 by adding 80 and 70, and dividing by 2. Is his approach correct? Explain.

3. **A list to meet certain conditions.**
    You might be asked to list numbers, dimensions, expressions, equations, etc.

Example: By looking, you should be able to tell that the average (mean) for 79, 80, 81 is 80. List three other sets of three scores that would also have an average of 80.

4. **A diagram to fit specific conditions.**

Example: On the grid, draw three figures (a triangle, a rectangle, a parallelogram) each with an area of 12 square units.

5. A description and/or extension of a pattern.

Example: Suppose this pattern were continued.

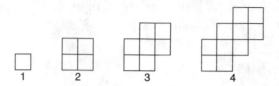

    A. Explain how the pattern is produced.
    B. How many small squares would be in the 100th diagram?

6. An indication of what will happen when a change is made in an existing situation.

Example: A rectangular prism (box) has dimensions of 8 cm × 4 cm × 2 cm. If you double each of the three dimensions, tell what happens to the volume of the box.

7. A diagram to enhance an explanation.

Example: Use a diagram to show that:

$$2\frac{1}{2} \times 2\frac{1}{2} = 6\frac{1}{4}$$

8. A process involving measurement with a follow-up task.

Example: Use a ruler to determine the lengths of the sides of the accompanying figure. Label the sides with the measurements you find. Use these measurements to find the perimeter and the area of the figure. Show all work clearly.

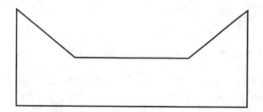

3. How are open-ended questions scored?

Beginning in 2005, the open-ended questions on the PSSA will each be worth four points. (The multiple-choice items are each worth one point). Partial credit is possible on the open-ended questions. You might receive a score of 4, 3, 2, 1, or 0. (An analytic approach is used based on the requirements of each problem.) In multi-part questions, for example, the four points a response could earn are distributed among the parts. The following examples show how the scoring could take place on different open-ended questions.

    The generic rubric used as a guide to develop specific scoring guides or rubrics for the open-ended items that appear on the PSSA is on page xiii.

Example 1: Suppose the coordinates of point A are (3, 1), the coordinates of point B are (10, 7), and the coordinates of point C are (3, 7). Sketch triangle ABC. Classify the triangle according to sides. Explain how you arrived at the classification.

Scoring:

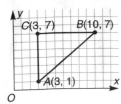

You would most likely earn one point for correctly locating the points.

You would most likely earn one point for correctly classifying the figure. (scalene)

You would most likely earn two points for an acceptable explanation of the classification. (i.e., use of ruler, properties of right triangle)

Example 2: Karin knows that the average test score in her class of 20 students is 80. If each student in the class receives an additional 5 points in extra credit, Karin believes the class average will be 85. Is Karin correct? Explain or prove your answer to someone who disagrees with you.

Scoring: You would most likely earn four points if you:

a. State that Karin is correct.

b. Support your response with an algebraic or arithmetic proof:

$$\frac{(20 \times 80) + (20 \times 5)}{20} = 85$$

c. Generalize your response in words: The sum will increase 100 points. The number of students remains constant. Hence, the change in the average is the increase divided by the number of students, or $100 \div 20 = 5$.

You would most likely receive three points if you state that Karin is correct and support your response with an arithmetic example, but do not generalize.

You would most likely receive two points if you state that Karin is correct but offer no explanation.

You would most likely receive zero points if you provide an unsatisfactory response that answers the question inappropriately.

4. What are some general guidelines for answering open-ended questions?

In answering open-ended questions, you will find the following suggestions helpful.

1. Write complete sentences.
2. Be concise, not wordy.
3. Make sure to explore different cases.
4. Make sure to answer each part of the question.
5. Make sure you answer the question that is being asked.
6. Use a diagram to enhance an explanation.
7. Label diagrams with dimensions.
8. As appropriate, give a clearly worked-out example with some explanation.
9. In problems involving estimation/approximation, make sure you do precomputational rounding.
10. Provide generalizations as requested.

11. When using a grid, follow specific instructions for the location of the origin, axes, etc.
12. Avoid assumptions that have no basis, such as assuming that a triangle is isosceles.
13. Double-check any computation needed within the open-ended response.
14. Be aware that a question may have more than one answer.

Holistic Scoring Guide for Mathematics Open-Ended Items (Generic Rubric)

4-Point Response

The response shows a student's advanced and complete understanding of the problem's essential mathematical concepts. The student arrives at the correct answer with correct procedures or calculations shown. The student provides a written explanation.

3-Point Response

The response shows a student's satisfactory understanding of the problem's essential mathematical concepts. The student arrives at the correct answer with a few minor errors made in the calculation. The student provides an incomplete explanation.

2-Point Response

The response shows a student's partial understanding of the problem's essential mathematical concepts. The student arrives at a correct answer with few or incorrect calculations shown or some explanation given. OR The student arrives at an incorrect answer with correct calculations shown and provides some or no explanation.

1-Point Response

The response shows a student's minimal understanding of the problem's essential mathematical concepts. The student arrives at a correct answer with incorrect calculations. OR The student arrives at an incorrect answer but shows partially correct calculations and provides some critical information showing that the student has read the problem.

0-Point Response

The response shows a student's insufficient understanding of the problem's essential mathematical concepts. The answer is incorrect with major errors in the calculation. The student provides an incorrect explanation. Calculations and explanation may be illegible.

Mathematics Formula Sheet

Permutations: $P(n, r) = \dfrac{n!}{(n - r)!}$

Combinations: $C(n, r) = \dfrac{n!}{r!(n - r)!}$

nth Term of an Arithmetic Sequence:

$$a_n = a_1 + (n - 1)d$$

nth Term of a Geometric Sequence:

$$a_n = a_1 r^{(n - 1)}$$

Sum of an Arithmetic Sequence:

$$S_n = \frac{n}{2}[2a_1 + (n - 1)d]$$

Sum of a Geometric Sequence:

$$S_n = \frac{a_1(1 - r^n)}{1 - r} \ \text{ or } \ S_n = \frac{a_1 - a_1 r^n}{1 - r}$$

Sum of an Infinite Geometric Series:

$$S = \frac{a_1}{1 - r}$$

Quadratic Formula:

If $ax^2 + bx + c = 0$, then

$$x = \frac{-b \pm \sqrt{b^2 - 4ac}}{2a}$$

Circle:

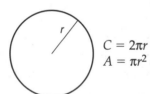

$C = 2\pi r$
$A = \pi r^2$

Rectangle:

$P = 2l + 2w$
$A = lw$

Parallelogram:

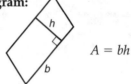

$A = bh$

Triangle:

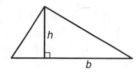

$$A = \frac{1}{2}bh$$

Trapezoid:

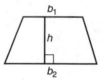

$$A = \frac{1}{2}(b_1 + b_2)h$$

Sphere:

$SA = 2\pi r^2 \qquad V = \dfrac{4}{3}\pi r^3$

Rectangular Parallelepiped:

$SA = 2lw + 2lh + 2wh$
$V = lwh$

Right Circular Cylinder:

$SA = 2\pi r^2 + 2\pi rh \qquad V = \pi r^2 h$

Distance Formula:

$$d = \sqrt{(x_2 - x_1)^2 + (y_2 - y_1)^2}$$

Pythagorean Formula:

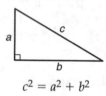

$$c^2 = a^2 + b^2$$

Law of Sines:

$$\frac{a}{\sin \angle A} = \frac{b}{\sin \angle B} = \frac{c}{\sin \angle C}$$

Law of Cosines:

$$c^2 = a^2 + b^2 - 2ab \cos \angle C$$

Trigonometric Ratios:

$$\sin \theta = \frac{\text{opp}}{\text{hyp}} \qquad \cos \theta = \frac{\text{adj}}{\text{hyp}}$$

$$\tan \theta = \frac{\text{opp}}{\text{adj}}$$

Simple Interest: $I = prt$

Compound Interest

(n times per year):

$$A = p\left(1 + \frac{r}{n}\right)^{nt}$$

Base Change Formula:

$$\log_b x = \frac{\log_c x}{\log_c b}$$

CHAPTER 1

Number Sense, Concepts, and Applications

1.1 Real Numbers

A *rational number* is any number that can be expressed as a ratio of two integers in the form $\frac{a}{b}$, with $b \neq 0$. This definition includes integers, fractions, and decimals.

In decimal form, a rational number is either a terminating decimal (such as 0.25; 0.165) or a repeating decimal (such as $0.3\overline{3}$; $4.\overline{31}$).

An *irrational number* in decimal form is neither a terminating decimal nor a repeating decimal. Examples of irrational numbers are 0.121221222 . . . ; $\sqrt{2} = 1.41421356$. . . . An irrational number cannot be written as a ratio of two integers.

The set of *real numbers* is formed by combining the set of rational numbers with the set of irrational numbers.

 MODEL PROBLEMS

1. Which of the following is NOT equal to the other three?

   A) $\frac{2}{10}$ B) $1.5 \div 7.5$ C) $1 \div \frac{1}{5}$ D) $\sqrt{\frac{1}{25}}$

Solution: Choice A: $\frac{2}{10} = \frac{1}{5}$

Choice B: $1.5 \div 7.5 = 0.2$ or $\frac{1}{5}$

Choice C: $1 \div \frac{1}{5} = 1 \times 5 = 5$

Choice D: $\sqrt{\frac{1}{25}} = \frac{1}{5}$

Answer: Choice C is not equivalent to the others.

2. Place the following rational numbers in order from LEAST to GREATEST:

$$-\frac{5}{2}, \frac{2}{5}, -3.2, 0.35$$

Solution: As you consider placement of rational numbers on a number line, numbers to the left are smaller than numbers to the right.

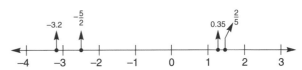

Answer: $-3.2, -\frac{5}{2}, 0.35, \frac{2}{5}$

3. Name an irrational number between 3 and 4.

Solution: There are an infinite number of irrational numbers between 3 and 4. To name one, it is necessary to write a decimal which is non-repeating and also non-terminating. Possible answers include 3.050050005 . . . ; $\sqrt{13}$; 3.929929992 . . . ; and π.

1. Arrange the following numbers in order from LEAST to GREATEST:

$$\frac{1}{3}, \frac{2}{5}, 0.6, 0.125$$

   A) $0.125, 0.6, \frac{1}{3}, \frac{2}{5}$ B) $0.125, \frac{1}{3}, \frac{2}{5}, 0.6$

   C) $0.125, \frac{1}{3}, 0.6, \frac{2}{5}$ D) $\frac{1}{3}, \frac{2}{5}, 0.125, 0.6$

2. For a series of eight football plays, a team had the following results:

   +4 yards, +3 yards, +9 yards, −4 yards,
   −5 yards, +10 yards, −5 yards, +8 yards

   What is the average yardage for this series of plays?

   E) 20   F) 6   G) 2.5   H) −2.5

3. Select the correct comparison between p and q.

   $$p = \frac{1}{3} \times \frac{1}{5} \times \frac{2}{7} \text{ and } q = \frac{2}{3} \times \frac{1}{5} \times \frac{1}{7}$$

   A) $p < q$
   B) $p > q$
   C) $p = q$
   D) The comparison cannot be determined without more information.

4. Which point on the number line could represent the product of the numbers P, Q, and R?

   E) S F) T G) U H) V

5. A fraction is equal to $\frac{1}{2}$. If its numerator is increased by 1 and its denominator is increased by 5, the value of the resulting fraction is $\frac{4}{9}$. Find the original fraction.

   A) $\frac{6}{12}$ B) $\frac{7}{13}$ C) $\frac{9}{18}$ D) $\frac{11}{22}$

6. The number 0.67667667 . . . is between which pair of rational numbers?

   E) $\frac{1}{2}$ and $\frac{2}{3}$ F) $\frac{1}{3}$ and $\frac{4}{7}$

   G) $\frac{2}{3}$ and $\frac{3}{4}$ H) $\frac{4}{7}$ and $\frac{5}{8}$

7. Which of the following sets contains the numbers 0.33, $-\frac{5}{6}$, and $\sqrt{5}$?

   A) Real numbers   B) Rational numbers
   C) Irrational numbers   D) Integers

8. If you know that $\frac{1}{8} = 0.125$, how can you use that fact to find the value of $\frac{7}{8}$?

9. Explain why the decimal 0.33 is not exactly equivalent to the fraction $\frac{1}{3}$.

10. How many ratios of two whole numbers are equivalent to $\frac{7}{10}$ and have a two-digit denominator?

1.2 Powers, Roots, Exponents, and Scientific Notation

Exponents

An *exponent* tells how many times a base is used as a factor.

$$3^4 = 3 \cdot 3 \cdot 3 \cdot 3 = 81$$

exponent → (pointing to the 4)

base → (pointing to the 3)

Rules of Exponents ($x \neq 0$):

Multiplication: $x^a \cdot x^b = x^{a+b}$

Division: $x^a \div x^b = x^{a-b}$

Powers: $(x^a)^b = x^{ab}$

Zero Exponent: $x^0 = 1$

Negative Exponent: $x^{-a} = \dfrac{1}{x^a}$

 MODEL PROBLEMS

1. In simplifying $\dfrac{5^5 \times 5^3}{5^6}$, Jessica is tempted to use her calculator to find 5^5, 5^3, and 5^6 individually prior to doing the multiplication and division. Explain how Jessica could use the laws of exponents to arrive at the result in a more efficient manner.

Solution: $5^5 \times 5^3 = 5^{5+3} = 5^8$

$\qquad 5^8 \div 5^6 = 5^{8-6} = 5^2 = 25$

2. Which of these three expressions

$\qquad$ I. 2^{12} $\quad$ II. 4^6 $\quad$ III. $2^3 \cdot 8^3$

is equivalent to the expression 16^3?

A) I, II, and III $\qquad$ B) only I and II
C) only II and III $\qquad$ D) only I

Solution: Since 16 is equivalent to 2^4, then 16^3 is equivalent to $(2^4)^3$ or 2^{12}.
Thus, I is an equivalent expression.

Since 16 is equivalent to 4^2, then 16^3 is equivalent to $(4^2)^3$ or 4^6.
Thus, II is an equivalent expression.

$2^3 \cdot 8^3$ is equivalent to $(2 \cdot 8)^3$ or 16^3.
Thus, III is an equivalent expression.

Answer: A

3. Simplify: $(-4)^{-3}$

Solution: By definition, $(-4)^{-3} = \dfrac{1}{(-4)^3} = \dfrac{1}{-64} = \dfrac{-1}{64}$.

Roots

A *root* is the inverse of a power.

If $b^2 = a$, then b is a square root of a. $\quad b = \sqrt{a}$

If $b^3 = a$, then b is a cube root of a. $\quad b = \sqrt[3]{a}$

Examples: $5^2 = 25 \rightarrow 5$ is a square root of 25. $\quad 5 = \sqrt{25}$

$\qquad\qquad (-5)^2 = 25 \rightarrow -5$ is a square root of 25. $\quad -5 = \sqrt{25}$

$\qquad\qquad 2^3 = 8 \rightarrow 2$ is a cube root of 8. $\quad 2 = \sqrt[3]{8}$

$\qquad\qquad 5^4 = 625 \rightarrow 5$ is a fourth root of 625. $\quad 5 = \sqrt[4]{625}$

$\qquad\qquad 3^5 = 243 \rightarrow 3$ is a fifth root of 243. $\quad 3 = \sqrt[5]{243}$

 MODEL PROBLEM

$x^4 = 16$, find two values of x so that the statement is true.

Solution: Since $2^4 = 16$ and $(-2)^4 = 16$, 2 and -2 are two values that satisfy the equation. Therefore, 2 and -2 are each fourth roots of 16.

Scientific Notation

A number in *scientific notation* is expressed as a product of two factors:

(first factor is between 1 and 10) $\times$ (second factor is an integral power of 10)

$$4,300,000 = 4.3 \times 10^6 \qquad 0.000043 = 4.3 \times 10^{-5}$$

 MODEL PROBLEM

Compute the product of $845,000 \times 0.0000045$ by using scientific notation for each factor.

Solution: $845,000 \times 0.0000045$

$\quad 8.45 \times 10^5 \times 4.5 \times 10^{-6}$

$\quad 8.45 \times 4.5 \times 10^5 \times 10^{-6}$

$\quad 8.45 \times 4.5 \times 10^{-1}$

$\qquad 38.025 \times 10^{-1} = 3.8025 \times 10 \times 10^{-1}$

$\qquad\qquad\qquad = 3.8025 \times 10^{1 + (-1)} = 3.8025 \times 10^0 = 3.8025$ **Answer**

1. Choose the correct comparison for the following two quantities: $p = 4^8$ and $q = 2^{15}$

   A) $p < q$ B) $p > q$ C) $p = q$
   D) The comparison cannot be determined without additional information.

2. Choose the correct comparison for the following two quantities: $p = (0.9)^3$ and $q = (0.9)^5$

   E) $p < q$ F) $p > q$ G) $p = q$
   H) The comparison cannot be determined without additional information.

3. Which of the following statements are always TRUE?

   I. $6^a = 2 \times 3^a$ II. $(0.9)^4 > (0.9)^3$

   A) I and II   B) I only   C) II only
   D) Neither statement is always true.

4. If the volume of a cube is 512 cubic inches, which of the following represents the length of an edge of the cube?

   E) $512 \div 3$ F) $\sqrt{512}$
   G) 512^3 H) $\sqrt[3]{512}$

5. Which of the following is NOT correct?

   A) $3^8 = (3^4)^2$ B) $3^4 \times 3^4 = 3^{16}$
   C) $3^4 \times 3^4 = 3^8$ D) $3^{10} \div 3^5 = 3^5$

6. Which of the following relations could you write in the blank to produce a true statement?

   $$2.5 \times 10^{-4} \underline{\quad} 3.4 \times 10^{-3}$$

   E) $>$ F) $<$ G) $=$
   H) The comparison cannot be determined without more information.

7. Which of the following would NOT represent a large number?

   A) 5.9×10^{24} B) 3.92×10^{-6}
   C) 7.37×10^{22} D) 2.279×10^8

8. Which of the following is NOT equivalent to 5^{-2}?

   E) -25 F) $\dfrac{1}{25}$ G) 0.04 H) $\left(\dfrac{1}{5}\right)^2$

9. If $3^\square = 9^4$, what exponent goes in the box?

10. What is the missing exponent? $\dfrac{r^{12}}{r^\square} = r^6$

11. Explain the difference between $a^3 \times a^5$ and $(a^3)^5$.

12. Show how scientific notation can be used to simplify the amount of computation in the following problem:

    $$52{,}000 \times 1{,}200{,}000$$

1.3   Logarithms

A *logarithm* is the exponent of the power to which a base number must be raised to equal a given number. For example, $y = \log_2 16$ can be translated to the exponential form $2^y = 16$. To solve the equation, y is the number that 2 is raised to so that it can be equivalent to 16. In this case, since $2^4 = 16$, $y = 4$.

Any logarithmic equation can be rewritten in exponential form. The following table contains examples.

Logarithmic Form	Exponential Form
$2 = \log_6 36$	$6^2 = 36$
$3 = \log_4 64$	$4^3 = 64$
$\dfrac{1}{2} = \log_{16} 4$	$16^{\frac{1}{2}} = 4$
$-1 = \log_{10} \dfrac{1}{10}$	$10^{-1} = \dfrac{1}{10}$

By observing the pattern in the table above, we can see that the general rule for logs and exponents is:

$$\log_b c = a \quad \leftrightarrow \quad b^a = c \text{ (such that } b > 0 \text{ and } b \neq 1)$$

Since logarithms are exponents, rules of exponents also apply to logarithms. The following table shows logarithmic rules and an example of each for all positive numbers m, n, and b, where $b \neq 1$.

	Logarithmic Rule	Example of Log Rule
Product	$\log_b mn = \log_b m + \log_b n$	$\log_b 20 = \log_b 2 + \log_b 10$
Quotient	$\log_b \dfrac{m}{n} = \log_b m - \log_b n$	$\log_b \dfrac{145}{12} = \log_b 145 - \log_b 12$
Power	$\log_b m^n = n\log_b m$	$\log_b 10^2 = 2\log_b 10$

The product rule of logarithms, in words, says that to find the logarithm of the product of two numbers, add the logarithms of both numbers together. For example,

$$\log_b (793 \cdot 915) = \log_b 793 + \log_b 915$$

$$\log_2 (16 \cdot 32) = \log_2 (2^4 \cdot 2^5) = \log_2 (2^{4+5}) = \log_2 (2^9) = 9 \log_2 2 = 9$$

The quotient rule of logarithms states that if the logarithm of the quotient of two numbers is taken, we would simply subtract the logarithm of the denominator from the logarithm of the numerator. For example,

$$\log_b \frac{57}{8} = \log_b 57 - \log_b 8 \qquad .$$

Finally, the power rule of logarithms states that to find the logarithm of a number raised to a power, take the product of the power and the logarithm of the number. For example,

$$\log_b 1{,}356^{\frac{1}{2}} = \frac{1}{2} \log_b 1{,}356$$

MODEL PROBLEMS

1. Solve for x: $x = \log_4 8$

Solution:

To solve for x, first write the equation in exponential form: $4^x = 8$. In this case, we need to solve for the exponent x, so we need to rewrite the equation to make the bases equal.

$$4^x = 8$$
$$2^{2x} = 2^3$$
$$2x = 3$$
$$x = \frac{3}{2}$$

Note: Remember that when bases of an exponential equation are equal, the exponents will also be equal.

2. The expression $\log_3 a^5 b$ is equivalent to

A) $5 \log_3 ab$ B) $5 \log_3 a + \log_3 b$

C) $\log_3 5ab$ D) $\log_3 5a + \log_3 b$

Solution:

Use the product rule for logarithms.

$$\log_3 a^5 b = \log_3 a^5 + \log_3 b$$

Use the power rule for logarithms.

$$= 5 \log_3 a + \log_3 b$$

Answer: B

Common Logarithms

The most often used *common logarithm* is an exponent to the base 10. When no base is written in the logarithmic form of a number, the base is understood to be 10, for example:

$$\log x = 2 \text{ is equivalent to } \log_{10} x = 2 \text{ or } 10^2 = x.$$
$$\log 6 = 0.7781512504 \text{ is equivalent to } \log_{10} 6 \text{ or } 10^{0.7781512504} = 6.$$

You can use the calculator to find the logarithm of a number with base 10. Depending on the calculator, you may need to press the log key first before entering the number. Check your calculator to see which method it uses.

MODEL PROBLEMS

1. If log 4.389 = a, which of the following would represent log 43.89?

   A) $10a + 10$ B) $1 + a$

   C) $a - 1$ D) $10a - 1$

Solution:

$$\log 43.89 = \log (10 \cdot 4.389)$$
$$= \log 10 + \log 4.389$$
$$= 1 + a$$

Answer: B

2. Use your calculator to solve for N: log N = 1.698970004

Solution: Rewrite log N = 1.698970004 in exponential form:

$$10^{1.698970004} = N.$$

On your calculator, press 2ND LOG, which is the 10^x function. Enter the value and press ENTER or EQUAL and you will get the answer 50.

Note: Depending on your calculator, you may need to enter the given value before pressing 2ND LOG.

Answer: 50

Solving Exponential Equations Using Logarithms

Recall that when solving exponential equations, it is necessary to have the bases equal to each other. Sometimes, however, the bases of the equation cannot be made equal to each other. For example, in $7^x = 80$, neither 7 nor 80 can be written as a power of the same base. In cases like this, we can use logarithms to solve for x.

MODEL PROBLEM

Solve $7^x = 80$ for x to the nearest hundredth.

Solution: Since $7^2 = 49$ and $7^3 = 343$, we can estimate that the value is between 2 and 3, but much closer to 2.

$$7^x = 80$$
$$\log 7^x = \log 80$$
$$x \log 7 = \log 80$$
$$x = \frac{\log 80}{\log 7}$$
$$x = 2.251916224$$
$$x \approx 2.25$$

Answer: x is approximately 2.25.

There are times when logarithms cannot be solved easily. For example, in $\log_3 64$, 3 cannot be raised to an integer power to arrive at 64. Since we know that the log function on the calculator is of base 10, and since it is possible to change from one base to another, we can use the *change of base formula*, which is:

$$\log_b x = \frac{\log_c x}{\log_c b}, \quad (b \neq 0 \text{ or } 1)$$

 ## MODEL PROBLEM

Compute $\log_3 64$ to the nearest thousandths.

Solution

Use the change of base formula.

$$\log_3 64 = \frac{\log 64}{\log 3}$$

$$= 3.785578521$$

$$\approx 3.786$$

Answer: $\log_3 64$ is approximately 3.786.

PRACTICE

1. If $\log_b 5 = a$ and $\log_b 2 = y$, then $\log_b 20$ can be represented by which of the following?

   A) $a + y^2$ B) $2ay$
   C) $a + 2y$ D) $2a + y$

2. If $\log_a 3 = m$ and $\log_a 6 = n$, express $\log_a \sqrt{\frac{1}{2}}$ in terms of m and n.

   E) $m - n$ F) $\frac{1}{2}mn$
   G) $\frac{1}{2}m - n$ H) $\frac{1}{2}(m - n)$

3. If $\log_2 a = \log_3 a$, then a equals:

   A) 0   B) 1   C) 2   D) 3

4. The expression $\log_5 \frac{a}{c^2}$ is equivalent to

   E) $\log_5 a - \frac{1}{2}\log_5 c$ F) $\frac{\log_5 c}{2 \log_5 c}$
   G) $2(\log_5 a - \log_5 c)$ H) $\log_5 a - 2 \log_5 c$

5. Solve for n: $\log_3 9 + \log_3 2 = \log_3 n$

   A) 18   B) 11   C) $\frac{9}{2}$ D) $\frac{2}{9}$

6. If $\log N = 2.5381$, find N to the nearest hundredth.

   E) 345.21   F) 345.22
   G) 345.25   H) 345.30

7. If $10^{3.7924} = a$, then $\log a$ is:

   A) 10   B) 0.37924
   C) 3.7924   D) 37,924

8. If $10^x = k$, which of the following is equivalent to 10^{x-1}?

   E) $k - 10$ F) $k - 1$

   G) $\dfrac{10}{k}$ H) $\dfrac{k}{10}$

9. If $N = \sqrt{\dfrac{5}{12}}$, then $\log N$ is equivalent to

   A) $\frac{1}{2}(\log 5 - \log 12)$ B) $\frac{1}{2}\log 5 - \log 12$

   C) $\frac{1}{2} \cdot \dfrac{\log 5}{\log 12}$ D) $\sqrt{\dfrac{\log 5}{\log 12}}$

10. If $K = \dfrac{\sqrt[3]{6}}{5^2}$, which of the following is equivalent to $\log K$?

   E) $3 \log 6 - 2 \log 5$ F) $\frac{1}{3} \log 6 - 2 \log 5$

   G) $\dfrac{\frac{1}{3} \log 6}{2 \log 5}$ H) $\dfrac{3 \log 6}{2 \log 5}$

In exercises 11–15, solve for x. Round to the nearest thousandth.

11. $x = \log_3 152$

12. $x = \log_6 513$

13. $12.3^x = 4{,}720$

14. $x = \log_5 426$

15. $x = \log_7 636$

1.4   Absolute Value

The **absolute value** (symbol $|\ \ |$) of a nonzero number is always positive. The absolute value of zero is zero: $|0| = 0$.

   We describe the absolute value of a nonzero number as a distance. Since the point representing $+3$ is a distance of 3 units from zero on a number line and the point representing -3 is also a distance of 3 units from zero, the absolute value of both $+3$ and -3 is 3.

   In symbols:

$$|+3| = 3 \qquad |-3| = 3 \qquad |+3| = |-3| = 3$$

 MODEL PROBLEMS

1. Simplify: $|-7| + |8| - |-9|$

Solution: $|-7| = 7$
$\qquad\qquad |8| = 8$
$\qquad\qquad |-9| = 9$
Therefore, $|-7| + |8| - |-9| = 7 + 8 - 9 = 6$

2. Solve for x: $|x| = 5$

Solution: Since $|x|$ is the distance x is from 0 on the number line, $x = 5$ or -5.

3. Solve for x: $|2x + 1| = 9$

Solution: If $|a| = 9$, then a must equal 9 or -9.
         Hence, $|2x + 1| = 9$ means

$$2x + 1 = 9 \quad \text{or} \quad 2x + 1 = -9$$
$$2x = 8 \qquad\qquad 2x = -10$$
$$x = 4 \qquad\qquad\quad x = -5$$

1. Place the following in order from LEAST to GREATEST:

$$-\frac{1}{2}, |-1|, -1.4, \left|-\frac{3}{8}\right|$$

A) $-1.4, -\frac{1}{2}, \left|-\frac{3}{8}\right|, |-1|$

B) $|-1|, \left|-\frac{3}{8}\right|, -\frac{1}{2}, -1.4$

C) $\left|-\frac{3}{8}\right|, -\frac{1}{2}, -1.4, |-1|$

D) $-1.4, \left|-\frac{3}{8}\right|, -\frac{1}{2}, |-1|$

2. If $|x - 4| = 3$, then x equals:

E) 7 only F) 1 only G) 7 or 1 H) 7 or -1

3. Which of the following would represent all of the real numbers at least 5 units away from 2 on the number line?

A) $|x| \geq 5$ B) $|x - 2| \geq 5$
C) $|x + 2| \geq 5$ D) $|x + 5| \geq 2$

4. Which of the following equations represents the situation: to qualify to be a member of the school's wrestling team, a student's weight (w) must be within 75 pounds of 180 pounds?

E) $w - 75 = 180$ F) $w - 180 < 75$
G) $|w - 75| < 180$ H) $|w - 180| < 75$

5. Simplify: $|12| - |-12|$

Properties of Arithmetic Operations and Equivalence Relations

Basic Properties of Operations		
	$+$	$\times$
Commutative	$a + b = b + a$	$ab = ba$
Associative	$(a + b) + c = a + (b + c)$	$(ab)c = a(bc)$
Identity	$a + 0 = a$	$a \cdot 1 = a$
Inverse	$a + (-a) = 0$	$a \cdot \frac{1}{a} = 1, a \neq 0$
Distributive	$a(b + c) = ab + ac$	

Note:

The Additive Inverse is also called the opposite and the Multiplicative Inverse is also called the reciprocal.

Properties of Equivalence Relations	
Reflexive	$A \circledR A$
Symmetric	If $A \circledR B$, then $B \circledR A$.
Transitive	If $A \circledR B$ and $B \circledR C$, then $A \circledR C$.
Note: $\circledR$ represents any relation.	

MODEL PROBLEMS

1. Which property has been applied to allow the product of 15(98) to be computed mentally?

$$15(98) = 15(100 - 2) = 1500 - 30 = 1470$$

A) Associative multiplication   B) Distributive

C) Associative addition   D) Inverse for addition

Solution: 98 is rewritten as the equivalent expression $100 - 2$ and then the 15 is distributed over the 100 and the 2. The difference can easily be found. The key is to rewrite the problem using numbers that make mental computation simple.

Answer: D

2. Which property or properties does the given relationship have?

"is congruent to" (for geometric figures)

E) Reflexive only   F) Symmetric only   G) Transitive only   H) All of the above

Solution: Since every figure is congruent to itself, the relationship is reflexive. If figure #1 is congruent to figure #2, then figure #2 is congruent to figure #1—so the relationship is symmetric. If figure #1 is congruent to figure #2 and figure #2 is congruent to figure #3, then figure #1 is congruent to figure #3. Therefore, "congruent to" is transitive.

Answer: H

PRACTICE

1. Which of the following does NOT have the transitive property?

   A) "is greater than"
   B) "has the same slope as"
   C) "is perpendicular to"
   D) "is less than"

2. Which of the following would NOT be commutative?

   E) Addition ($p + q$ and $q + p$)
   F) Exponentiation (p^q and q^p)
   G) Multiplication (pq and qp)
   H) All of the above are commutative.

3. For the following relationship, which properties would be TRUE?

"is perpendicular to" (for lines)

   A) Reflexive only
   B) Symmetric only
   C) Transitive only
   D) Reflexive, symmetric, and transitive

4. For which of the following could the distributive property be used to rewrite the expression?

   E) $a + (b - c)$ F) $a(b - c)$
   G) $a - (b \div c)$ H) $ab - c$

5. Which relation has all three equivalence properties?

   A) "has the same grandmother as"
   B) "is in the same time zone as"
   C) "has at least as many calories as"
   D) "lives across the street from"

6. Deanne bought 6 tee shirts at $8.95 each. She figured out her total purchase by using a shortcut: $6 \times \$9 - 6 \times \$0.05 = \$53.70$. Her shortcut is an illustration of which property?

1.6 Primes, Factors, and Multiples

Numbers can be classified as *prime* or *composite*.
   A *prime number* is a whole number greater than 1 with exactly two factors, 1 and the number.

$$2, 3, 5, 7, 11, 13, \ldots$$

A *composite number* is a whole number greater than 1 with more than two factors.

$$4, 6, 8, 9, 10, 12, \ldots$$

One number is a *factor* of another number if it evenly divides that number.
Thus, 6 is a factor of 18, since $18 \div 6 = 3$.
But 8 is not a factor of 18, since $18 \div 8$ is not equal to a whole number.
Two or more numbers may share common factors.
The largest shared common factor is called the *greatest common factor* (*GCF*).
The GCF of 18 and 48 is 6.
   A *multiple* of a number is the product of that number and any other whole number.
Thus, 20 is a multiple of 5, since $4 \times 5 = 20$.
But 18 is not a multiple of 4, since no whole number times 4 equals 18.
Two or more numbers may share a common multiple.
The smallest shared common multiple is called the *least common multiple* (*LCM*). The LCM of 12 and 15 is 60.

MODEL PROBLEMS

1. Mr. Smart likes to describe his age in the following way: "If you divide my age by 7, the remainder is 1. If you divide my age by 2, the remainder is 1. If you divide my age by 3, the remainder is 1. My age is not divisible by 5 and is less than 100. Now you know my age." How old is Mr. Smart?

Solution:

If Mr. Smart's age is divisible by 7, 2, and 3, his age would be $7 \cdot 3 \cdot 2 = 42$

To obtain a remainder of 1 on each division, his age must be $42 + 1$ or 43.

No other possible age fits the conditions.

Answer: 43

2. The members of the Decorating Committee for a school dance have 36 red carnations, 48 white carnations, and 60 pink carnations. They want to form identical centerpieces, using all of the carnations, so that each one has the same combination of colors as the other centerpieces. What is the largest number of centerpieces they can make?

Solution: Factor each number.

red: 36: (1, 2, 3, 4, 6, 9, 12, 18, 36)

white: 48: (1, 2, 3, 4, 6, 8, 12, 16, 24, 48)

pink: 60: (1, 2, 3, 4, 5, 6, 10, 12, 15, 20, 30, 60)

common factors: (1, 2, 3, 4, 6, 12)

Answer: GCF = 12

3. What is the least number of pencils that could be packaged evenly in groups of 8 pencils OR groups of 12 pencils?

Solution:

packages of 8 could hold: (8, 16, 24, 32, 40, 48, . . .)

packages of 12 could hold: (12, 24, 36, 48, 60, . . .)

Answer: Least number possible is 24.

PRACTICE

1. Which of the numbers below has all the following characteristics?

- It is a multiple of 12.
- It is the least common multiple of two one-digit even numbers.
- It is not a factor of 36.

A) 12   B) 24   C) 36   D) 48

2. Which of the following is NOT a correct statement?

E) If a is a multiple of b, then b is a factor of a.

F) If b is a factor of a, then b is a multiple of a.

G) Any two numbers can have a common multiple.

H) If a is a multiple of b and b is a multiple of c, then a is a multiple of c.

3. 48 is NOT a multiple of 36 because:

   A) 12 is the greatest common factor of 48 and 36.
   B) 9 is a factor of 36 but not a factor of 48.
   C) 48 is not a prime number.
   D) No whole number multiplied by 36 will give a product of 48.

4. 18 is NOT a factor of 84 because:

   E) 84 is not prime.
   F) 18 is not prime.
   G) 6 is not a factor of 84.
   H) 9 is not a factor of 84.

5. What is the smallest three-digit number divisible by 3?

6. If 2, 3, and 5 are factors of a number, list three other factors of the number.

7. Lisa believes that a characteristic of a prime number is that prime numbers are odd. Explain why Lisa's generalization is incorrect.

8. If 2 is not a factor of a number, why can't 6 be a factor of the same number?

9. One rectangle has an area of 48 cm². Another rectangle has an area of 80 cm². The dimensions of each rectangle are whole numbers. If each rectangle is to have the same length, what is the greatest possible dimension, in centimeters, the length can be?

10. Jack believes that the larger a number is, the more factors the number has. Write an argument in support or contradiction of Jack's belief.

11. Chen believes that the LCM of two numbers is always greater than either number. Write an argument in support or contradiction of Chen's belief.

12. Stan and John begin a race at the same time. John runs a lap of the track in 8 minutes. Stan runs the same lap in 6 minutes. When is the first time that John and Stan will complete a lap together?

1.7 Ratio and Proportion

A *ratio* is a comparison of two numbers by division.
The ratio of two numbers a and b (where $b \neq 0$) can be expressed as:

$$a \text{ to } b \quad \text{or} \quad a : b \quad \text{or} \quad \frac{a}{b}$$

A ratio that compares two unlike quantities is called a *rate*.

To Find a Unit Rate:
1. Set up a ratio comparing the given units.
2. Divide to find the rate for one unit of the given quantity.

A *proportion* is a statement that two ratios are equal.
In a proportion, the *cross products* are equal.

$$\text{Example:} \quad \frac{2}{3} = \frac{8}{12}$$
$$2 \times 12 = 3 \times 8$$

MODEL PROBLEMS

1. Find the unit rate if you travel 150 miles in 2.5 hours.

Solution: $\dfrac{\text{miles} \rightarrow}{\text{hours} \rightarrow} \dfrac{150}{2.5} = \dfrac{1{,}500}{25} = \dfrac{60}{1}$

Answer: The rate is 60 mph.

2. A store has a 10-oz package of oat cereal for $2.29 and a 15-oz package of the same cereal for $2.89. Which is the better buy?

Solution:

$$\dfrac{\text{price} \rightarrow}{\text{oz} \rightarrow} \dfrac{2.29}{10} = \dfrac{0.229}{1} = 0.229 \text{ cent/oz}$$

$$\dfrac{\text{price} \rightarrow}{\text{oz} \rightarrow} \dfrac{2.89}{15} = \dfrac{0.193}{1} = 0.193 \text{ cent/oz}$$

Answer: The 15-oz package is the better buy.

3. Solve: $\dfrac{1.2}{1.5} = \dfrac{x}{5}$

Solution: $(1.5)(x) = (1.2)(5)$

$$1.5x = 6$$
$$x = \dfrac{6}{1.5}$$

Answer: $x = 4$

4. In the scale on a map, 1 cm represents 250 km. What is the actual distance represented by a length of 1.75 cm?

Solution: $\dfrac{\text{cm} \rightarrow}{\text{km} \rightarrow} \dfrac{1}{250} = \dfrac{1.75}{x}$

$$x = (1.75)(250)$$

Answer: $x = 437.5$ km

5. Dominic traveled an average of 60 mph for 3 hours and 15 minutes. How far did he travel?

Solution: 15 minutes is $\dfrac{15}{60} = 0.25$ of an hour.

3 hours and 15 minutes is 3.25 hours. Using the formula, $d = rt$, Dominic traveled:

$$d = 60 \cdot 3.25$$
$$d = 195 \text{ miles}$$

Answer: Dominic traveled 195 miles.

Scale Drawings

Scale drawings involve the principles of both ratio and proportion. For example, in order to draw the plans for a building to scale, an architect must choose a particular ratio. In a drawing of a room, the scale might be 1 inch = 1 foot. Then the drawing of the room would be 12 inches by 14 inches to represent an actual room that is 12 feet by 14 feet.

A proportion is set up with the *scale ratio* to determine the actual size of objects represented by a scale drawing. The formula for the scale ratio is:

$$\text{Scale ratio} = \dfrac{\text{scaled measurements}}{\text{actual measurements}}$$

MODEL PROBLEM

In the drawing below, the scale is 2 cm = 3 feet. What are the actual measurements of the figure?

```
┌──────────────────────┐
│                      │ 6 cm
└──────────────────────┘
        18 cm
```

Solution:

To find the width, let w = width.

Use: $\dfrac{2 \text{ cm}}{3 \text{ ft}} = \dfrac{6 \text{ cm}}{w \text{ ft}}$

Then $2w = 18$ and $w = 9$.

To find the length, let ℓ = length.

Use: $\dfrac{2 \text{ cm}}{3 \text{ ft}} = \dfrac{18 \text{ cm}}{\ell \text{ ft}}$

Then $2w = 54$ and $w = 27$.

Answer: The actual dimensions are 9 feet by 27 feet.

PRACTICE

1. In a class of 25 students, there are 13 boys. What is the ratio of girls to boys?

   A) 12 : 13   B) 12 : 25   C) 13 : 12   D) 13 : 25

2. John is paid at the rate of $8.50 an hour for the first 40 hours a week that he works. He is paid time and a half for any hours over 40. What would John's gross pay be for a week in which he worked 48 hours?

   E) $340   F) $408   G) $442   H) $610

3. A basketball player makes 3 out of every 5 of her foul shots. At this rate, if she attempts 55 foul shots, how many will she miss?

   A) 50   B) 40   C) 33   D) 22

4. If three students share $180 in the ratio of 1 : 2 : 3, how much is the largest share?

   E) $30   F) $60   G) $90   H) $120

5. In a recipe, 4 eggs are used to make 36 muffins. How many eggs are needed to make 90 muffins?

   A) 8   B) 9   C) 10   D) 12

6. If 30 cards can be printed in 40 minutes, how many hours will it take to print 540 cards at the same rate?

   E) 6 hours   F) 9 hours
   G) 12 hours   H) 15 hours

7. Which proportion does NOT represent the given question?

   If 48 oz cost $1.89, what will 72 oz cost?

   A) $\dfrac{48}{1.89} = \dfrac{72}{x}$ B) $\dfrac{48}{72} = \dfrac{1.89}{x}$

   C) $\dfrac{1.89}{72} = \dfrac{x}{48}$ D) $\dfrac{1.89}{48} = \dfrac{x}{72}$

8. With which roll of film would the cost of a single exposure be less? By how much less would it be?

   a roll of 20-exposure film for $2.30
   a roll of 12-exposure film for $1.50

   E) 20 exposures, $0.08
   F) 20 exposures, $0.01
   G) 12 exposures, $0.80
   H) 12 exposures, $0.01

9. Which of the following is a better buy? Explain why.

    a 3-pack of blank videotapes for $8.85

    a 2-pack of blank videotapes for $5.95

10. Which of the following situations represents a better salary offer? Explain why.

    a salary of $504.50 per week

    $12.50 per hour for 40 hours

11. One car travels 468 miles on 18 gallons of gas. Will 40 gallons of gas be enough for the car to travel 1,200 miles? Explain.

12. Solve the given proportion: $\dfrac{28}{32} = \dfrac{x}{40}$

13. The scale on a map is $\dfrac{1}{2}$ inch = 55 miles. How far apart are two cities that are shown as being 5 inches apart on the map?

14. A city map has scale of 3 inches = 2 kilometers. If a distance of the map is 15 inches, what is the actual distance?

15. The drawing below shows the actual dimensions of a rectangular floor. Ben uses a scale of 2 inches = 8 feet to make a scale drawing. What length would he make each of the following parts in the drawing?

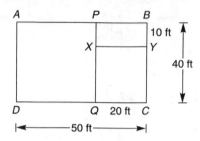

A. $\overline{XY}$ B. $\overline{AD}$ C. $\overline{PX}$

1.8 Percent

Percent means per hundred $\left(\% \text{ symbol} = \dfrac{1}{100}\right)$. A percent is a ratio that compares a number to 100.

    A percent can be written as a fraction or as a decimal.

$$25\% = 0.25 = \dfrac{1}{4}$$

> **Key Percents to Remember:**
> _____
> 100% is all.
> 50% is one-half.
> 25% is one-quarter.
> 10% is one-tenth.
> 1% is one-hundredth.
> 200% is double.

 MODEL PROBLEM

Barry's restaurant check for dinner totaled $18 before the tip. He wanted to leave a 15% tip. Explain how Barry would be able to compute the tip mentally.

Solution: 15% = 10% + 5%

    10% of $18 = $1.80   5% of $18 = $\dfrac{1}{2}$ of 10% of $18 = $0.90

Answer: 15% of $18 = $2.70

In general, percent applications involve three terms:

percentage: part of the total   *rate:* percent   *base:* total amount

To solve percent problems, use the formula: *percentage* = *rate* × *base*

 # MODEL PROBLEMS

1. At a sale, Dan paid $59 for a sweater whose price had been reduced 20%. What was the original price?

Solution:

20% reduction → sale price is
           80% of original price

59 is 80% of original price

$$p = r \times b$$
$$59 = 0.80 \times b$$
$$\frac{59}{0.80} = b$$

Answer: $73.75 = b$

2. The price of a shirt increased from $20 to $25. Find the percent of increase.

Solution:

$$\text{percent increase} = \frac{\text{increase}}{\text{original amount}},$$
$$\text{expressed as a percent}$$

$$\text{percent increase} = \frac{25 - 20}{.20}$$

$$= \frac{5}{20} = \frac{1}{4} = 25\%$$

Answer: $\frac{1}{4}$ expressed as a percent is 25%.

Calculating Interest

The principles of percents are used when calculating interest. *Interest* is a charge for money that is borrowed. You are charged interest when you take a loan from the bank. The bank pays you interest when you deposit money into an account, because the bank uses your money to carry on its business.

The *principal, p,* represents the amount of money that is invest or borrowed.

The *interest rate, r,* represents the percent charge or earned.

There are two general forms of interest, simple interest and compound interest. The formula for *simple interest* is $I = prt$, where p represents the *principal,* that is, the amount of money that is invested or borrowed, r represents the interest rate, and t represents time in years. In simple interest, the principal and amount of interest earned each year stay the same.

The formula for *compound interest* is Amount $= p\left(1 + \dfrac{r}{n}\right)^{nt}$, where p represents the principal amount, r represents the interest rate, n represents the number of times the interest is compounded per year, and t represents the time in years.

MODEL PROBLEMS

1. Robert has $500 in his savings account. If the bank pays 5% simple interest per year, how much will Robert have in his account:

   A. 1 year from now?
   B. 5 years from now?

Solutions:

A. Using the simple interest formula, $I = prt$:

   $I = (\$500)(0.05)(1)$
   $I = \$25$

Answer:
   Total amount = $500 + $25 = $525

B. Using the simple interest formula, $I = prt$:

   $I = (\$500)(0.05)(5)$
   $I = \$125$

Answer:
   Total amount = $500 + $125 = $625

2. Jessica deposited $2,500 in a bank account earning 5.25% interest compounded quarterly. How much will Jessica have in her account in 10 years?

Solution: The interest is compounded quarterly, which means 4 times a year, so $n = 4$. Using the compound interest formula,

$$\text{Amount} = p\left(1 + \frac{r}{n}\right)^{nt}:$$

$$= \$2,500\left(1 + \frac{0.525}{4}\right)^{4 \times 10}$$

Answer: $4,211.74

PRACTICE

1. The number of students in the senior class is 240. This figure is 112% of what it was the previous year. This means that:

   A) 12 more students are in the senior class now.
   B) The number of students in the senior class decreased from last year to this year.
   C) The total population of the school increased.
   D) The number of seniors increased from last year to this year.

2. Which of the following is NOT a correct statement?

   E) 63% of 63 is less than 63.
   F) 115% of 63 is more than 63.
   G) $\frac{1}{3}$% of 63 is the same as $\frac{1}{3}$ of 63.
   H) 100% of 63 is equal to 63.

3. On a math test of 25 questions, Mary scored 72%. How many questions did Mary get wrong?

   A) 7   B) 9   C) 18   D) 20

4. Laura bought a softball glove at 40% off the original price. This discount saved her $14.40. What was the original price of the glove?

   E) $5.76   F) $20.16   G) $36   H) $50.40

5. The sale price of a chair is $510 after a 15% discount has been given. Find the original price.

   A) $76.50 B) $433.50 C) $586.50 D) $600

6. The regular price of an exercise bike is $125. If it is on sale for 40% off the regular price, what is the sale price?

   E) $90   F) $80   G) $75   H) $48

7. The Sound System Store is selling AM-FM radios for $\frac{1}{3}$ off the regular price of $63. Murphy's Discount Store is selling the same radios at 25% off the regular price of $60. What is the lower sale price for the radio?

   A) $35   B) $42   C) $45   D) $48

8. Jan deposited $900 into a savings account that pays an annual 6.5% interest compounded monthly. How much money will Jan have after 2 years?

   E) 958.50   F) $1,000.00
   G) $1,017.00   H) $1,024.59

9. Mrs. Jeffrey borrowed $3,500 at 9% interest yearly. She paid back the loan after 9 months. How much did she repay in all?

   A) $6,335.00   B) $5,862.50
   C) $3,736.25   D) $3,657.50

10. If a price is doubled, it is increased by ___%.

11. If you needed to compute $33\frac{1}{3}$% of $45 without a calculator, would it be better to represent $33\frac{1}{3}$% as a fraction or a decimal? Explain your response.

12. When the sales-tax rate decreased from 7% to 6%, how much less in sales tax did you pay when purchasing an item priced at $480?

13. To obtain a score of 75% on a test containing 40 questions, how many questions must Juan get correct?

14. On a 10 × 10 grid, 31 squares are shaded. How many squares would have to be shaded on a 5 × 10 grid in order to have the same percent of the total squares shaded?

15. The cost of a first-class stamp increased from 32¢ to 37¢. Find the percent of increase.

16. The enrollment in a school went from 750 students to 600 students over a 10-year period. Find the percent of decrease.

17. Using the simple interest formula, $I = prt$, what is the interest on $400 borrowed at 6% for 2 years?

18. Norma received a commission of 5% on her sales. Her gross sales for November were $12,500. How much more would she receive if her commission were raised to 7%?

19. Is there a difference between buying an item at 50% off the regular price versus buying an item reduced by 30%, and then reduced by an additional 20%? Give examples to justify your answer.

20. Jackson and Lisa each deposited $1,500 into a savings account. Jackson's bank pays 6% interest yearly. Lisa's bank pays 7.5% interest compounded monthly. After 2 years,

    A. who will have more money in his or her account?
    B. what will the difference be between the two savings accounts?

1. Which of the following types of numbers would solve the equation $x^2 = 45$?

   A) Whole numbers   B) Rational numbers
   C) Integers   D) Irrational numbers

2. Which equation below represents the following situation? To qualify to be a member of the school's math team, a student's cumulative points on a qualifying exam must be within 15 points of 275.

   E) $|x - 15| \leq 275$ F) $x - 275 \leq 15$
   G) $x - 15 \leq 275$ H) $|x - 275| \leq 15$

3. Which of the following represents a commutative operation?

   A) $a * b = a^2 - b$ B) $a * b = 4(a + b)$
   C) $a * b = a^b$ D) $a * b = a \div (3b)$

4. Which of the following is NOT equal to the other three?

   E) 1.5×10^1 F) $\dfrac{15}{10}$ G) 150% H) $\sqrt{2.25}$

5. Which of the following numbers is between $\dfrac{1}{10,000}$ and $\dfrac{1}{100,000}$, and is also correctly expressed in scientific notation?

   A) 4.5×10^{-3} B) 4.5×10^3
   C) 4.5×10^{-4} D) 4.5×10^{-5}

6. A $32 sweater is reduced by 25% for a holiday sale. By what percent must the sale price of the sweater be multiplied to restore the price to the original price before the sale?

   E) $133\frac{1}{3}\%$ F) 125% G) 25% H) 8%

7. The members of the Decorating Committee for a school dance have 24 red carnations, 32 white carnations, and 40 pink carnations. They want to form as many identical centerpieces as possible, using all of the carnations so that each centerpiece has the same combination of colors as all of the other centerpieces. How many pink carnations will each centerpiece have?

   A) 4   B) 5   C) 8   D) 10

8. Which of the following is NOT a way to find 120% of a number?

   E) Multiply the number by 1.20.
   F) Divide the number by 5 and add the result to the number.
   G) Divide the number by 5 and multiply the result by 6.
   H) Multiply the number by 0.20 and multiply the result by 5.

9. On some days, a bakery packages cupcakes 4 to a box. On other days, cupcakes are packaged in boxes of 6 or 8. On a given day, after the cupcakes were packaged, there was one cupcake left over. Which of the following could NOT be the number of cupcakes baked on that day?

   A) 22   B) 25   C) 49   D) 97

10. There are three times as many girls as boys in the Spanish Club of Central High School. If there are 36 members in the club, how many of them are boys?

    E) 9   F) 12   G) 15   H) 27

11. Light travels at a speed of about 186,281.7 miles per second. How far would light travel in 365 days?

    A) 5.87×10^{12} miles   B) 6.79×10^7 miles
    C) 7.05×10^{13} miles   D) 9.7×10^{10} miles

12. Mr. Kim, a salesperson, is paid $300 a week plus commission. His commission is 5% of his weekly sales. In the month of January, his weekly sales totals were:

Week 1	Week 2	Week 3	Week 4
$8,576	$9,500	$7,362	$10,567

What was his average weekly commission?

E) $429   F) $450   G) $528   H) $1,800

13. Knowing that $2^3 = 2 \times 2 \times 2 = 8$, what number in the box would make the following TRUE?

$$8^6 = 2^\square$$

A) 9   B) 15   C) 18   D) 24

14. Miranda earns $7.50 an hour for the first 40 hours a week she works. She earns time and a half for any hours over 40 she works during the week and double time for hours worked on the weekend. Her time card for one week is shown below. How much did Miranda earn?

Mon.	Tues.	Wed.	Thurs.	Fri.	Sat.
$8\frac{1}{2}$	9	$9\frac{1}{2}$	8	7	$3\frac{1}{2}$

E) $341.25   F) $361.88
G) $375   H) $382.50

15. A fraction is equivalent to $\frac{3}{8}$. The sum of the numerator and denominator is 33. What is the fraction?

16. Suppose you visited Canada and took $325 to spend. The rate of currency exchange was $1.1515 Canadian dollars per U.S. dollar. To the nearest dollar, how many Canadian dollars would you get for the exchange?

17. Helene is paid at the rate of $6.50 an hour for the first 40 hours a week that she works. She is paid time and a half for any hours over 40. How much more will Helene make working 50 hours compared with working 46 hours?

18. If five students share $450 in the ratio 1 : 2 : 3 : 4 : 5, how much is the largest share?

19. A baseball player's batting average is the ratio of the number of hits to the official number of times at bat. A player had 150 hits during a season and wound up with a batting average of .300. What was the total number of times he was at bat for the season?

20. A printer charges 4.2 cents per copy of a standard size original. There is an additional charge of one-half cent for each copy on colored paper. How much would you pay for 100 copies of an original on white paper and 100 copies on blue paper?

21. Ground beef sells for $2.19 per pound. If a package of ground beef costs $4.25, what is the weight of the package to the nearest hundredth of a pound?

22. Because of a printer malfunction, Harold could not read some of the information on the monthly statement from his checking account. From the information given, find the closing balance of Harold's account.

Account Summary			
Number 00-537-387-5			
Beginning balance 08/01		875.45	
3 deposits/credits		xxxxxxx	
3 checks/debits		xxxxxxx	
service charge		xxxxxxx	
Ending balance 08/31			
Date	**Amount**	**Date**	**Amount**
08/02	135.00+	08/22	35.92−
08/05	163.50−	08/25	214.35+
08/11	14.75−	08/29 printing checks	11.45−
		08/31 interest	3.45+

23. Mary puts $1,500 in a bank certificate that pays an annual rate of 4.5% compounded annually. No withdrawals or deposits are made. How much will the certificate be worth (to the nearest dollar) at the end of 7 years?

24. If a principal of $1,000 is saved at an annual yield of 8% and the interest is kept in the account, in how many years will the principal double in value?

25. The cost of a hamburger goes from $2.00 to $2.25. Determine the percent of increase. Explain your approach.

26. In York City, the sales-tax rate is increased from 7% to 7.25%. Under this change, how much additional tax would you pay for an item priced at $800? Show your process in determining the answer.

27. The scale on a map is $\frac{1}{2}$ inch = 80 miles. How far apart are two cities that are $4\frac{3}{4}$ inches apart on the map? Explain your answer and approach.

28. If 4, 5, and 7 are factors of a number, list four other numbers that would also be factors of the number.

OPEN-ENDED QUESTIONS

29. Your friend applies the Distributive Property to multiplication and determines 2(3 × 5) = 2(3) × 2(5). Write a paragraph explaining how you would convince your friend that he is incorrect.

30. Every Monday at Capri Pizza, lucky customers can get free slices of pizza and free soda. Every 10th customer gets a free plain slice of pizza and every 12th customer gets a free cup of soda. On the first Monday of March, Capri Pizza had 211 customers.

    A. How many free pizza slices were given away? How many cups of soda were given away?

    B. When Jackie came into Capri Pizza, the owner told her that she was the first person to get both free items (the free slice of pizza and the free soda). What number customer must Jackie have been? How many other customers (from the 211 customers) would also get both free items?

    C. Suppose that the owner also decides to give away free bag of potato chips to every 7th customer. Would any of the 211 customers be lucky enough to get all three free items? Explain.

31. Your local supermarket offers two brands of cheese sticks:

    Brand A: 12-ounce package for $2.49

    Brand B: 15-ounce package for $3.19

    A. Which is the better buy? Show how you arrived at your answer.

    B. Suppose the one that is a better buy now has a 10% price increase. Is it still the better buy? Explain.

32. Given: $0.4 < A < 0.5$
    $$0.7 < B < 0.9$$
    $$0 < C < 0.1$$
    $$1 < D < 2$$
    $$4 < E < 5$$

    If $X = A + B$, note that the number line shows a possible location of X.

    Using the number line below, insert a mark and a capital letter to show one possible location for each of the following:

    - P if $P = A \times B$
    - Q if $Q = B^2$
    - R if $R = 3C - 3D$
    - S if $S = \sqrt{E}$

    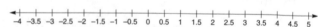

    Explain your locations for any two of the four questions.

CHAPTER 2

Spatial Sense and Geometry

2.1 Geometric Terms

Term	Illustration	Definition
point	$\cdot A$	a basic undefined term (A point has no dimensions.)
line ($\overleftrightarrow{AB}$)	A B	a basic undefined term (A line has one dimension.)
ray ($\overrightarrow{AB}$)	A B	the part of line AB that contains point A and all the points of AB that are on the same side of point A as point B
line segment ($\overline{AB}$)	A B	two points and all the points between them that lie on the line containing the two points
midpoint	M A B	the point on a line segment that divides it into two equal lengths
plane		a basic undefined term (A plane has two dimensions.)
polygon		a closed figure in a plane formed by three or more sides that are line segments with common endpoints (Each side intersects exactly two other sides, but only at their endpoints.)

Term	Illustration	Definition
vertex of a polygon		a point where two adjacent sides meet
diagonal of a polygon		a segment joining nonconsecutive vertices of the polygon
polyhedron		a closed 3-dimensional figure made up of flat polygonal regions
vertex		in a polyhedron, where three or more edges intersect
edge		in a polyhedron, a line segment in which a pair of faces intersect
face		in a polyhedron, the flat polygonal surfaces that intersect to form the edges of the polyhedron
angle (∠ABC)		two rays that share a common endpoint
acute angle		an angle that measures between 0° and 90°
obtuse angle		an angle that measures between 90° and 180°
right angle		an angle that measures 90°
straight angle		an angle that measures 180°

Term	Illustration	Definition
angle bisector		a ray that divides an angle into two congruent angles
adjacent angles		two angles that have the same vertex and a common side between them $\angle 1$ and $\angle 2$ are adjacent. $\angle 2$ and $\angle 3$ are adjacent. $\angle 1$ and $\angle 3$ are not adjacent.
vertical angles		a pair of congruent angles, formed by two intersecting lines, that have a common vertex and are not adjacent $\angle 1 \cong \angle 3$ $\angle 2 \cong \angle 4$
complementary angles		two angles whose measures have a sum of 90°
supplementary angles		two angles whose measures have a sum of 180°

MODEL PROBLEMS

1. Draw and label a figure to illustrate the following situation. Planes *A* and *B* intersect. Planes *B* and *C* intersect, but planes *A* and *C* do not intersect.

Solution:

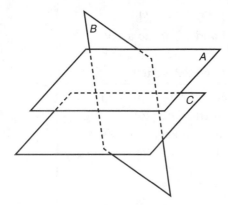

2. The measures of two supplementary angles are in the ratio of 2 : 3. What is the degree measure of the larger angle?

Solution:

$$2x + 3x = 180°$$
$$5x = 180°$$
$$x = 36°$$

The larger angle is $3x$, so $3(36°) = 108°$.

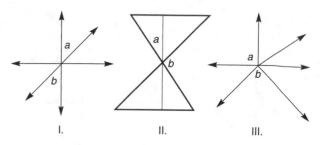

PRACTICE

1. What is the measure of the complement of the complement of an angle of 30°?

   A) 30°
   B) 60°
   C) 120°
   D) 250°

2. The measures of two supplementary angles are in the ratio of 4 : 5. What is the degree measure of the smaller angle?

   E) 20°
   F) 80°
   G) 100°
   H) 160°

3. In which of the following diagrams are $\angle a$ and $\angle b$ vertical angles?

   I.   II.   III.

   A) I only   B) I and II
   C) I and III   D) I, II, and III

4. Which of the following statements is always TRUE?

   E) Vertical angles are supplementary.
   F) The complement of an obtuse angle is acute.
   G) The supplement of an obtuse angle is acute.
   H) Complementary angles are congruent.

5. Draw and label the following figure. Planes P and Q intersect each other. They both intersect plane R.

6. If D is the midpoint of $\overline{AC}$ and C is the midpoint of $\overline{AB}$, what is the length of $\overline{AB}$ if $BD = 12$ cm?

7. If $\overrightarrow{BD}$ is the angle bisector of $\angle ABC$ and $\overrightarrow{BE}$ is the angle bisector of $\angle ABD$, what is m$\angle ABC$ if m$\angle DBE = 36$?

8. If a polyhedron has 8 faces and 12 vertices, how many edges will it have?

9. A polygon has 9 diagonals. How many sides does it have?

10. Find the measure of the angle made by the hands of a clock at 4:30.

2.2 Properties of Geometric Figures

Polygons

A *polygon* is a closed figure in a plane formed by three or more sides that have common endpoints. Each side intersects exactly two other sides but only at their endpoints.

Polygons may be classified by number of sides:

3—triangle	7—heptagon
4—quadrilateral	8—octagon
5—pentagon	9—nonagon
6—hexagon	10—decagon

n—n-gon

A *regular polygon* is a convex polygon with all sides congruent and all angles congruent.

The sum of the measures of the interior angles of a convex polygon with n sides is $S = 180°(n - 2)$.

 MODEL PROBLEM

ABCDE is a regular pentagon. What is the measure of each interior angle of the figure?

Solution: Since a pentagon has 5 sides, $n = 5$. Therefore, to find the sum of the measures of the interior angles of the pentagon, use the formula $S = 180°(n - 2)$

$$= 180°(5 - 2)$$
$$= 180°(3) = 540°$$

Since the pentagon is regular, all angles are equal. Therefore, to find the measure of each interior angle, divide 540 by 5. Each interior angle equals 108 degrees.

Triangles

In a triangle, the sum of the lengths of any two sides must be greater than the length of the third side. The sum of the interior angles of a triangle is 180°.

Classification of Triangles:	

1. *by number of congruent sides:*
    no sides congruent: *scalene triangle*
    two sides congruent: *isosceles triangle*
    all sides congruent: *equilateral triangle*
	2. *by types of angles:*
	    one right angle: *right triangle*
	    one obtuse angle: *obtuse triangle*
	    all acute angles: *acute triangle*

 MODEL PROBLEMS

1. In $\triangle ABC$, $m\angle A = 52$ and $m\angle B = 12$. Classify $\triangle ABC$ as acute, right, or obtuse.

Solution: The sum of the angles of the triangle is 180°.

$52 + 12 = 64$

$180 - 64 = 116$

$m\angle C = 116$. $\angle C$ is an obtuse angle.

Answer: $\triangle ABC$ is an obtuse triangle.

2. If two sides of a triangle have lengths of 4 cm and 7 cm, what is the range of lengths that is possible for the third side?

Solution: The sum of the measures of any two sides of the triangle must be greater than the third side.

CASE 1: 7 cm represents the longest side.

the third side + 4 cm > 7 cm

the third side > 3 cm

CASE 2: The third side is the longest side.

7 cm + 4 cm > the third side

11 cm > the third side

Answer: 3 cm < the third side < 11 cm

Quadrilaterals

Special quadrilaterals are classified on the basis of lengths of sides, angle measure, and parallel sides.

Name	Illustration	Characteristics
parallelogram		quadrilateral with both pairs of opposite sides parallel and congruent quadrilateral with both pairs of opposite angles congruent
rectangle		parallelogram with right angles
rhombus		parallelogram with all sides congruent
square		rhombus with right angles
trapezoid		quadrilateral with one pair of opposite sides parallel
isosceles trapezoid		trapezoid with congruent legs

1. Which of the following statements is true?

   A) All rectangles are parallelograms.
   B) All parallelograms are rectangles.
   C) All quadrilaterals are trapezoids.
   D) All trapezoids are parallelograms.

Solution: A rectangle is a special parallelogram with right angles. Therefore, any rectangle must be a parallelogram.

Answer: A

2. A quadrilateral *ABCD* has vertices *A*(0, 0), *B*(6, 0), *C*(7, 5), *D*(1, 5). What is the best name for quadrilateral *ABCD*?

   E) Rectangle   F) Trapezoid
   G) Parallelogram   H) Rhombus

Solution: Plot the points (all of which are in the first *quadrant*) and examine the properties of the resulting figure.

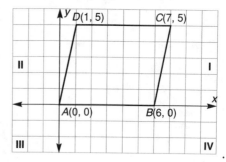

Since both pairs of opposite sides are parallel, the figure is a parallelogram. Since adjacent sides are not congruent, it is not a rhombus. Since there are no right angles, it is not a rectangle.

Answer: G

Circles

A *circle* is a closed plane figure that represents all of the points a specified distance from a point called the *center*.

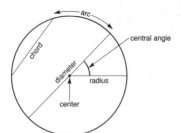

The *radius* of a circle is a line segment with one endpoint at center of the circle and the other on the circle. The length of the radius, *r*, is $\frac{1}{2}$ the diameter, *d*. $\left(r = \frac{1}{2}d \right)$

A *chord* is a line segment with both endpoints on the circle.

The *diameter* of a circle is a chord that passes through the center of the circle. The length of the diameter, *d*, is twice the length of the radius, *r*. ($d = 2r$)

The *central angle* of a circle is an angle formed by two radii. The radii intercept an arc.

An *arc* is a part of a circle. A *major arc* is an arc whose measure is greater than 180°. A *minor arc* is an arc whose measure is less than 180°.

A *tangent* to a circle is a line, ray, or line segment that is drawn outside of the circle and touches the circle at only one point.

A *secant* of a circle is a line that intersects the circle in two points

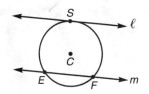

ℓ is a tangent to circle C.
m is a secant on circle C.

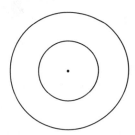

If two or more cicles have the same center, they are known as *concentric circles*.

MODEL PROBLEM

A circle with a center at (5, 0) passes through the point (1, 0). What is the length of a diameter of the circle?

Solution: Since the center is at (5, 0) and (1, 0) is on the circle, the length of a radius is the distance from (5, 0) to (1, 0), or 4 units.

Answer: A diameter has a length of 8 units.

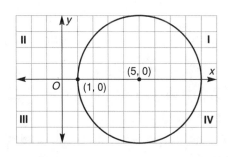

PRACTICE

1. Which of the following sets of lengths does NOT represent a triangle?

   A) 1, 1, 1   B) 3, 4, 5
   C) 4, 4, 8   D) 5, 12, 13

2. If the measure of one angle of a triangle is equal to the sum of the measures of the other two, then the triangle is always:

   E) acute   F) obtuse
   G) right   H) isosceles

3. Which of the following cannot exist?

   A) Isosceles right triangle
   B) Isosceles obtuse triangle
   C) Scalene right triangle
   D) Right obtuse triangle

4. The measures of the angles of a triangle are in the ratio of 2 : 2 : 5. What type of triangle is it?

   E) Isosceles triangle   F) Acute triangle
   G) Right triangle   H) Scalene triangle

5. In parallelogram *ABCD*, what is the measure of ∠C?

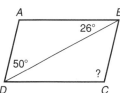

   A) 76°   B) 86°   C) 100°   D) 104°

6. Quadrilateral *ABCD* has vertices at $A(-2, 2)$, $B(-2, -4)$, $C(5, -8)$, $D(5, 6)$. What is the most specific name for the quadrilateral?

   E) Parallelogram   F) Isosceles trapezoid

   G) Trapezoid   H) Rectangle

7. Triangle *ABC* has vertices $A(1, 6)$, $B(10, 3)$, $C(1, 3)$. Which of the following must be TRUE concerning $\angle A$ and $\angle B$?

   A) They are congruent.

   B) They are supplementary.

   C) One is twice as large as the other.

   D) They are complementary.

8. A circle has its center at $(4, 0)$ and a radius of 5 units. Which quadrant(s) does the circle pass through?

   E) I only   F) I and II

   G) I and IV   H) All four

9. Which of the following statements is TRUE?

   I. A rhombus with right angles is a square.

   II. A rectangle is a square.

   III. A parallelogram with right angles is a square.

   A) I only   B) II only

   C) III only   D) I and III

10. A pentagon has two right angles. What is the sum of the measures of the other three angles?

    E) 108°   F) 360°   G) 450°   H) 540°

11. Which of the following could NOT be the sum of the measures of the interior angles of a polygon?

    A) 720°   B) 1,080°   C) 1,900°   D) 1,980°

12. A circle with its center at *P* has a radius of 5 cm. Line segment *PQ* measures 6 cm and line segment *PR* measures 5.1 cm. Which of the following is a TRUE statement?

    E) Points *Q* and *R* are inside the circle.

    F) Points *Q* and *R* are on the circle.

    G) Points *Q* and *R* are outside the circle.

    H) The distance from point *R* to point *Q* is 0.9 cm.

13. Three concentric circles are shown. The diameter of the largest circle is 16 units. The diameter of the middle circle is 12 units and the diameter of the smallest circle is 10 units. What is the distance between the smallest circle and the middle circle?

    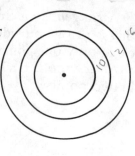

    A) 1   B) 2   C) 4   D) 6

14. A circular swimming pool has a diameter of 20 feet. Two poles for a volleyball net are each placed 15 feet from the center of the pool and as far apart as possible. What is the length of net needed to be strung tautly between the two poles? (Assume the net extends pole to pole.)

15. In quadrilateral *ABCD*, $A(0, 0)$, $B(0, 5)$, $C(4, 11)$, $D(4, k)$. What value of *k* will make *ABCD* a parallelogram?

16. There are 50 paper quadrilaterals in a box. If 18 are rectangles, 30 are rhombuses, and 7 are squares, how many of the quadrilaterals would be of a type other than rectangle, rhombus, or square?

17. Two vertices of a triangle are $(0, 0)$ and $(6, 0)$. List four possible sets of coordinates for the third vertex such that the triangle would be a right scalene triangle.

18. Explain why the measure of $\angle a$ equals the measure of $\angle c$.

    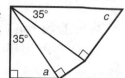

19. Draw the diagram resulting from the following directions. Rectangle *ABCD* has side *AD* removed. Segments drawn from *A* and *D* meet at point *E*, outside the rectangle, such that $m\angle E = 100$. What type of polygon is *ABCDE*? What is the sum of the measures of $\angle EAB$ and $\angle EDC$? Explain your justification for the answer to this last question.

20. Two sides of a triangle each measure 8 cm.

 A. Divide the following list of integers into two groups.

 1, 2, 3, 8, 10, 12, 18, 20, 30

 Group 1: possible lengths for the third side of the triangle

 Group 2: lengths that are not possible for the third side of the triangle.

 B. What is the smallest positive integer that cannot represent the length of the third side?

 C. For the triangles that are possible, with sides of integral lengths, draw and label the lengths of the sides for one acute triangle and one obtuse triangle.

21. One angle of a triangle has a measure equal to half the measure of each of the other two angles.

 A. Classify this triangle according to sides.

 B. Write an equation (using x as a variable) you could use to find the measures of the angles of the triangle.

 C. What are the measures of the three angles of this triangle?

 D. Explain why you cannot find the perimeter of this triangle.

22. If two circles have unequal radii, there are different configurations that can be drawn to show how these circles might intersect. Here is a configuration in which the two circles intersect in two points.

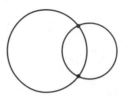

 A. Draw as many different diagrams as necessary to show all other possible ways the two circles can be pictured in terms of points of intersection.

 B. A circle has center at (0, 0) and a radius of 5 units. A second circle has a center at (0, 7) and a radius of 4. Show a sketch of these circles in order to determine the number of points of intersection between them.

2.3 Geometric Relationships

Lines

In a plane, distinct lines will either *intersect* or be *parallel*. **Perpendicular lines** intersect at right angles.

 Lines will be parallel if certain relationships exist between pairs of angles formed when the lines are cut by a third line, called a **transversal.**

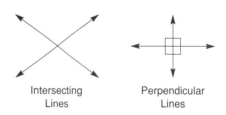

Intersecting Lines   Perpendicular Lines

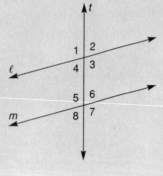

1. alternate interior angles are congruent.

∠4 and ∠6, ∠3 and ∠5 are alternate interior angles.

2. corresponding angles are congruent.

∠1 and ∠5, ∠2 and ∠6, ∠4 and ∠8, ∠3 and ∠7 are corresponding angles.

3. interior angles on the same side of the transversal are supplementary.

∠4 and ∠5, ∠3 and ∠6 are interior angles on the same side of the transversal.

Conversely, if you know the lines are parallel, then you know that the angle relationships are true.

Skew lines are lines that do not intersect and are not in the same plane.

 # MODEL PROBLEMS

1. Line *a* is parallel to line *b*. Line *c* is perpendicular to line *b*. Line *d* is parallel to line *c*. Line *e* is perpendicular to line *d*. How is line *a* related to line *e*?

Solution: Draw a diagram to determine the relationship.

Answer:

Line *e* is parallel to line *a*.

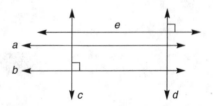

2. In the given diagram, ∠5 is congruent to ∠13 (in symbols, ∠5 ≅ ∠13). Based on that information, what pairs of lines can you conclude are parallel?

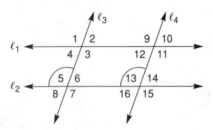

Solution: ∠5 and ∠13 are corresponding angles formed by ℓ_3 and ℓ_4 being cut by ℓ_2. Since ∠5 ≅ ∠13, $\ell_3 \parallel \ell_4$. Since no additional information is provided about angles, you cannot conclude that ℓ_1 is parallel to ℓ_2.

3. $\ell \parallel m$. Find the measure of *x*.

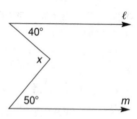

Solution: Draw in line *r* such that $r \parallel \ell$ and $r \parallel m$. m∠1 = 40 and m∠2 = 50 by alternate interior angle relations. Hence, *x* = 40 + 50 = 90.

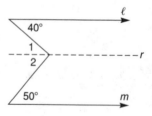

1. How many pairs of skew lines are represented by the edges of a cube?

   A) 0   B) 6   C) 12   D) 24

2. *ACDF* is a rectangle divided into two squares. How many pairs of line segments in the diagram are perpendicular?

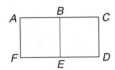

   E) 3   F) 4   G) 6   H) 14

3. If ray *AB* is perpendicular to ray *AC*, what is the measure of $\angle EAG$?

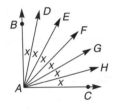

   A) 15°   B) 30°   C) 36°   D) 60°

4. Based on the diagram, which of the following may be FALSE?

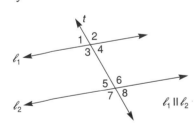

   E) $\angle 1 \cong \angle 4$
   F) $\angle 1 \cong \angle 5$
   G) $\angle 1$ is supplementary to $\angle 3$
   H) $\angle 1 \cong \angle 7$

5. Given $\overleftrightarrow{AB} \perp \overleftrightarrow{CD}$ and $\overline{FG} \parallel \overline{EH}$, which of the following would be true about triangles *EOH* and *GOF*?

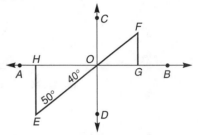

   A) The two triangles are congruent.
   B) The two triangles are congruent right triangles.
   C) The two triangles are isosceles.
   D) The two triangles are similar right triangles.

6. In the diagram, if $\ell_1 \parallel \ell_2$, $\ell_2 \parallel \ell_3$, and $\ell_1 \perp \ell_4$, which of the following statements must be true?

   I. $\ell_1 \parallel \ell_3$ II. $\ell_2 \perp \ell_4$ III. $\ell_3 \perp \ell_4$

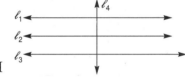

   E) I only
   F) II only
   G) I and II
   H) I, II, and III

7. How many pairs of parallel lines are shown?

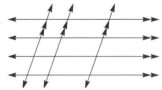

8. For this diagram, you are told that $m\angle 3 = m\angle 5$. How does the appearance of the diagram contradict the given information? Write out an explanation.

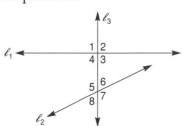

2.4 Inductive and Deductive Reasoning

Deductive reasoning is a system of reasoning used to reach conclusions that must be true whenever the assumption on which the reasoning is based is true.

  Inductive reasoning is reasoning that uses a number of specific examples to arrive at generalizations or predictions.

 MODEL PROBLEMS

1. Here is a deductive proof that the measure of an exterior angle of a triangle is equal to the sum of the two nonadjacent interior angles.

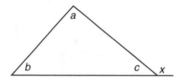

$m\angle a + m\angle b + m\angle c = 180$	measures of angles of a triangle total 180°
$m\angle c + m\angle x = 180$	supplementary angles
$m\angle a + m\angle b + m\angle c = m\angle c + m\angle x$	substitution
$m\angle a + m\angle b = m\angle x$	subtraction property of equality

If you wanted to explore this theorem through inductive reasoning, discuss the approach you would use.

Solution:

Draw several different triangles with one exterior angle shown. Using a protractor, measure the exterior angle and the two nonadjacent interior angles in each of the triangles. Compare the sum of the two interior angles with the measure of the exterior angle. Conclude they are the same.

2. Given that $\angle A$ and $\angle C$ are complementary angles and $\angle B$ and $\angle C$ are complementary angles, which of the following conclusions follows?

  A) $\angle A$ and $\angle B$ are complementary   B) $\angle A \cong \angle B$ C) $\angle A \cong \angle B \cong \angle C$
  D) $\angle A, \angle B, \angle C$ are supplementary

Solution:

If $\angle A$ and $\angle C$ are complementary then, $m\angle A + m\angle C = 90$.

If $\angle B$ and $\angle C$ are complementary then, $m\angle B + m\angle C = 90$.

It follows that $m\angle A + m\angle C = m\angle B + m\angle C$. Therefore, $m\angle A = m\angle B$ and $\angle A \cong \angle B$.

Answer: B

PRACTICE

1. Using a ruler and grid paper or an automatic drawing program, give evidence of the following theorem:

   "A point on the perpendicular bisector of a line segment is equidistant from the endpoints of the segment."

2. Use induction to show evidence of the following theorem:

   "If two parallel lines are cut by a transversal, then each pair of corresponding angles is congruent."

3. Determine if the given conjecture is true or false. Explain your answer and give a *counterexample* (a false example) if the conjecture is false.

   Given: $ABCD$ is a rectangle.
   Conjecture: $AB = BC$ and $CD = DA$

4. If $\triangle PQR$ is equilateral then $m\angle P = 60$. If $m\angle P \neq 60$, then what can you conclude?

5. Does the conclusion follow from the given argument? If yes, explain why; if no, explain why not.

   If three angles of a triangle are acute, then the triangle is acute. In $\triangle DEF$, angle D and angle F are acute. Therefore, $\triangle DEF$ is acute.

2.5 Logic

Open and Closed Sentences

Logic is an example of deductive reasoning, which is the process of using mathematical sentences to arrive at conclusions. A simple declarative sentence that states a complete idea is called a *mathematical sentence*.

A *statement* is a sentence that can be either true or false. The truth value of a statement can be easily determined. Sentences that can neither be true nor false are not statements; these include questions, commands, and exclamations. If the sentence does not contain variables or replacement pronouns, it is a *closed sentence*, for example, "Every hour has sixty minutes." This statement is true.

Open sentences contain unknown pronouns, such as *he, she, they, it,* or variables. Unlike closed sentences, the truth value of an open sentence cannot be determined until the unknown or variable is replaced. Otherwise, open sentences can be neither true nor false; they will have no truth value. A *solution set* for an open sentence is the set of all replacements for the pronouns that will make the sentence true. For example:

Sentence	Unknown	Solution Set
1. $x + 5 = 9$	The variable x.	{4}
2. He was the twenty-sixth president of the United States.	The unknown pronouns is *he*.	{Theodore Roosevelt}

Truth Tables

Most explanations of logical relationships assign letters to statements because it is a helpful shorthand for writing them. The letters most commonly used are p, q, and r. For example, if p represents "Philadelphia is in Pennsylvania," then we can say that p is a true statement.

When we need to study all the possible truth values assigned to a statement, we would use a truth table. A *truth table* is a compact way of listing all of the possible truth values for a statement that is represented by the letter assigned to it.

Negations

A statement and its negation have opposite truth values. For example, if the statement "It is sunny out" is true, then its *negation*, "It is not sunny out," is false.

The shorthand symbol for negation is ~ . If p in the example above is a true statement, then $\sim p$ is a false statement. On the other hand, if p is false, then $\sim p$ is true.

A double negation means the same as the original statement. For example, "It is not true that it is not raining out" has the same meaning as "It is raining out."

The truth values for a statement and its negation can be shown in a truth table.

 MODEL PROBLEM

Let p represent the original statement: "An orange is fruit." It's negation would be represented by $\sim p$: "An orange is not a fruit."

Solution: Set up a table listing all the possible truth values for the original statement, p, in the first column. List all the possible truth values for the negation of the original statement, $\sim p$, in the second column.

p	$\sim p$
T	F
F	T

Conjunctions and Disjunctions

A compound statement is formed by combining simple statements with connectives such as *and*, *or*, and *if/then*. Take, for example, these two simple statements:

It is cold outside.

I wear a sweater.

Three basic compound statements can be formed with these two statements.

- It is cold outside *and* I wear a sweater.
- It is cold outside *or* I wear a sweater.
- *If* it is cold outside, *then* I wear a sweater.

A compound sentence that is formed by connecting two simple statements using the word *and* is called a **conjunction**. The shorthand symbol for the word *and* is $\wedge$. A sentence *p and q* can be represented symbolically as $p \wedge q$.

p: Today is Wednesday.

q: I have hockey practice.

$p \wedge q$: Today is Wednesday *and* I have hockey practice.

In order for a conjunction to be true, both parts that form the statement must be true. The conjunction is false if either or both parts are false. For example,

p: Bananas are fruits.	(true statement)
q: Chocolate is a vegetable.	(false statement)
$p \wedge q$: Bananas are fruits *and* chocolate is a vegetable.	(false statement)

A compound sentence that is formed by connecting two simple sentences using the word *or* is called a **disjunction**. The shorthand symbol that represents the word *or* is $\vee$. Symbolically, the sentence *p or q* can be represented as $p \vee q$. For the disjunction to be false, both parts of the compound sentence must be false. When either part or both parts of the compound sentence are true, the disjunction is true.

Let us now observe how the truth values differ in a compound sentence when the word *and* is replaced with the word *or*. We can do this by using the example we used for conjunctions.

p: Bananas are fruits.	(true statement)
q: Chocolate is a vegetable.	(false statement)
$p \vee q$: Bananas are fruits *or* chocolate is a vegetable.	(true statement)

A truth table can be constructed to summarize the truth values for conjunctions and disjunctions.

p	*q*	$p \wedge q$	$p \vee q$
T	T	T	T
F	T	F	T
T	F	F	T
F	F	F	F

MODEL PROBLEM

The truth values for the first two sentences of the three sentences are given below. Determine the truth value of the third sentence.

Jack likes fish and Jennifer likes steak.   (False)

Jack likes fish.   (True)

Jennifer likes steak.   (?)

Solution:

Step 1   Represent the sentences by using symbols and indicate their truth values.

$p \wedge q$ (False):   Jack likes fish and Jennifer likes steak.

p (True):   Jack likes fish.

q (?):   Jennifer likes steak.

Step 2   Construct a truth table for the conjunction. Cross out the rows of the truth table that do not agree with the information given.

p	q	$p \wedge q$
~~T~~	~~T~~	~~T~~
T	F	F
~~F~~	~~T~~	~~F~~
~~F~~	~~F~~	~~F~~

Notice that there is only one case where $p \wedge q$ is false and where p is true. Since the only case occurs in row 2 of the truth table, the truth value of q in row 2 is false. Therefore, you can conclude that the sentence q, "Jennifer likes steak," is false.

Answer: "Jennifer likes steak" is false.

Conditionals

A conditional is a compound sentence that is formed by combining two simple sentences using the words *If . . . then*. The *If* part of the sentence is called the *premise*, the **hypothesis**, or the **antecedent**. The *then* part of the sentence is called the *conclusion* or the *consequent*. A conditional statement can be represented symbolically as $p \rightarrow q$ and is read "If p then q" or "p implies q." For example,

Hypothesis (p):   I wear a hat.

Conclusion (q):   It is cold out.

Conditional ($p \rightarrow q$):   *If* I wear a hat, *then* it is cold out.

Statements not written in *If . . . then* form can often be rephrased. For example,

A quadratic equation can be solved easily if it is factored.

Conditional form: *If* a quadratic equation is factored, *then* it can be solved easily.

Hypothesis: A quadratic equation is factored.

Conclusion: It can be solved easily.

A conditional statement has a false truth value if and only if the hypothesis is true and the conclusion is false. For example,

p:	Today is Monday.	(true statement)
q:	Tomorrow is Thursday.	(false statement)
$p \rightarrow q$:	If today is Monday, then tomorrow is Thursday.	(false statement)

 **MODEL PROBLEM**

Both parts of the statement "If John lives in Florida, then he lives in Orlando" are true. Choose the statement that is *false*.

A) If John doesn't live in Florida, then he doesn't live in Orlando.
B) If John lives in Orlando, then he lives in Florida.
C) If John doesn't live in Orlando, then he doesn't live in Florida.
D) If John lives in Orlando, he does not live in Florida.

Answer: D In this case the hypothesis is true and conclusion is false. Therefore, the conditional is false.

Converses, Inverses, and Contrapositives

Converses, inverses, and contrapositives are formed from a given conditional statement. For example, we are given the conditional statement:

If it is morning, the sun is out.

Hypothesis: It is morning.

Conclusion: The sun is out.

If the hypothesis and conclusion are interchanged, the *converse* of the conditional is formed:

If the sun is out, then it is morning.

The *inverse* of a conditional statement is formed by negating both is hypothesis and its conclusion:

If it is not morning, then the sun is not out.

The *contrapositive* of a conditional statement is formed by interchanging the hypothesis and conclusion of the inverse of the conditional statement:

If the sun is not out, then it is not morning.

The truth values of these three new conditionals can best summarized in a truth table, where p is the hypothesis and q is the conclusion. The truth value of each conditional is determined by the truth value of its components.

p	q	$\sim p$	$\sim q$	Conditional $p \rightarrow q$	Converse $q \rightarrow p$	Inverse $\sim p \rightarrow \sim q$	Contrapositive $\sim q \rightarrow \sim p$
T	T	F	F	T	T	T	T
T	F	F	T	F	T	T	F
F	T	T	F	T	F	F	T
F	F	T	T	T	T	T	T

When two statements always have the same truth value, they are *logically equivalent*. Notice that in the above table, the truth values in the conditional and contrapositive columns are always the same. The truth values in the converse and inverse columns are also always the same. Therefore, the conditional and contrapositive of a statement are logically equivalent, and the converse and inverse of a statement are logically equivalent.

 # MODEL PROBLEM

For the conditional statement below, form the converse, inverse, and contrapositive.

If the polygon has only five sides, then the polygon is a pentagon.

Solution:

Hypothesis: The polygon has only five sides.

Conclusion: The polygon is a pentagon.

Converse: If the polygon is a pentagon, then the polygon has only five sides.

Inverse: If the polygon does not have only five sides, then the polygon is not a pentagon.

Contrapositive: If the polygon is not a pentagon, then the polygon does not have only five sides.

Biconditional

A *biconditional* is a compound statement formed by the conjunction of a conditional statement and the converse of the conditional. In word form, the biconditional is written using *if and only if*. Symbolically, a biconditional is represented by the symbol $\leftrightarrow$.

Example:

Conditional $(p \rightarrow q)$:   If two lines do not intersect, then they are parallel.

Converse $(q \rightarrow p)$:   If two lines are parallel, then they do not intersect.

Biconditional $(p \leftrightarrow q)$:   Two lines do not intersect *if and only if* they are parallel.

A biconditional statement is true only when both original statements have the same truth value—that is, when they are both true or both false. If the original statements have different truth values, the biconditional is false. The truth table below summarizes the truth values for the biconditional.

p	q	$p \rightarrow q$	$q \rightarrow p$	$p \leftrightarrow q$
T	T	T	T	T
T	F	F	T	F
F	T	T	F	F
F	F	T	T	T

 MODEL PROBLEM

Construct a truth table for the following biconditional:

$(p \rightarrow q) \leftrightarrow (\sim p \vee q)$

p	q	$\sim p$	$p \rightarrow q$	$\sim p \vee q$	$(p \rightarrow q) \leftrightarrow (\sim p \vee q)$
T	T	F	T	T	T
T	F	F	F	F	T
F	T	T	T	T	T
F	F	T	T	T	T

Note: A compound sentence that is always true, no matter what truth values are assigned to the simple sentences within the compound sentence, is called a *tautology*. Observe that the last column of the truth table above is all true; therefore, the compound sentence is a tautology.

1. Which whole number, when substituted for a, will make the following sentence true?

   $(a + 4 > 9) \wedge (a < 7)$

   A) 5   B) 6   C) 7   D) 8

2. What is the converse of the statement "If it snowed, the ground is wet?"

   E) If the ground is not wet, it did not snow.
   F) If the ground is wet, it snowed.
   G) If it did not snow, the ground is not wet.
   H) The ground is wet if and only if it snowed.

3. The sentence $q \vee r$ is false if and only if

   A) q is false and r is true
   B) both q and r are false
   C) q is true and r is false
   D) both q and r are true

4. If $r \leftrightarrow s$ is true, which sentence is also true?

   E) $r \rightarrow s$ F) $r \wedge s$
   G) $r \vee s$ H) $\sim r \wedge s$

5. Given the true statement "If Christina does not set her alarm, she will be late for school," which statement must also be true?

   A) If Christina is late for school, she did not set her alarm.
   B) If Christina set her alarm, she will not be late for school.
   C) If Christina is not late for school, then she did set her alarm.
   D) If Christina is late for school, then she set her alarm.

6. If a statement is true, what is the truth value of the negation of its negation?

   E) True
   F) False
   G) No truth value
   H) Cannot be determined

7. Which has the same truth value as the sentence "If Bill won, then Grace lost"?

   A) If Grace lost, then Bill won.
   B) If Bill did not win, then Grace did not lose.
   C) If Grace lost, then Bill did not win.
   D) If Grace did not lose, then Bill did not win.

8. What is the inverse of the sentence "If it is March, then Justina will go on vacation?"

   E) If Justina will go on vacation, then it is March.
   F) If it is not March, then Justina will not go on vacation.
   G) If it is March, then Justina will not go on vacation.
   H) If Justina will not go on vacation, then it is not March.

9. Which sentence is always false?

   A) $s \vee \sim s$ B) $t \wedge \sim t$
   C) $s \wedge \sim t$ D) $t \vee \sim s$

10. Which of the following sentences is equivalent to $\sim(p \wedge \sim q)$?

    E) $\sim p \wedge \sim q$ F) $\sim p \vee q$
    G) $\sim p \vee \sim q$ H) $\sim p \rightarrow \sim q$

11. For the conditional statement "If I don't go to band practice, I will not be in the concert"

    A. Write the converse.
    B. Write the inverse.
    C. Write the contrapositive.

12. For the given statement "The measures of congruent segments are equal"

    A. rewrite the statement as a conditional and state its truth value.
    B. write the converse and state its truth value.

13. For the conditional statement "If Josh plays on the football team, he runs track"

   A. write the converse.
   B. Using the conditional and converse, write a biconditional statement.

14. Write the biconditional statement of "If $x = \sqrt{48}$, then $x = 4\sqrt{3}$."

15. Construct a truth table for $(p \wedge q) \leftrightarrow (\sim q \rightarrow p)$.

 2.6 # Spatial Relationships

Common Three-Dimensional Figures		
Type	**Illustration**	**Description**
pyramid		a polyhedron in which the base is a polygon and the lateral faces are triangles with a common vertex
prism		a solid with two faces (bases) formed by congruent polygons that lie in parallel planes and whose other faces are rectangles
cone		a solid consisting of a circular base and a curved lateral surface that extends from the base to a single point called the vertex
cylinder		a solid with congruent circular bases that lie in parallel planes.
sphere		the set of all points a given distance from a given point

To Visualize or Represent a Figure:

1. Make a drawing—use grid paper or isometric dot paper.
2. Think about a physical model.
3. Create a physical model.

MODEL PROBLEMS

1. Which of the following pieces of cardboard cannot be folded along the dotted lines to make a closed box?

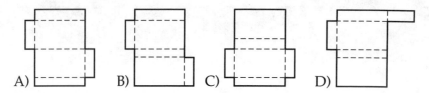

A)   B)   C)   D)

Solution: METHOD 1: Copy the four patterns onto paper or cardboard. Cut them out and fold on dotted lines to determine which would work and which would not work.

METHOD 2: Envision the folds and the relationships of the different faces.

Answer: Choice A would not make a closed box because opposite faces would not turn out to be congruent.

2. A plane passing through a solid gives a cross section of the solid. Determine the cross section of a cone if a plane passes through the cone parallel to the base.

Solution: You can combine the strategy of drawing a diagram with the strategy of thinking about a physical model.

Think of a traffic cone being cut by a piece of cardboard parallel to the base. What do you see when the vertex has been cut off the cone?

Answer: The top of the cone is a circle.

3. From the views given below make a model and then draw a corner view.

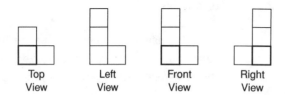

| Top View | Left View | Front View | Right View |

Solution: If you use cubes to represent the views, then the top view tells us that the base has three blocks and that the figure has columns of different heights. The left view shows blocks flush with the surface. The left back must be three blocks high. From the front and right views it is clear the other columns are one block high. Hence, the figure should look like this:

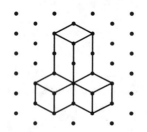

1. Which of the following patterns will NOT fold to form a cube?

A)   B)   C)   D)

2. Which figure will be formed by folding the given pattern along the dotted lines?

E) Hexagonal prism
F) Hexagonal pyramid
G) Cone
H) Triangular prism

3. A plane passing through a solid gives a cross section of the solid. Which of the following plane figures can be a cross section of a triangular prism?

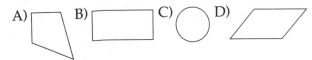

A)   B)   C)   D)

4. If rectangular region *ABCD* is rotated 360° about $\overline{BC}$, which of the following three-dimensional solids is formed?

E) Cone   E) Pyramid
G) Prism   H) Cylinder

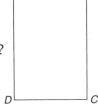

5. Given the three views of the cube below, what shape is opposite the triangle?

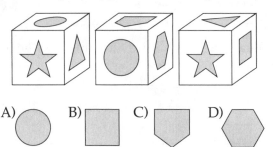

A)   B)   C)   D)

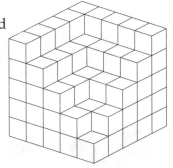

6. How many cubes are needed to build the given figure?

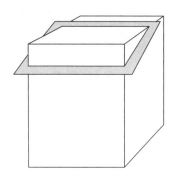

7. What would the cut surface of the following solid look like?

8. Explain why the diagram shown cannot be folded along the dotted lines to make a closed box. Suggest a modification in the diagram to allow the folding to result in a closed box.

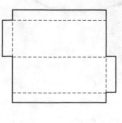

9. Draw the solid figure described by the given views.

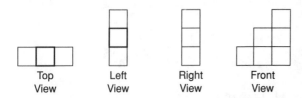

Top View   Left View   Right View   Front View

10. For the given solid, sketch the top, left, right, and front views.

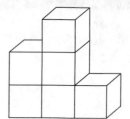

2.7 Congruence

Congruent figures have the same size and the same shape. The symbol for congruence is ≅ .

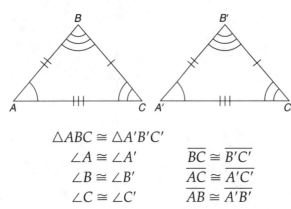

$$\triangle ABC \cong \triangle A'B'C'$$
$$\angle A \cong \angle A' \qquad \overline{BC} \cong \overline{B'C'}$$
$$\angle B \cong \angle B' \qquad \overline{AC} \cong \overline{A'C'}$$
$$\angle C \cong \angle C' \qquad \overline{AB} \cong \overline{A'B'}$$

Characteristics of Congruent Polygons:

1. Corresponding angles are congruent.
2. Corresponding sides are congruent.

Proving Triangles Congruent

There are five different ways to prove triangles congruent.

- **Side-side-side: SSS ≅ SSS.** Two triangles are congruent if three sides of one triangle are congruent to the corresponding sides of the other triangle.

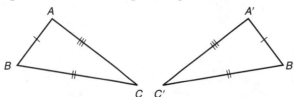

- **Side-angle-side: SAS ≅ SAS.** Two triangles are congruent if two sides of one triangle and the included angle (the angle between them) are congruent, respectively, to the two sides and included angle of the other.

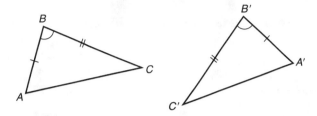

- **Angle-side-angle: ASA ≅ ASA.** Two triangles are congruent if two angles and the included side of one triangle are congruent, respectively, to two angles and the included side of the other.

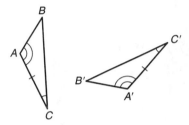

- **Angle-angle-side: AAS ≅ AAS.** Two triangles are congruent if two angles and a non-included side of one triangle are congruent, respectively, to two angles and corresponding side of the other.

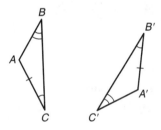

- **Hypotenuse-leg: HL ≅ HL** (This applies to right triangles only.) Two right triangles are congruent if the hypotenuse and the leg of one triangle are congruent to the hypotenuse and a leg of the other triangle.

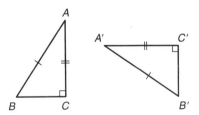

1. Give a set of coordinates for point Q so that parallelogram $ABCD$ will be congruent to parallelogram $MNPQ$.

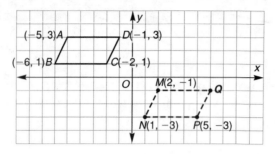

Solution:

If parallelogram $ABCD \cong$ parallelogram $MNPQ$, $\overline{AD} \cong \overline{MQ}$.

Since $AD = 4$ units, MQ must be 4 units.

Answer: Point Q must be located at $(6, -1)$.

2. Determine whether $\triangle I$ and $\triangle II$ are congruent. Explain your answer.

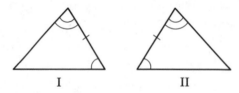

              I   II

Answer: $\triangle I$ is congruent to $\triangle II$ by angle-side-angle.

Note: If any two pairs of corresponding angles of a triangle are congruent, then their measures have to the same sum. The third angle must then also be congruent, so that the sum of all of the interior angles is 180°.

1. Quadrilateral $ABCD \cong$ quadrilateral $PQRS$. Which of the statements below does NOT follow?

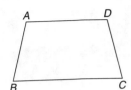 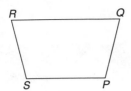

A) $\overline{AB} \cong \overline{PQ}$

B) $\overline{AD} \cong \overline{RS}$

C) $\overline{BC} \cong \overline{QR}$

D) $\overline{CD} \cong \overline{RS}$

2. Which of the following everyday applications is an illustration of congruence?

E) Obtaining an enlargement of a picture

F) Duplicating a key

G) Preparing a scale drawing

H) Buying a scale model of a sports car

3. $\triangle DAB \cong \triangle CBA$. Which angle is congruent to $\angle BDA$?

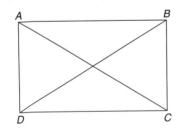

A) $\angle ACB$

B) $\angle BAC$

C) $\angle ABC$

D) $\angle CAB$

4. Which statement is TRUE?

I. If two circles have the same area, the circles are congruent.

II. If two squares have the same area, the squares are congruent.

III. If two rectangles have the same area, the rectangles are congruent.

E) II only

F) III only

G) I and II only

H) II and III only

For 5–7 refer the five pairs of triangles below.

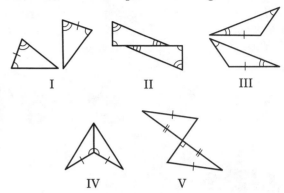

I   II   III

IV   V

5. Which pair of triangles are congruent by SAS?

A) I

B) III

C) IV

D) V

6. The pair of triangles in I are congruent by

E) SSS

F) AAS

G) ASA

H) SAS

7. Which pair of triangles are NOT congruent?

A) II

B) III

C) IV

D) V

8. $\triangle ABC \cong \triangle EFG$, $m\angle A = 40$, $m\angle F = 105$. What is the measure of $\angle C$?

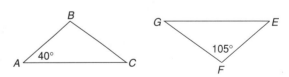

9. What is the x-coordinate of point Z such that trapezoid $ABCD \cong$ trapezoid $WXYZ$?

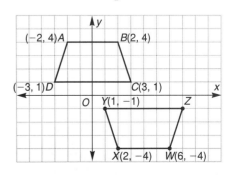

10. Take a regular octagon. Draw all the diagonals from one vertex. How many pairs of congruent triangles are formed?

11. Bob thinks that if the angles of one triangle are congruent to the angles of another triangle, then the two triangles must be congruent. Do you agree with Bob? Explain. Give an example to support your answer.

12. Draw two triangles that meet each of the given conditions. Be sure to label the dimensions on the triangles.

 A. The two triangles have equal areas and are congruent.

 B. The two triangles have equal areas and are not congruent.

2.8 Similarity

Similar figures have the same shape. The symbol for similar is ~.

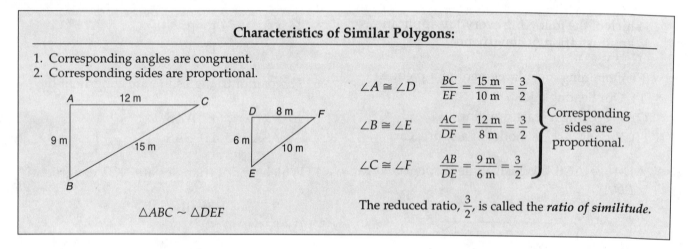

Characteristics of Similar Polygons:

1. Corresponding angles are congruent.
2. Corresponding sides are proportional.

$$\angle A \cong \angle D \qquad \frac{BC}{EF} = \frac{15 \text{ m}}{10 \text{ m}} = \frac{3}{2}$$

$$\angle B \cong \angle E \qquad \frac{AC}{DF} = \frac{12 \text{ m}}{8 \text{ m}} = \frac{3}{2}$$

$$\angle C \cong \angle F \qquad \frac{AB}{DE} = \frac{9 \text{ m}}{6 \text{ m}} = \frac{3}{2}$$

Corresponding sides are proportional.

$\triangle ABC \sim \triangle DEF$

The reduced ratio, $\frac{3}{2}$, is called the *ratio of similitude*.

Proving Triangles Similar

The following are three different ways to prove triangles similar.

- **Side-side-side: SSS.** Two triangles are similar if all three pairs of corresponding sides are in proportion. In the example below, $\triangle ABC \sim \triangle A'B'C'$ because $\frac{a}{a'} = \frac{b}{b'} = \frac{c}{c'}$.

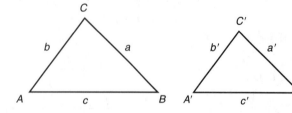

- **Side-angle-side: SAS.** Two triangles are similar if two pairs of corresponding sides are in proportion and the included angles are congruent. In the example below, $\angle B \cong \angle S$ and $\dfrac{AB}{RS} = \dfrac{BC}{ST}$ or $\dfrac{15}{3} = \dfrac{25}{5}$, so $\triangle ABC \sim \triangle RST$.

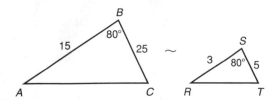

- **Angle-angle: AA.** Two triangles are similar if two pairs of corresponding angles are congruent. In the example below, $\triangle ABC \sim \triangle A'B'C'$ because each has a 80° angle and a 40° angle. For the sum of the angles to equal 180°, the third angle is each 60°. Therefore, all three pairs of angles are congruent.

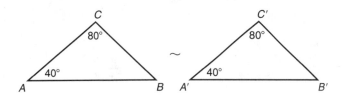

1. Quadrilateral $ABCD \sim$ quadrilateral $PQRS$. Find x, y, z.

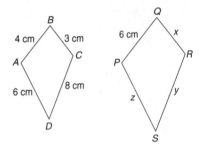

Solution: In similar quadrilaterals, corresponding sides are in proportion.

$$\frac{AB}{PQ} = \frac{BC}{QR} \quad \frac{AB}{PQ} = \frac{CD}{RS} \quad \frac{AB}{PQ} = \frac{AD}{PS}$$

$$\frac{4}{6} = \frac{3}{x} \quad \frac{4}{6} = \frac{8}{y} \quad \frac{4}{6} = \frac{6}{z}$$

$$4x = 18 \quad 4y = 48 \quad 4z = 36$$

Answer: $x = 4.5$ cm $\quad y = 12$ cm $\quad z = 9$ cm

Note: Since $\overline{PQ}$ and $\overline{AB}$ are corresponding sides and the length of $\overline{PQ}$ is one and one-half times the length of $\overline{AB}$, the missing sides in the larger quadrilateral must be one and one-half times the corresponding sides in the smaller quadrilateral.

2. A person 6′ tall is standing near a tree. If the person's shadow is 4′ long and the tree's shadow is 10′ long, what is the height of the tree?

Solution: During the day, two objects that are near each other have shadows whose measures are proportional to the heights of the objects, resulting in similar triangles.

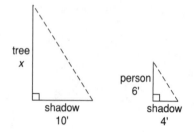

Write a proportion:

$$\frac{\text{tree}}{\text{tree's shadow}} = \frac{\text{person}}{\text{person's shadow}}$$

$$\frac{x}{10} = \frac{6}{4}$$

$$4x = 60$$

$$x = 15$$

Answer: The tree is 15′ high.

3. For the following pair of triangles, determine whether $\triangle ABC$ and $\triangle DEF$ are similar. Explain your answer.

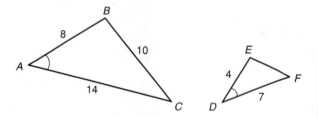

Answer: $\triangle ABC$ is similar to $\triangle DEF$ by side-angle-side (SAS).

1. Which of the following statements about similar figures is TRUE?

   A) All squares are similar.
   B) All right triangles are similar.
   C) All rhombuses are similar.
   D) All hexagons are similar.

2. $\triangle ABC \sim \triangle DEF$. What is the measure of $\overline{DF}$?

   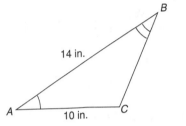

   E) 5 in.   F) 11 in.   G) 17 in.   H) 20 in.

3. Rectangle $ABCD \sim$ rectangle $PQRS$. If $AD = 3$ mi and $PS = 5$ mi, which of the quantities that follow would NOT be in the ratio $3 : 5$?

   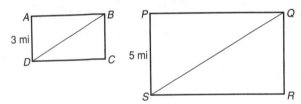

   A) AB and PQ
   B) BD and QS
   C) $m\angle A$ and $m\angle P$
   D) The perimeter of $ABCD$ and the perimeter of $PQRS$

4. The pair of triangles below are similar by

   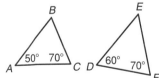

   E) SAS
   F) SSS
   G) AA
   H) The triangles are not similar.

5. A tree casts a 20-m shadow at the same time that a 6-m pole casts an 8-m shadow. Find the height of the tree.

6. The wing of a model of a glider is a right triangle with sides 3 inches, 4 inches, and 5 inches. In the actual glider, the hypotenuse is 35. Find the perimeter of the wing on the actual glider.

7. Triangle ABC has vertices $A(-4, 1)$, $B(-1, 1)$, $C(-4, 3)$. Triangle PQR is to be drawn similar to the first triangle. If two vertices of the second triangle are $P(2, 1)$ and $Q(8, 1)$, find the positive y-coordinate for the vertex R if the x-coordinate is 8.

8. If these two triangles are similar, explain why $m\angle x$ must be equal to $m\angle y$.

   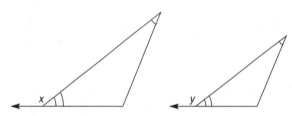

9. After takeoff, a plane ascends at a constant rate. At a ground distance of 240 meters from takeoff, the plane's altitude is 80 meters. Find its altitude at a ground distance of 960 meters from takeoff. Draw a diagram to support your solution.

10. $\triangle ABC$ has vertices $A(0, 0)$, $B(6, 0)$, $C(3, 3)$. If the coordinates of each vertex are multiplied by 2, will the new figure be similar to the original figure? Give the coordinates of the new vertices. Plot the coordinates and draw both triangles on the grid.

11. Jennifer knows that two rectangles are similar and that the ratio of corresponding sides is $2 : 5$. She also knows that the ratio of the perimeters of the two rectangles is $2 : 5$. Because of this, she thinks that the ratio of the areas of the two rectangles is $2 : 5$. Using grid paper, draw approximate rectangles to prove or disprove Jennifer's thinking.

2.9 Geometric Proofs

Geometric proofs are examples of deductive reasoning. A geometric proof is used to demonstrate the validity of specific geometric statements. A sequence of true statements, which includes the given, definitions, postulates, and theorems, are linked by sound reasoning from one to another until the desired conclusion is reached.

An example of a formal proof is a two-column proof. There are five parts in the proof: the diagram, the given statement, the prove statement, the statements, and the reasons. The left column is for the statements and the right column is for the reasons why the statements are true.

The following is a table of postulates, that are commonly used in geometric proofs.

Postulate	Definition	Example
Addition Property (If $a = b$, and $c = d$, then $a + c = b + d$.)	If equal quantities are added to equal quantities, the sums are equal.	If $AB = DE$, and $BC = EF$, then $AB + BC = DE + EF$.
Subtraction Property (If $a = b$, and $c = d$, then $a - c = b - d$.)	If equal quantities are subtracted from equal quantities, the differences are equal.	If $m\angle ABG = m\angle DEH$, and $m\angle 1 = m\angle 2$, then $m\angle ABG - m\angle 1 = m\angle DEH - m\angle 2$.
Multiplication Property (If $a = b$, and $c = d$, then $ac = bd$.)	If equal quantities are multiplied by equal quantities, the products are equal.	If $AB = CD$, $RS = 2AB$, and $LM = 2CD$, then $RS = LM$.
Division Property (If $a = b$, and $c = d$, then $\dfrac{a}{c} = \dfrac{b}{d}$, where $c \neq 0$ and $d \neq 0$.)	If equal quantities are divided by nonzero equal quantities, the quotients are equal.	If $\overline{AB} \cong \overline{DC}$, $AF = \dfrac{1}{2}AB$, $EC = \dfrac{1}{2}DC$, then $AF \cong EC$.
Substitution (If $a = b$, then a can be substituted for b.)	A quantity may be substituted for its equal in any expression.	If $AB = 2AD$ and $AD = DB$, then $AB = 2DB$.
Reflexive Property of Equality ($a = a$.)	A quantity is equal to itself.	In $\triangle ABC$, $AB = AB$, $BC = BC$, and $AC = AC$.
Symmetric Property of Equality (If $a = b$, then $b = a$.)	An equality may be expressed in either order.	If $AB = CD$, then $CD = AB$.
Transitive Property of Equality (If $a = b$ and $b = c$, then $a = c$.)	If quantities are equal to the same quantity, they are equal to each other.	If $AB \cong CD$, and $CD \cong EF$, then $AB \cong EF$.

MODEL PROBLEM

Given: $\angle 2 \cong \angle 3$

Prove: $\angle 1 \cong \angle 4$

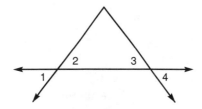

Solution:

Statements	Reasons
1. $\angle 1 \cong \angle 2$	1. Vertical angles are congruent.
2. $\angle 2 \cong \angle 3$	2. Given.
3. $\angle 1 \cong \angle 3$	3. Transitive Property.
4. $\angle 3 \cong \angle 4$	4. Vertical angles are congruent.
5. $\angle 1 \cong \angle 4$	5. Transitive Property.

Direct and Indirect Proofs

In a direct proof, the argument proceeds directly from hypothesis to conclusion. In an indirect proof, you begin by assuming the hypothesis is true and also assuming the negation of the conclusion. Then you proceed to show that this assumption leads to a contradiction.

To construct an indirect proof, keep in mind the following:

- Accept that the given information is true.
- Assume that the opposite of what you want to prove is true. That is, assume that the negation of the conclusion is true.
- Continue with your argument until you obtain a contradiction of a known fact, such as the given information or a theorem.
- Conclude that the initial assumption is false.
- Conclude that the statement to be proved must be true.
- Use an indirect proof when there seems to be no clear way to prove a statement directly.

Given: Triangle *ABC*

Prove: Triangle *ABC* can contain at most one right angle

Solution:

Statements	Reasons
1. Triangle *ABC*	1. Given.
2. Triangle *ABC* contains more than one right angle. Call the angles $\angle A$ and $\angle B$.	2. Assumed.
3. $m\angle A = m\angle B = 90$	3. Definition of a right angle.
4. $m\angle A + m\angle B + m\angle C > 180$	4. Since $m\angle A = m\angle B = 90°$, the sum of $m\angle A + m\angle B$ is already 180°, to add to it the $m\angle C$, the sum of the three angles will be greater than 180°.
5. $\angle A$ and $\angle B$ are not both right angles.	5. Contradiction from statement 4. The sum of the angles of a triangle is 180°. Therefore, the assumption in statement 2 is false and the conclusion is true. Triangle *ABC* can contain at most one right angle.

PRACTICE

1. Given: $\angle 1 \cong \angle 3$

   Prove: $\angle 2 \cong \angle 3$

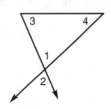

2. Given: Ray *EB* bisects $\angle CEF$.

   Prove: $\angle 1 \cong \angle 3$

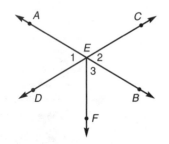

For problems 3 and 4, assume that each of the following is a statement that is to be proven. If you were to use an indirect proof, how would you begin your proof?

3. Triangle *ABC* is isosceles.

4. $\overline{HE} \perp \overline{LP}$.

5. Copy and complete the partial proof below for the accompanying diagram by providing reasons for steps, 3, 6, 8, and 9.

Given: $\overline{AFCD}$

$\overline{AB} \perp \overline{BC}$

$\overline{DE} \perp \overline{EF}$

$\overline{BC} \parallel \overline{FE}$

$\overline{AB} \cong \overline{DE}$

Prove: $\overline{AC} \cong \overline{FD}$

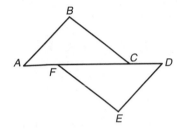

Statements	**Reasons**
1. $\overline{AFCD}$	1. Given.
2. $\overline{AB} \perp \overline{BC}, \overline{DE} \perp \overline{EF}$	2. Given.
3. $\angle B$ and $\angle E$ are right angles.	3. _____
4. $\angle B \cong \angle E$	4. All right angles are congruent.
5. $\overline{BC} \parallel \overline{FE}$	5. Given.
6. $\angle BCA \cong \angle EFD$	6. _____
7. $\overline{AB} \cong \overline{DE}$	7. Given.
8. $\triangle ABC \cong \triangle DEF$	8. _____
9. $\overline{AC} \cong \overline{FD}$	9. _____

6. Given: $\overline{HE} \perp \overline{WL}$

$\angle HEW \cong \angle A$

Prove: $m\angle A = 90$

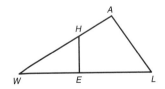

7. Given: $\triangle RST$, Q is a point on $\overline{RS}$ and P is a point on $\overline{RT}$ such that $\overline{QP} \parallel \overline{ST}$.

Prove: $\triangle RQP \sim \triangle RST$

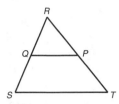

8. Given: $AD = AB$

$AE = \dfrac{AD}{3}$

$AF = \dfrac{AB}{3}$

Prove: $AE = AF$

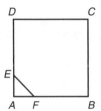

9. Given: $m\angle x = 40$

$m\angle y = 40$

Prove: $m\angle x = m\angle y$

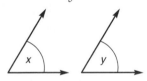

10. Given: $\overline{AB} \cong \overline{DC}$

$AF = \dfrac{1}{2}AB$

$EC = \dfrac{1}{2}DC$

Prove: $\overline{AF} \cong \overline{EC}$

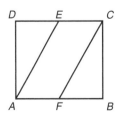

2.10 Transformations

Reflection and Line Symmetry

When you look in a mirror, you see your reflected image. A *reflection* is a flipping of a geometric figure about a line to obtain its mirror image.

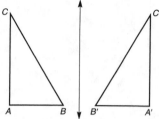

Note that under a reflection, the *orientation* of the figure is changed. For example, point A is to the left of B in the original figure, or *preimage*, but, in the image, point A' is to the right of B'.

If a line can be drawn through a figure so that the part of the figure on one side of the line is the mirror image of the part on the other side of the line, the figure has *line symmetry*.

 ## MODEL PROBLEMS

1. Draw the reflection of △ABC over the x-axis. State the coordinates of the vertices of the image.

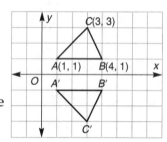

Solution: Point A has coordinates (1, 1). Since point A is 1 unit above the reflecting line, point A' will be 1 unit below the line. Since point B(4, 1) is also 1 unit above the reflecting line, point B' will be 1 unit below the line. Since point C(3, 3) is 3 units above, point C' will be 3 units below.

Answer: point A(1, 1) → point A'(1, −1)
point B(4, 1) → point B'(4, −1)
point C(3, 3) → point C'(3, −3)

2. How many lines of symmetry does a square have?

Solution:

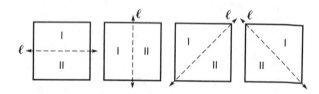

In each of the above figures, line ℓ is a line of symmetry. If the square is folded on line ℓ, then region I will exactly coincide with region II.

Answer: There are four lines of symmetry.

Rotation and Rotational Symmetry

A *rotation* is a turning of an object about a point through a specified angle measure.

A figure will be rotated either clockwise or counterclockwise.

Rotational symmetry exists when a figure is rotated a number of degrees (less than 360°) about a fixed point and the image coincides with the figure.

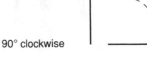

90° clockwise

MODEL PROBLEMS

1. Rotate △*ABC* 90° clockwise using (0, 0) as the point of rotation. Identify the coordinates of the vertices of the image.

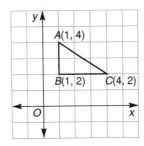

2. Given this square with a fixed point at its center, determine the rotations that would show the presence of rotational symmetry.

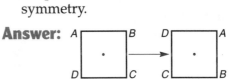

Answer:

90° clockwise

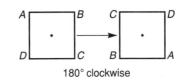

180° clockwise

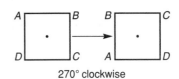

270° clockwise

Solution: Trace △*ABC* on grid paper. Locate (0, 0) and draw a ray away from the origin and along the negative branch of the *x*-axis. Hold the paper with pencil point at (0, 0) and rotate the paper 90° clockwise, moving the ray from the *x*-axis to the *y*-axis.

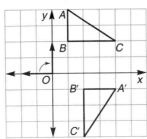

$A(1, 4) \rightarrow A'(4, -1)$

$B(1, 2) \rightarrow B'(2, -1)$

$C(4, 2) \rightarrow C'(2, -4)$

Translation

A *translation* is a sliding of a geometric figure, without turning, from one position to another.

 MODEL PROBLEMS

1. Translate $\triangle ABC$ right 3 units. State the coordinates of the vertices of the image of $\triangle ABC$.

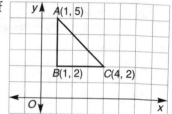

Solution:

The image of A under the translation 3 units right is A'. Add 3 to the x-coordinate of point A.

$$A(1, 5) \rightarrow A'(1 + 3, 5) \rightarrow A'(4, 5)$$

Repeat for points B and C.
$B(1, 2) \rightarrow B'(4, 2)$
$C(4, 2) \rightarrow C'(7, 2)$

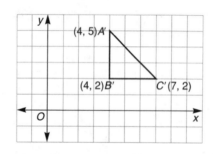

2. Explain the translation used to produce the given image of trapezoid $ABCD$.

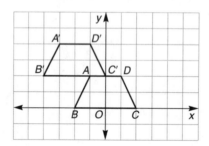

Solution:
$$\begin{aligned}
A(-1, 2) &\rightarrow A'(-3, 4) \\
B(-2, 0) &\rightarrow B'(-4, 2) \\
C(2, 0) &\rightarrow C'(0, 2) \\
D(1, 2) &\rightarrow D'(-1, 4)
\end{aligned}$$

Both the x- and y-coordinates changed, indicating that the figure was moved both vertically and horizontally. Since -2 was added to the x-coordinates, the x-coordinates were moved 2 units left. Since 2 was added to the y-coordinates, the y-coordinates were moved 2 units up.

Answer: The image of trapezoid $ABCD$ was formed by translating the figure left 2 units and up 2 units.

Dilation

A *dilation* is a transformation that reduces or enlarges a figure. In a dilation, every image is similar to its preimage. Every dilation has a point known as the *center of dilation* and a *scale factor* k. If $k > 1$, the dilation is an enlargement. If $0 < k < 1$, the dilation is a reduction. If k is written as a fraction, it represents the ratio of similitude between the image and preimage.

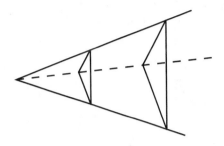

 MODEL PROBLEMS

1. Using the diagram, identify the dilation and find its scale factor.

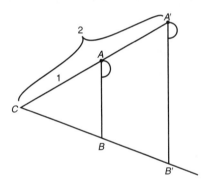

   Solution: The dilation is an enlargement because the scale factor is greater than 1. $\dfrac{CA'}{CA} = \dfrac{2}{1}$

2. Draw a dilation of rectangle $PQRS$ with vertices $P(2, 2)$, $Q(4, 2)$, $R(4, 3)$, $S(2, 3)$. Use the origin as the center and a scale factor of 3. How does the perimeter of the preimage compare to the perimeter of the image?

   Solution: With center at $(0, 0)$ you find the image of each vertex by multiplying its coordinates by the given scale factor.

   $P(2, 2) \rightarrow P'(6, 6)$

   $Q(4, 2) \rightarrow Q'(12, 6)$

   $R(4, 3) \rightarrow R'(12, 9)$

   $S(2, 3) \rightarrow S'(6, 9)$

   From the graph it follows the perimeter of $PQRS = 6$ and the perimeter of $P'Q'R'S' = 18$. The perimeter was enlarged by a scale factor of 3.

1. A figure undergoes a transformation. The preimage and the image are not congruent. What type of transformation took place?

   A) Dilation
   B) Reflection
   C) Rotation
   D) Translation

2. A polygon is dilated with center at the origin and scale factor 3.5. The image is then dilated with center at the origin and scale factor x. What value of x would cause the second image to be congruent to the original polygon?

   E) 3.5
   F) 1
   G) $\frac{2}{7}$
   H) -3.5

3. Which of the following polygons has 36° rotational symmetry?

   A) Equilateral triangle
   B) Regular pentagon
   C) Regular octagon
   D) Regular decagon

4. What would the coordinate of point A' be if $\triangle ABC$ located at $A(1, 1)$, $B(4, 1)$, $C(2, 3)$ was translated left 3 units?

   E) $(4, 1)$ F) $(-2, 1)$ G) $(-2, 2)$ H) $(1, 2)$

5. If the line segment joining $A(-2, 3)$ and $B(1, 6)$ is rotated 90° clockwise about point A, the coordinates of the image of B are:

   A) $(1, 0)$ B) $(1, 6)$ C) $(-2, 0)$ D) $(-2, 6)$

6. Which of the following figures has NO lines of symmetry?

   E)   F)   G)   H)

7. What are the coordinates of the image of $(5, 0)$ under a rotation of 90° clockwise about the origin?

   A) $(-5, 0)$
   C) $(0, -5)$
   B) $(0, 5)$
   D) $(5, -5)$

8. Which of the following could be the image of $\triangle ABC$ reflected over the x-axis?

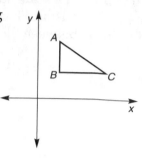

E)

F)

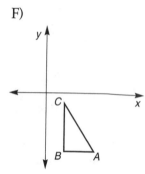

G)

H)

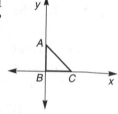

9. Which figure below could be a translation of $\triangle ABC$?

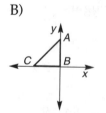

A)

B)

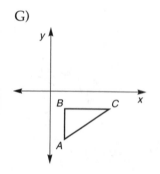

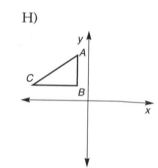

C)

D)

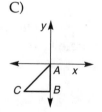

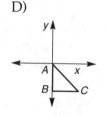

10. If $\triangle ABC$ with vertices $A(-2, 0)$, $B(-2, -2)$, $C(-4, -2)$ is reflected over the x-axis and then the image is reflected over the y-axis, which coordinates would represent the final image of point A?

E) $(-2, 0)$ F) $(2, 0)$ G) $(0, 2)$ H) $(0, -2)$

11. If the x-axis is the line of reflection, what would be the coordinates of the reflected image of $P(6, 1)$?

A) $(6, -1)$ B) $(-6, 1)$
C) $(-6, -1)$ D) $(6, 1)$

12. Which of the following could be the reflected image of **B** over a vertical line?

E) ʙ F) 8 G) **B** H) ᗺ

13. Which figure could be a translation of **R** ?

A) ᴚ B) ꓤ C) **R** D) Я

14. Which of the following transformations could be a rotation?

15. Which of the following would NOT represent a translation?

A) $(x, y) \to (x + 7, y + 1)$
B) $(x, y) \to (x, y - 3)$
C) $(x, y) \to (x + 7, y)$
D) $(x, y) \to (-x, -y)$

16. $\triangle ABC$ has been rotated clockwise about point $(0, 0)$ to produce the image $\triangle A'B'C'$. Through how many degrees was $\triangle ABC$ rotated?

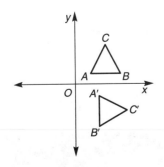

17. Point A is reflected over the x-axis and then the image is reflected over the y-axis, resulting in the point A'' with coordinates $(-3, -7)$. What was the y-coordinate of the original point A?

18. The word MATH when written in column form has a vertical line of symmetry. Find two other words that have a vertical line of symmetry when written in column form.

19. The point $(2, 1)$ is rotated $270°$ clockwise about point $(0, 0)$. What is the y-coordinate of the image?

20. If $\triangle RST$ is translated up 6 units, what will the y-coordinate of point S' be?

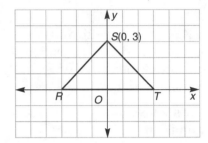

21. Parallelogram $ABCD$ was translated down 2 units and right 5 units, resulting in the given image. What was the x-coordinate of point B?

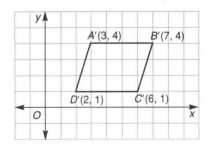

22. Triangle OAB with vertices $O(0, 0)$, $A(-3, 0)$, and $B(-3, -4)$ is rotated $180°$ clockwise about point O. Draw the image of triangle OAB and state the coordinates of the image.

23. If a line ℓ parallel to the y-axis at $x = 4$ is drawn on the given plane and $\triangle ABC$ is reflected over the y-axis and then over line ℓ, what single transformation could have been used to arrive at the final image?

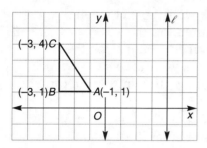

24. $\triangle ABC$ with vertices at $A(-1, 1)$, $B(0, 4)$, and $C(-3, 3)$ is rotated 180° clockwise about the origin. What are the vertices of the image of $\triangle ABC$?

25. In $\triangle ABC$, $A(-1, -2)$, $B(0, 3)$, $C(1, 1)$, the image of A under a translation is $A'(-3, 5)$. What would the image of B and C be under the same translation?

26. A Ferris wheel's motion is an example of a rotation.

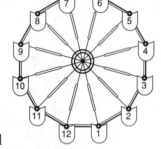

   A. What is the measure of the angle of rotation if seat 1 of a 12-seat Ferris wheel is moved to the seat 6 position?

   B. If seat 1 of a 12-seat Ferris wheel is rotated 240°, find the seat whose position it now occupies.

27. On a coordinate plane, graph the given vertices. Using the origin as the center of the dilation and a scale factor of 2, draw the dilation image. $A(2, 3)$, $B(4, 8)$, $C(-3, 5)$

28. $\triangle ABC$ is mapped onto $\triangle A'B'C'$. Find the scale factor and state if the dilation is a reduction or an enlargement.

   $AB = 6$ cm $BC = 8$ cm $AC = 10$ cm
   $A'B' = 24$ cm $B'C' = 32$ cm $A'C' = 40$ cm

29. $AB = 5$ mm. The measure of its dilated image is 7.5 mm. What is the value of the scale factor?

30. $\triangle MNP$ was translated down 4 units and right 3 units to form $\triangle M'N'P'$. $\triangle M'N'P'$ was translated up 6 units and left 6 units to form $\triangle M''N''P''$. Explain how $\triangle M''N''P''$ could have been obtained directly from $\triangle MNP$ under a single translation.

31. If the figure on the right is a dilation image of the figure on the left, what is the scale factor for the dilation?

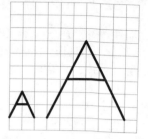

32. A figure $WXYZ$, a dilation center, and an image point Y' are given. Copy the diagram and complete the dilation.

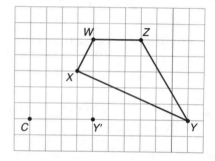

33. A triangle with vertices at $(0, 2)$, $(4, 2)$, and $(0, 4)$ is reflected over the line $y = 5$. The image of the triangle is then reflected over the line $y = 11$.

   A. Give the coordinates of the vertices of the triangle resulting from the second reflection.

   B. What single transformation would also give you the final resulting triangle obtained by the two successive reflections? (Be specific with your answer.)

34. Wrapping paper often consists of a design that is translated over and over to create a pattern. Create an original pattern for wrapping paper by translating a hexagon and an equilateral triangle.

35. Plot the given points to form a figure and its image. Is this an example of a reflection? Explain why or why not.

   figure: $A(-2, 9)$, $B(-2, 2)$, $C(-5, 2)$
   image: $A'(9, 2)$, $B'(2, 2)$, $C'(2, 5)$

2.11 Coordinate Geometry

Every point in the coordinate system can be represented as an ordered pair (x, y).

The rectangular coordinate system can be used to represent geometric situations and solve related problems. Major coordinate geometry topics are midpoint, slope, and distance.

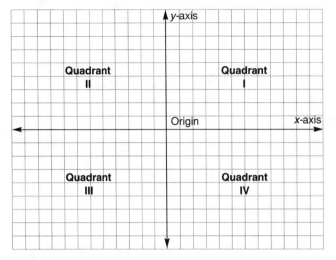

Midpoint of a line segment with endpoints at (x_1, y_1) and (x_2, y_2):

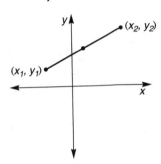

Midpoint: $\left(\dfrac{x_1 + x_2}{2}, \dfrac{y_1 + y_2}{2} \right)$

Note:

The coordinates of the midpoint are the respective averages of the x- and y-coordinates of the endpoints of the segment.

 MODEL PROBLEM

A line segment has a midpoint at (3, 4). If one endpoint has coordinates (6, 0), find the coordinates of the other endpoint.

Solution:

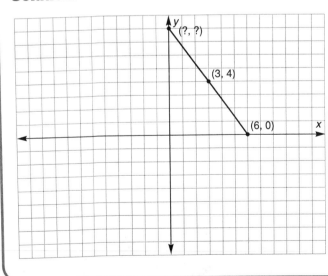

Missing endpoint (x_1, y_1)

Using the midpoint formula

$$3 = \frac{x_1 + 6}{2} \qquad 4 = \frac{y_1 + 0}{2}$$

$$x_1 + 6 = 6 \qquad y_1 + 0 = 8$$

$$x_1 = 0 \qquad y_1 = 8$$

The endpoint has coordinates (0, 8).

Slope, or steepness, of a line with points at (x_1, y_1) and (x_2, y_2):

$$\text{slope} = \frac{y_2 - y_1}{x_2 - x_1}$$

To describe the steepness of a roof, you determine the *vertical rise* compared to the *horizontal run*.

To describe the slope of a straight line, you choose two points on the line and determine the rise and run.

$$\text{Slope} = \frac{\text{rise}}{\text{run}} = \frac{\text{vertical change}}{\text{horizontal change}} = \frac{\text{difference of }y\text{-coordinates}}{\text{difference of }x\text{-coordinates}}$$

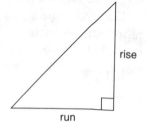

 MODEL PROBLEM

Show that two different segments on the line $y = x$ have the same slope.

Solution:

Select two points on the line:
   (0, 0) and (5, 5)

$$\text{slope} = \frac{5 - 0}{5 - 0} = 1$$

Select two different points on the line:
   (3, 3) and (−2, −2)

$$\text{slope} = \frac{3 - (-2)}{3 - (-2)} = \frac{5}{5} = 1$$

The two segments have the same slope, 1.

The slope of the line $y = x$ is the same value, 1, everywhere on the line.

The slope of a line is always a constant value and is the same as the slope of any segment on the line.

If a line is parallel to the x-axis, the line has no steepness. Its slope is zero.

If a line is parallel to the y-axis, the line has an undefined slope.

If a line rises from left to right, its slope is positive.

If a line falls from left to right, its slope is negative.

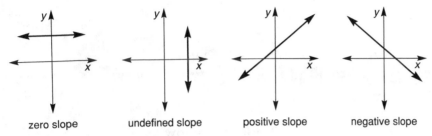

zero slope   undefined slope   positive slope   negative slope

Slopes of parallel lines are equal.

Slopes of perpendicular lines are negative reciprocals of each other.

 MODEL PROBLEM

A quadrilateral has vertices at $A(0, 0)$, $B(8, 0)$, $C(11, 3)$, $D(3, 3)$. Show that the quadrilateral is a parallelogram.

Solution: For the quadrilateral to be a parallelogram, both pairs of opposite sides must be parallel. For lines to be parallel, they must have the same slope.

Since $\overline{AB}$ and $\overline{DC}$ are both horizontal lines, the slope of each line is 0. Thus, $\overline{AB} \parallel \overline{DC}$.

slope $\overline{AD} = \dfrac{3 - 0}{3 - 0} = 1$ slope $\overline{BC} = \dfrac{3 - 0}{11 - 8} = 1$ Thus, $\overline{AD} \parallel \overline{BC}$.

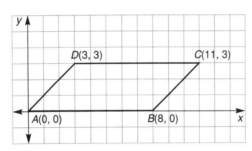

$ABCD$ is a parallelogram because slopes show that both pairs of opposite sides are parallel.

Distance can be determined in one of two ways.

1. If the segment joining the two points is either horizontal or vertical, the distance between the points is found by subtraction.
2. If the two points are the endpoints of an oblique segment, the distance (length) is found by using the Pythagorean Relation ($a^2 + b^2 = c^2$).

MODEL PROBLEMS

1. Find the distance from (2, 0) to (6, 3).

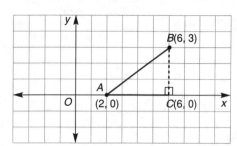

Solution: Draw $\overline{BC}$ to form a right triangle.

$$(AC)^2 + (BC)^2 = (AB)^2$$
$$4^2 + 3^2 = (AB)^2$$
$$16 + 9 = (AB)^2$$
$$25 = (AB)^2$$

Answer: $AB = 5$ units

Note: Using the distance formula,

$$d = \sqrt{(x_2 - x_1)^2 + (y_2 - y_1)^2}$$

is the same as using the Pythagorean Relation.

2. Plot the following points on a grid:

$$A(1, 0), B(1, 3), C(5, 3), D(5, 0)$$

What is the length of $\overline{BD}$?

Solution:

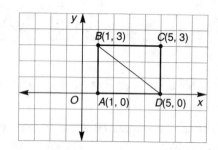

$$AB = 3 \text{ units}$$
$$AD = 4 \text{ units}$$
$$(BD)^2 = 3^2 + 4^2$$
$$= 9 + 16$$
$$= 25$$

Answer: $BD = 5$ units

1. Segment *AB* is horizontal. What must be the coordinates of point *B* if the length of $\overline{AB}$ is 10 units?

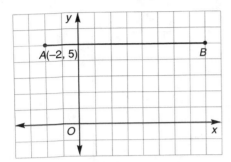

   A) (10, 0)   B) (10, 5)   C) (8, 5)   D) (12, 5)

2. If you plot the following points on a grid, what kind of triangle is formed?

   A(0, 0), *B*(8, 0), *C*(10, 5)

   E) Right   F) Acute
   G) Obtuse   H) Isosceles

3. A rectangle located in the first quadrant has two vertices at (0, 0) and (0, 6). Where would the other two vertices be if the area of the rectangle is 30 square units?

   A) (0, 5) and (6, 5)   B) (5, 0) and (6, 5)
   C) (5, 0) and (5, 6)   D) (9, 0) and (9, 6)

4. What is the best name for quadrilateral *ABCD* defined by *A*(0, 0), *B*(8, 0), *C*(10, 5), *D*(2, 5)?

   E) Rectangle   F) Trapezoid
   G) Isosceles trapezoid   H) Parallelogram

5. If a line passes through the points (3, 5) and (1, *k*) and has a slope of 2, what must be the value of *k*?

6. Two vertices of a triangle are *A*(0, 0), and *B*(6, 0). The third vertex in the first quadrant is (6, *k*). The area of triangle *ABC* is 30 square units. Find the value of *k*.

7. Find the slope of the line.

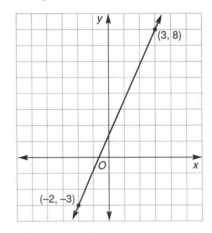

8. Find the coordinates of point *C* on the line *y* = 4 such that $\overline{CD} \parallel \overline{AB}$. Explain your procedure.

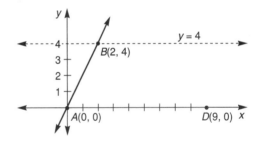

9. Line segment *AB* has *A*(2, 3) and *B*(10, −3). Point *M* is the midpoint of *AB* and point *P* is the midpoint of segment *AM*. What are the coordinates of point *P*?

10. Given *A*(1, 5), *B*(1, −1), *C*(9, −1).

    A. Plot the points on a grid, and form a figure.
    B. Give the best name for the figure formed.
    C. Find the area.

2.12 Coordinate Geometry Proofs

Like all kinds of proofs, coordinate geometry proofs should be arranged in an orderly step-by-step format. A conclusion should be clearly stated at the end of the algebraic or arithmetic procedures. The following table gives the general methods of proof and formulas used in proving basic properties of geometric figures.

To Prove	Formula to Use
that line segments are congruent, show that the lengths are equal.	Distance formula $d = \sqrt{(x_2 - x_1)^2 + (y_2 - y_1)^2}$
that line segments bisect each other, show that the midpoints are the same.	Midpoint formula $M = \left(\dfrac{x_1 + x_2}{2}, \dfrac{y_1 + y_2}{2} \right)$
that lines are parallel, show that the slopes are equal.	Slope formula $m = \dfrac{y_2 - y_1}{x_2 - x_1}$ $m_1 = m_2$
that lines are perpendicular, show that the slopes are negative reciprocals.	Product of slopes $= -1$ $m_1 \cdot m_2 = -1$ or $m_1 = -\dfrac{1}{m_2}$

The table below gives methods that can be used to prove that a quadrilateral belongs to a specific category.

To Prove a Figure Is a	Methods
Parallelogram	Show *one* of the following: • The diagonals bisect each other. • Both pairs of opposite sides are parallel. • Both pairs of opposite sides are congruent. • One pair of opposite sides is congruent and parallel.
Rectangle	Show that the figure is a parallelogram **and** *one* of the following: • The figure has one right angle. • The diagonals are congruent.
Rhombus	Show that the figure is a parallelogram **and** *one* of the following: • The diagonals are perpendicular. • Two adjacent sides are congruent.
Square	Show that the figure is a rectangle **and** two adjacent sides are congruent. **or** Show the figure is a rhombus **and** one angle is a right angle.
Trapezoid	Show that the quadrilateral has only *one* pair of opposite sides parallel.

MODEL PROBLEM

If the coordinates of the vertices of quadrilateral *STAR* are $S(-1, 0)$, $T(2, 3)$, $A(4, 1)$, and $R(1, -2)$, prove that *STAR* is a rectangle.

Solution:

To prove that a quadrilateral is a rectangle we first have to show that it is a parallelogram and either the figure has one right angle or the diagonals are congruent. To do so, we have to show that (1) the diagonals of the figure bisect each other and (2) the lengths of the diagonals are congruent.

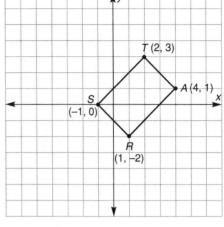

(1) Use the midpoint formula to find the midpoint M of diagonal $\overline{TR}$ and midpoint N of diagonal $\overline{SA}$.

$$M = \left(\frac{x_1 + x_2}{2}, \frac{y_1 + y_2}{2} \right)$$

$$M = \left(\frac{2 + 1}{2}, \frac{3 + (-2)}{2} \right) = \left(\frac{3}{2}, \frac{1}{2} \right)$$

$$N = \left(\frac{4 + (-1)}{2}, \frac{1 + 0}{2} \right) = \left(\frac{3}{2}, \frac{1}{2} \right)$$

Since midpoints M and N are the same, the diagonals bisect each other, and quadrilateral *STAR* is a parallelogram.

(2) To find the lengths of the diagonals, use the distance formula.

$$d = \sqrt{(x_2 - x_1)^2 + (y_2 - y_1)^2}$$

$$d_{TR} = \sqrt{(2 - 1)^2 + [3 - (-2)]^2} = \sqrt{1 + 25} = \sqrt{26}$$

$$d_{SA} = \sqrt{[4 - (-1)]^2 + (1 - 0)^2} = \sqrt{25 + 1} = \sqrt{26}$$

Answer: Since the diagonals $\overline{TR}$ and $\overline{SA}$ are congruent, parallelogram *STAR* is a rectangle.

1. If the midpoints of the four vertices of a rectangle, $(-1, -2)$, $(5, -2)$ $(5, 2)$, and $(-1, 2)$, are joined in order, what kind of quadrilateral is formed?

   A) Rectangle
   B) Rhombus
   C) Square
   D) Trapezoid

2. To prove that a quadrilateral is a square, you must show that:

   E) the figure is a parallelogram and the diagonals are congruent.
   F) one pair of opposite side is congruent and parallel.
   G) the figure is a rhombus and one angle is a right angle.
   H) it has only one pair of opposite sides parallel.

3. The slope of line PQ is $\dfrac{3}{5}$ and the slope of line RS is $\dfrac{10}{k}$. If $PQ \perp RS$, what is the value of k?

   A) $-16\dfrac{2}{3}$
   B) -6
   C) 6
   D) $16\dfrac{2}{3}$

4. Quadrilateral $CARD$, with vertices $C(-1, 0)$, $A(3, 3)$, $R(5, 0)$, and $D(3, -3)$, is a:

   E) rectangle
   F) rhombus
   G) square
   H) trapezoid

5. To prove a quadrilateral is a trapezoid, you must show that:

   A) both pairs of opposite sides are congruent.
   B) two adjacent sides are congruent.
   C) the diagonals bisect each other.
   D) it has only one pair of opposite sides parallel.

6. If the vertices of right triangle JAR are $J(-1, 2)$, $A(3, 8)$, and $R(5, -2)$, prove that point M, the midpoint of the hypotenuse, is equidistant from all three vertices of the triangle.

7. The vertices of $\triangle BED$ are $B(-4, 3)$, $E(1, 8)$, and $D(6, 3)$. Show that $\triangle BED$ is an isosceles right triangle.

8. The coordinates of $\triangle DOG$ are $D(1, 3)$, $O(8, 4)$, and $G(4, 7)$. Using slopes, show that $\triangle DOG$ is a right triangle.

9. The coordinates of the vertices of quadrilateral $BETH$ are $B(-3, -1)$, $E(3, 1)$, $T(7, 5)$, and $H(1, 3)$. Using slopes only, show that

   A. $BETH$ is a parallelogram.
   B. $BETH$ is or is not a rhombus.

10. The coordinates of rhombus $DAVE$ are $D(2, 1)$, $A(6, -2)$, $V(10, 1)$, and $E(6, 4)$. Find the following:

    A. length of a side of $DAVE$.
    B. coordinates of the point of intersection of the diagonals.
    C. area of $DAVE$.

2.13 Perimeter and Circumference

The *perimeter* of a figure is the total distance around the outside of the figure. Perimeter is measured in linear units.

For a circle, the distance around the outside is called *circumference* instead of perimeter.

Formulas can be used to find the perimeters of common geometric figures.

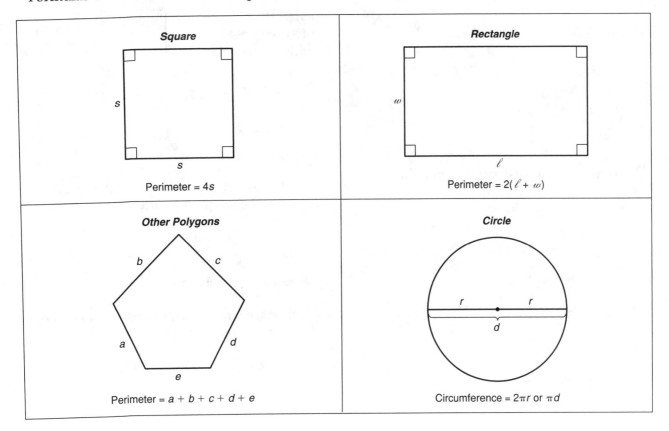

Square

s
s

Perimeter = $4s$

Rectangle

w
ℓ

Perimeter = $2(\ell + w)$

Other Polygons

b c
a d
e

Perimeter = $a + b + c + d + e$

Circle

r r
d

Circumference = $2\pi r$ or πd

MODEL PROBLEMS

1. A rectangle with a width of 5 cm has the same perimeter as an equilateral triangle with a side of 12 cm. Find the length of the rectangle.

Solution: Draw a diagram to help.

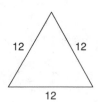 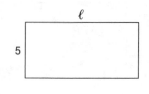

Perimeter is the distance around the outside.

$$P_{\text{triangle}} = 12 + 12 + 12 = 36$$
$$P_{\text{rectangle}} = 2(\ell + w)$$
$$P_{\text{triangle}} = P_{\text{rectangle}}$$
$$36 = 2(\ell + 5)$$
$$36 = 2\ell + 10$$
$$26 = 2\ell$$
$$13 = \ell$$

Answer: 13 cm

2. A circle is inscribed in a square with a perimeter of 24 cm. What is the circumference of the circle?

Solution: Draw a picture to help with the solution.

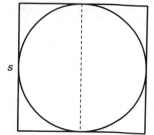

$$P_{\text{square}} = 4s$$
$$24 = 4s$$
$$6 = s$$

A side of the square is 6 cm.
The length of a diameter of the circle is equal to the length of a side of the square.

$$C = \pi d$$
$$C = \pi 6$$

Answer: $C = 6\pi$ cm

Note: If a single-number answer is needed, use $\pi = 3.14$ to simplfy:

$$6\pi = 6(3.14) = 18.84 \text{ cm}$$

PRACTICE

1. The perimeter of rectangle *ABCD* is 40 units and its length is 15 units.

Find the number of units in the perimeter of the square.

A) 20   B) 25   C) 40   D) 60

2. A rectangle has three vertices at $(-2, 3)$, $(10, 3)$, and $(10, 6)$. What is the perimeter of the rectangle?

E) 22   F) 26
G) 30   H) 36

3. If the circumference of a circle is increased from 30π inches to 50π inches, by how many inches is the length of the radius increased?

A) 10   B) 10π C) 20   D) 20π

4. Six congruent squares are shown. Squares added to the figure must share an existing side. What is the minimum number of squares that needs to be added to the diagram in order to increase the perimeter to 18 units?

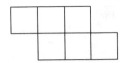

5. A regular pentagon and a regular decagon each have sides with a length of 8 cm. What is the difference between the two perimeters?

6. To the nearest centimeter, what is the perimeter of trapezoid *ABCD*?

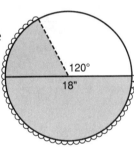

7. A garden hose lies coiled in a circular pile about 2 ft across. If there are 6 coils, estimate the length of the hose.

8. A circular piece of plywood is to be decorated to form a wall hanging. Elena wants to place lace completely around the shaded sector of the circle.

To the nearest inch, how much lace will she need if the diameter of the plywood piece is 18 inches and the measure of the central angle is 120°?

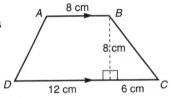

9.

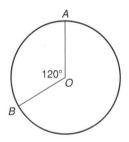

For the given diagram, what happens to the total perimeter of the shape if you remove the following squares? Explain your answers.

A. square 3 only
B. square 2 only
C. Which other square could you remove and have the same effect as in part A?
D. Which other square could you remove and have the same effect as in part B?
E. Draw a diagram to show how you could add three squares to the original figure and thereby change the perimeter from the original 10 units to 14 units.

10. Use a centimeter ruler to determine the length of the radius of the given circle. Using this measurement, find the length of the 120° arc of the circle (to the nearest tenth of a centimeter). Explain how you go about finding the length of this arc.

2.14 Area

Area is the number of square units needed to cover a surface.
Formulas can be used to find the areas of common geometric figures.

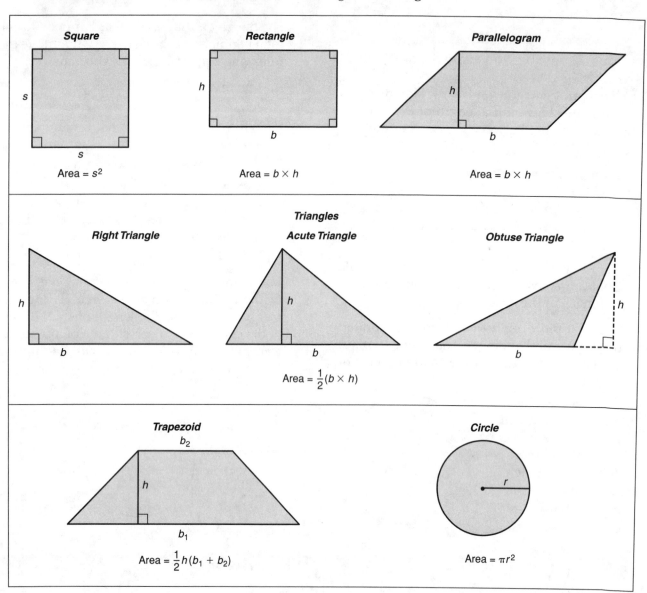

Square

Area = s^2

Rectangle

Area = $b \times h$

Parallelogram

Area = $b \times h$

Triangles

Right Triangle **Acute Triangle** **Obtuse Triangle**

Area = $\frac{1}{2}(b \times h)$

Trapezoid

Area = $\frac{1}{2}h(b_1 + b_2)$

Circle

Area = πr^2

MODEL PROBLEMS

1. Arrange the three figures in INCREASING order of area.

    I. a rectangle with dimensions of 6 in. by 8 in.

    II. a square with a side of 7 in.

    III. a right triangle with sides of 5 in., 12 in., and 13 in.

    A) rectangle, square, triangle

    B) rectangle, triangle, square

    C) triangle, rectangle, square

    D) square, rectangle, triangle

Solution: Find the areas by using the appropriate formulas.

$$\text{Area (rectangle)} = bh \qquad \text{Area (square)} = s^2$$
$$A = (6)(8) \qquad\qquad A = 7^2$$
$$A = 48 \text{ sq in.} \qquad\qquad A = 49 \text{ sq in.}$$

$$\text{Area (triangle)} = \frac{1}{2}bh$$
$$A = \frac{1}{2}(5)(12)$$
$$A = 30 \text{ sq in.}$$

In increasing order: triangle, rectangle, square

Answer: C

2. A right triangle is inscribed in a circle as shown. Write an expression involving π for the area of the shaded region.

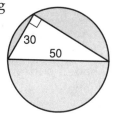

Solution: Since the triangle is a right triangle, the missing leg can be found by the Pythagorean Relation.

$$c^2 = a^2 + b^2$$
$$50^2 = 30^2 + b^2$$

Recognize that these numbers are a multiple of the triple 3, 4, 5.
The missing side is 10(4) or 40 units.

$$\text{area of shaded region} = \text{area of circle} - \text{area of triangle}$$
$$A = \pi r^2 - \frac{1}{2}bh$$
$$A = \pi(25)^2 - \frac{1}{2}(30)(40)$$

Answer: $A = 625\pi - 600$

Using a calculator, you can express the answer as 1,362.5 square units.

1. The area of a rectangle is 200 sq cm and one dimension is 15 cm. Find the length of a diagonal of the rectangle.

   A) 13.3 cm   B) 20.1 cm
   C) 28.3 cm   D) 48.1 cm

2. If a radius of a circle is tripled, then the area is:

   E) increased by 3
   F) multiplied by 9
   G) tripled
   H) cubed

3. If you draw a square with an an area equal to the area of triangle ABC, how long will each side of the square be?

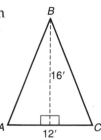

   A) A little less than 7 ft
   B) A little less than 10 ft
   C) A little more than 10 ft
   D) A little less than 14 ft

4. What is the area of the shaded portion of the triangle?

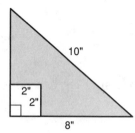

   E) 8 sq in.
   F) 20 sq in.
   G) 36 sq in.
   H) 44 sq in.

5. If A_L represents the area of the triangle on the left and A_R represents the area of the triangle on the right, which of the following is a correct comparison of the areas?

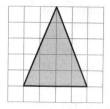
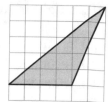

   A) $A_L < A_R$ B) $A_L > A_R$ C) $A_L = A_R$
   D) You cannot make the comparison without additional information.

6. A circle has a diameter with endpoints at $(5, 0)$ and $(-5, 0)$. How many square units are in the area of the circle?

   E) 5π F) 25   G) 25π H) 100π

7. In the figure, each side of the square has been divided into four equal segments. What is the ratio of the shaded area to the total area?

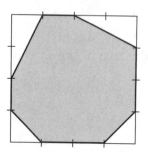

   A) $\dfrac{3}{16}$ B) $\dfrac{13}{16}$ C) $\dfrac{3}{8}$ D) $\dfrac{5}{8}$

8. A trapezoid has three sides each with a length of 5 units. If the height of the trapezoid is 4 units, what is the area of the trapezoid?

9. In a town, the property tax is $0.06 per square foot of land. What would the tax be on the plot of ground pictured?

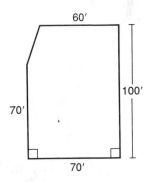

10. If there are 100 square units in the grid, what is the area, in square units, of the shaded figure?

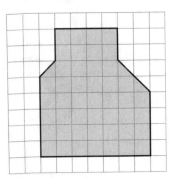

11. The length of a rectangle is increased by 20% and its width is decreased by 10%. Explain how to determine what happens to the area in terms of percent increase or percent decrease. Would the new area be the same if the original length were increased 10% and the original width were decreased 20%? Explain.

12. An isosceles trapezoid in the first quadrant has a lower base with endpoints at (0, 0) and (8, 0). The upper base has endpoints at (r, 6) and (t, 6) where r and t are whole numbers and $r < t$.

A. What values for r and t would give the largest area for the isosceles trapezoid?

B. What is this largest area? Show your process for finding the area.

C. Explain why the perimeter of the trapezoid cannot be a whole number. (You may need the Pythagorean theorem to answer part C. See page 98.)

2.15 Volume

The *volume* of a solid figure is the number of cubic units that fit inside the solid.
Formulas can be used to find the volumes of common solid figures.

Volume of Solid Figures		
Cube $V = e^3$	**Rectangular Prism** $V = \ell \cdot w \cdot h$	**Pyramid** $V = \frac{1}{3}(B \cdot h)$
Cylinder $V = \pi r^2 h$	**Cone** $V = \frac{1}{3}\pi r^2 h$	**Sphere** $V = \frac{4}{3}\pi r^3$

MODEL PROBLEMS

1. Which of the following rectangular prisms does NOT have a volume of 48 cubic units?

A)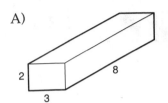

B)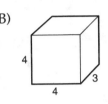

C)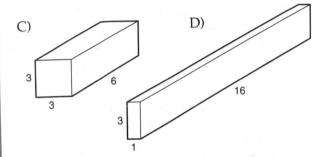

D)

Solution: Use V = area of base × height.
For rectangular prism, $V = lwh$.
Prism A: $V = 2 \times 3 \times 8 = 48$ cu units
Prism B: $V = 4 \times 4 \times 3 = 48$ cu units
Prism C: $V = 3 \times 3 \times 6 = 54$ cu units
Prism D: $V = 3 \times 1 \times 16 = 48$ cu units

Answer: C

2. The Air Puff Popcorn Company is considering the three designs shown as new containers for their popcorn.

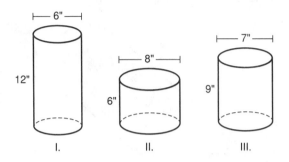

I.   II.   III.

Which container holds the most popcorn?

Solution: The container that holds the most popcorn is the one with the greatest volume.

$$V = \pi r^2 h$$

Container I: $V = 3.14(3)^2 \cdot (12) = 339.12$ in.³
Container II: $V = 3.14(4)^2 \cdot (6) = 301.44$ in.³
Container III: $V = 3.14(3.5)^2 \cdot (9) = 346.185$ in.³

Answer: Container III holds the most popcorn.

PRACTICE

1. If the edge of a cube is doubled, the volume is multiplied by:

A) 2   B) 3   C) 6   D) 8

2. Which of the following has a volume different from the other three volumes?

E) A cylinder with a radius of 4 cm and a height of 9 cm

F) A cylinder with a radius of 5 cm and a height of 6 cm

G) A cylinder with a radius of 2 cm and a height of 36 cm

H) A cylinder with a radius of 6 cm and a height of 4 cm

3. The measure of a radius of a cone is doubled and the measure of the height remains the same. The volume is multiplied by:

   A) 2   B) 4   C) 6   D) 8

4. An ice cream log is packaged as a semicircular cylinder as shown. What is the volume of the package in cubic inches?

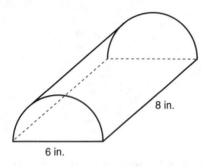

8 in.

6 in.

   E) 18π   F) 24π   G) 36π   H) 72π

5. What is the volume of this right triangular prism?

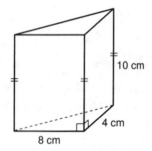

10 cm

4 cm

8 cm

6. Find the number of cubic centimeters in the volume of the solid shown.

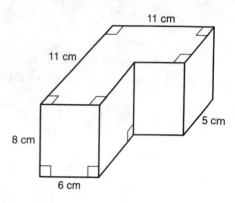

11 cm

11 cm

5 cm

8 cm

6 cm

7. Two cylinders have the same height. If the base of one of the cylinders has a diameter that is three times the diameter of the other base, how do the volumes of the two cylinders compare?

8. A structure is formed with a cone attached to a cylinder. Find the volume of the structure. Show your use of formulas. Give your answer to the nearest cubic inch.

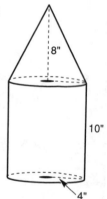

8"

10"

4"

9. You have 80 blocks, each one a cube with a volume of 1 cubic centimeter. List the dimensions of all the different rectangular prisms you can build using all the blocks for each prism. Explain why none of these prisms turns out to be a cube.

2.16 Surface Area

The *surface area* of a solid is the sum of the areas of all the surfaces of the solid.
Surface area is measured in square units.

To find the surface area of a solid:

- Visualize the unfolded pattern made up of the faces of the solid.
- Find the area of each face of the solid.
- Find the sum of the areas.

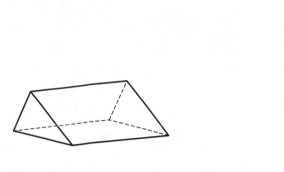

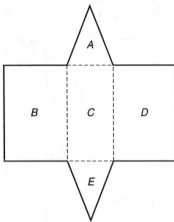

Surface area of the triangular prism = Area A + Area B + Area C + Area D + Area E

MODEL PROBLEMS

1. Find the surface area of the triangular prism shown.

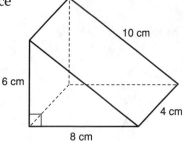

10 cm

6 cm

4 cm

8 cm

Solution: The surface area of the prism equals the area of two triangular faces plus the area of three rectangular faces.

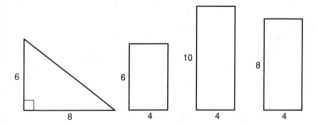

6

8

6

4

10

4

8

4

$A = \frac{1}{2}bh$ $A = bh$ $A = bh$ $A = bh$

$= \frac{1}{2}(8)(6)$ $= (6)(4)$ $= (10)(4)$ $= (8)(4)$

$= 24$ $= 24$ $= 40$ $= 32$

surface area of prism $= 2(24) + 24 + 40 + 32$

Answer: 144 cm^2

2. If the surface area of the cube is 24 cm^2, what is the length of an edge of the cube?

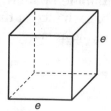

e

e

Solution: Surface area of cube $= 6 \cdot$ area of a face

$$24 = 6 \cdot e^2$$
$$4 = e^2$$
$$2 = e$$

Answer: An edge is 2 cm.

PRACTICE

1. Find the surface area of a cube whose edge has a length of 5 cm.

   A) 100 cm^2 B) 120 cm^2
   C) 125 cm^2 D) 150 cm^2

2. Which of the following applications would require finding surface area?

   E) Finding the amount of packing material needed to fill a box
   F) Finding the amount of ribbon needed to tie a bow on a gift box
   G) Determining the amount of wrapping paper needed for a gift box
   H) Determining the amount of water needed to fill a fish tank

3. The diagram shows a structure made with eight cubes. If each cube has an edge of 1 cm, what is the surface area of the structure?

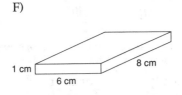

A) 22 cm²   B) 26 cm²
C) 28 cm²   D) 30 cm²

4. Of the following solids, which one has the greatest surface area?

E)

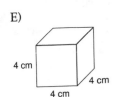

4 cm
4 cm
4 cm

F)

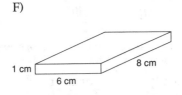

1 cm
6 cm
8 cm

G)

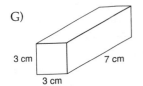

3 cm
3 cm
7 cm

H)

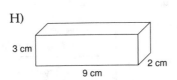

3 cm
9 cm
2 cm

5. The volume of a cube is 27 cubic inches. Find the surface area.

6. The bottom of a box meaures 18 cm by 20 cm. The box is 10 cm high and has no top. What is the surface area of the box?

7. Find x such that the total surface area of the prism is 132 square inches.

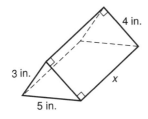

4 in.
3 in.
x
5 in.

8. Two rectangular prisms have the same volume. Show that it is not necessary for them to have the same surface area. Use a diagram with your explanation.

9. A rectangular solid has a surface area of 42 square units. If the dimensions are each tripled, find the new surface area. Explain your procedure and generalize the relationship between the original surface area and the surface area after the dimensions are tripled.

10. Sketch the figure that the net shown folds into.

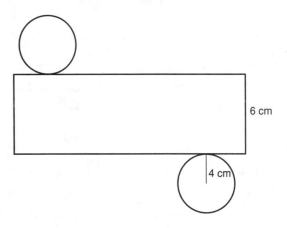

6 cm
4 cm

A. What is the solid called?
B. Find its volume. Show your process.
C. Find its surface area. Show your process.
D. Suppose the "6 cm" and "4 cm" on the figure above were switched. What change would result in the surface area?

Standard and Non-Standard Units of Measure

Measurement Systems

The *metric system* of measurement is a decimal system. The basic unit for length is the *meter*, for weight is the *gram*, and for capacity is the *liter*.

To convert from a larger unit to a smaller unit, multiply the larger unit by an appropriate power of 10. To convert from a smaller unit to a larger unit, divide the smaller unit by an appropriate power of 10.

Here is the relationship of the units in the metric system to the basic unit:

1000	100	10	1	0.1	0.01	0.001
kilo-	*hecto-*	*deka-*	*unit*	*deci-*	*centi-*	*milli-*

The chart shows the most commonly used units of measure in the *customary system* of measures.

To change from a larger unit to a smaller unit, multiply the larger unit by the appropriate conversion factor. To change from a smaller unit to a larger unit, divide the smaller unit by the appropriate conversion factor.

Length	Weight (Mass)	Liquid (Capacity)
Customary System: 1 foot (ft) = 12 inches (in.) 1 yard (yd) = 36 inches 1 yard = 3 feet 1 mile (mi) = 5,280 feet	Customary System: 1 pound (lb) = 16 ounces (oz) 1 ton (T) = 2,000 pounds	Customary System: 1 cup (c) = 8 fluid ounces 1 pint (pt) = 2 cups 1 quart (qt) = 2 pints 1 gallon (gal) = 4 quarts
Metric System: 1 meter (m) = 100 cm 1 kilometer (km) = 1000 m	Metric System: 1 gram (g) = 1000 mg 1 kilogram (kg) = 1000 g	Metric System: 1 liter (l) = 1000 ml

MODEL PROBLEMS

1. A rectangle has a length of 85 cm and a width of 53 cm. What is the perimeter of the rectangle in meters?

Solution:

$P = 2(l + w)$

$P = 2(85 \text{ cm} + 53 \text{ cm}) = 2(138 \text{ cm}) = 276 \text{ cm}$

To change to meters, divide by 100 since 1 cm = 0.01 meter.

Answer: $P = 2.76$ m

2. Bob purchased two packages of ground beef for hamburgers. One package weighed 2.5 pounds and the other package weighed 3.75 pounds. How many four-ounce hamburgers can Bob make from the two packages?

Solution: Total number of pounds purchased = 2.5 lb + 3.75 lb = 6.25 lb. Since 1 pound equals 16 ounces, 4 ounces equal $\frac{1}{4}$ of a pound. In 6 pounds, you have 24 four-ounce hamburgers and 0.25 lb equals another four-ounce hamburger.

Answer: 25 hamburgers can be made.

Converting Units

In the customary measurement system, 60 miles per hour (mph) is considered a unit of rate. Sometimes it is necessary to convert a unit of rate to an equivalent unit.

To convert unit rates:

- Write the given unit in fraction form.
- Write one or more conversion fractions.
- Multiply and cancel.

MODEL PROBLEM

Convert 60 mph to ft/min.

Solution: Since 60 mph can be written as $\frac{60 \text{ miles}}{1 \text{ hour}}$, the conversion can be accomplished by selecting conversion fractions (each equal to 1) to lead to the goal of ft/min.

1 mile = 5,280 feet

1 hour = 60 minutes

$$\frac{60 \text{ mi}}{1 \text{ hr}} \times \frac{5,280 \text{ ft}}{1 \text{ mi}} \times \frac{1 \text{ hr}}{60 \text{ min}} = \frac{5,280 \text{ ft}}{1 \text{ min}} \quad \textbf{Answer}$$

Strategies of Estimation

Rounding numbers is a common method of estimating. When you round a number, you change the exact value to an approximate value. A number is rounded to a specific *place value* depending on the problem and how much accuracy is needed.

There are a few things you need to remember when you are rounding a number:

(1) Decide how much accuracy is needed, that is, to what place value you will round the number.

(2) Underline the number that in the place value.

(3) Look at the number to the right of the underlined number.

- If the number to the right is greater than or equal to 5, add 1 to the underlined number and substitute zeros for all the numbers to the right of the underlined number.

- If the number to the right of the underlined number is less than 5, leave the underlined number as it is and substitute zeros for all the numbers to the right of the underlined number.

 ## MODEL PROBLEM

What is 482 rounded to the nearest hundreds place?

  A) 300   B) 400   C) 480   D) 500

Solution: Underline 4 in 4̲82, since that is in the hundreds place. The number to the right of 4 is 8, and 8 > 5. Therefore, add 1 to the 4, which makes 5. Then substitute zeros for all the numbers that were to the right of 4. 482 rounded to the nearest hundreds place is 500.

Answer: D

Estimation can be used to solve problems in which the exact answer is not needed. Remember that you must first use the given information.

MODEL PROBLEM

In a forest, an area measuring 1,000 square yards contains 700 trees. Estimate how many trees are in each area measuring 1,400 square yards.

Solution: Since 1,000 square yards contains 700 trees, 2,000 square yards would contain twice that number: 1,400 trees. Halfway between 1,000 and 2,000 is 1,500 square yards, and halfway between 700 and 1,400 would be 1,050 trees. Since 1,400 square yards is a little less than 1,500 square yards, you can estimate that there would be a little less than 1,000 trees in 1,400 square yards.

Answer: any number that is a little less than 1,000

Once you have calculated an answer, or if you are looking at possible answers, be sure to check to see if the answer is reasonable. For example, if the it takes 3 days to wash 10 windows, something is probably wrong. If the answer to a problem indicates that a man would be 13 feet tall or that a customers would pay $2.50 for a 10-carat diamond ring, something is wrong. When this happens, redo the problem, looking for a mistake.

MODEL PROBLEM

Michael is 50 years younger than his uncle Paul. Which of the following cannot be Uncle Paul's age?

  A) 47   B) 64   C) 80   D) 103

Solution: Uncle Paul could not be 47 years old, since that would make Michael −3 years old, which is impossible.

Answer: A

Estimating Measurements

In working with measurements, you can judge the reasonableness of results better if you know how common units of measure relate to familiar objects.

Length	
inch:	distance between the joints of your index finger
foot:	length of a sheet of notebook paper
yard:	distance from the tip of your nose to the tip of your middle finger with your arm outstretched
meter:	a little more than a yard
centimeter:	a little less than half an inch
Weight/Mass	
gram:	weight of a paper clip
kilogram:	weight of a hammer
ounce:	weight of a slice of bread
pound:	weight of a loaf of bread

 MODEL PROBLEM

Which of the following is the best estimate for the measure of the diameter of an NBA basketball?

    A) 4 in.   B) 8 in.   C) 13 in.   D) 24 in.

Solution: 4 inches and 8 inches would be too small.
              24 inches would be much too large.

Answer: 13 inches is a reasonable estimate.

Accuracy of Measurements

In measuring length using an inch ruler, it is necessary to determine the degree of precision required.

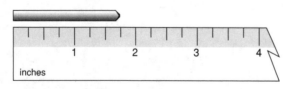

The pencil is 2 inches long to the nearest inch.

The pencil is $1\frac{1}{2}$ inches long to the nearest half inch.

The pencil is $1\frac{3}{4}$ inches long to the nearest quarter inch.

MODEL PROBLEM

Find the length of the straw to the nearest half inch.

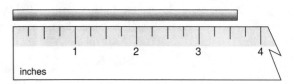

Solution: The length of the straw is between 3 and 4 inches. To find the length to the nearest half inch, you need to see if it is closer to 3, $3\frac{1}{2}$, or 4. Since it is closer to $3\frac{1}{2}$, the length is $3\frac{1}{2}$ inches.

Error in Measurement

Sometimes even when great care is taken in measuring an object, an error occurs. Inaccurate measurement is often caused by the limitations of the measuring equipment. For example, we can use a ruler to measure something to the nearest $\frac{1}{4}$ inch or with a steady eye to the nearest $\frac{1}{8}$ inch. However, if we used the ruler to measure a pen that is exactly $6\frac{3}{70}$ inches long, we would be able to say only that the length of the pen is very close to 6 inches. The $\frac{3}{70}$ of an inch is too small to measure; therefore, our measurement of the pen has an error of $\frac{3}{70}$.

The *margin of error* describes the maximum difference expected between a measurement and the truth value. A margin of error is sometimes written with a plus-or-minus sign ($\pm$). A smaller margin of error implies that the measurement is more exact. For the ruler that we used in the example above, the margin of error might be $\pm\frac{1}{32}$ inch.

MODEL PROBLEM

The population of a town is 5,470 when rounded to the nearest 10 people. What is the range of numbers for the actual population? What is the margin of error?

Solution:

If there were 5,465 people, 5,465 would be rounded up to 5,470: $5{,}470 - 5{,}465 = 5$

If there were 5,474 people, 5,474 would be rounded down to 5,470: $5{,}474 - 5{,}470 = 4$

The range for the population is from 5,465 to 5,474. The maximum possible error is 5, so the margin of error is ± 5.

1. A tree grows 1.4 cm each day. In 120 days, how many METERS will the tree have grown?

   A) 0.168 m   B) 1.68 m
   C) 16.8 m   D) 168 m

2. Which of the following is a correct measurement of the length of the crayon?

   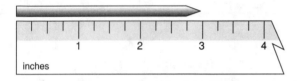

   E) 2 inches to the nearest inch

   F) $2\frac{1}{2}$ inches to the nearest half inch

   G) $2\frac{1}{2}$ inches to the nearest quarter inch

   H) 3 inches to the nearest half inch

3. Which of the conversions below would be done using the following procedure?

   $$6 \text{ mi} \times \frac{5{,}280 \text{ ft}}{1 \text{ mi}} \times \frac{12 \text{ in.}}{1 \text{ ft}}$$

   A) Miles to feet
   B) Feet to miles
   C) Miles to inches
   D) Inches to miles

4. Which of the following is a correct reading of the voltage?

   E) 4 volts to the nearest volt
   F) 3.5 volts to the nearest volt
   G) 3.5 volts to the nearest $\frac{1}{2}$ volt

   H) 3.5 volts to the nearest $\frac{1}{4}$ volt

5. Each side of a regular decagon (10-sided figure) has a length of 4.25 inches. Find the perimeter.

   A) 3 ft 6.5 in.   B) 3 ft 8 in.
   C) 3 ft 11 in.   D) 4 ft

6. Approximately what percent of a yard is an inch?

   E) 3%   F) 10%   G) 33%   H) 36%

7. At 6:00 A.M., the temperature in Nome, Alaska, was 15° below zero Fahrenheit. The average increase in temperature per hour was 3°. What was the temperature at noon?

   A) −12°F   B) −3°F   C) 3°F   D) 33°F

8. For which of the following objects would 180 cm be a good estimate of its length?

   E) The length of a driveway
   F) The length of a dining room table
   G) The height of a kindergarten child
   H) The length of a city block

9. For which of the following objects would 6 pounds be a good estimate of its weight?

   A) A box of cereal
   B) Three apples
   C) Two math textbooks
   D) A case of 24 packages of copy paper

10. Choose the best comparison of the two indicated weights:

    p = weight of a 5-pound bag of potatoes
    q = weight of a 1-kilogram box of sugar

    E) $p > q$ F) $p < q$ G) $p = q$
    H) You cannot complete the comparison based on the given information.

11. Christopher's family bought a new rug to cover part of the their living room floor. The rug measures 108 square feet. Which could not be the measurements of their living room?

    A) 12 feet by 10 feet
    B) 8 feet by 10 feet
    C) 13 feet by 15 feet
    D) 14 feet by 12 feet

12. Justin polled the entire freshman class to learn about their opinion on two versions of a dress code. The poll indicated that 35% preferred dress code A, 45% preferred dress code B, and 20% were undecided. The poll had a margin of error of ±5%. Which of the following is a possibility for the true results of the poll?

E) 40% for dress code A, 30% for dress code B, and 30% undecided

F) 40% for dress code A, 40% for dress code B, and 20% undecided

G) 50% for dress code A, 40% for dress code B, and 10% undecided

H) 50% for dress code A, 25% for dress code B, and 25% undecided

13. Using a ruler, measure the sides of the given figure to the nearest $\frac{1}{8}$ in. Record all measurements. What is the perimeter of the figure to the nearest eighth of an inch?

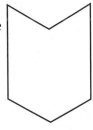

14. How many times does a person's heart beat in one day if it beats an average of 68 times per minute?

15. Temperature can be measured in either of two systems: *Celsius* (0° freezing point of water; 100° boiling point of water) and *Fahrenheit* (32° freezing point of water; 212° boiling point of water). The two systems are related by the formula:

$$F = \frac{9}{5}C + 32°$$

20°C is considered an appropriate measure for room temperature. Express this measure in degrees Fahrenheit.

16. Use an inch ruler to determine the lengths of the sides of the figure shown. Use your measurements to find the area of the figure.

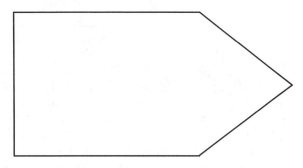

2.18 Pythagorean Theorem

If you know the lengths of two sides of a right triangle, a special formula can be used to find the length of the third side.

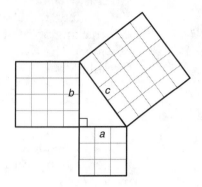

The number of square units in the square on the hypotenuse, c, is equal to the sum of the number of square units in the squares on both legs, a and b.

$$c^2 = a^2 + b^2$$

 ## MODEL PROBLEMS

1. A ladder is 6 meters long. If the ladder is leaning against a wall and the bottom of the ladder is 3 meters from the base of the wall, how far up the wall does the ladder reach?

Solution:
Let h = height of the wall.

$c^2 = a^2 + b^2$
$6^2 = 3^2 + h^2$
$36 = 9 + h^2$
$27 = h^2$
$h = \sqrt{27}$

Answer: $h \approx 5.2$ meters

2. Is a triangle with sides of lengths 5, 9, and 10 a right triangle?

Solution: If the triangle is a right triangle, the lengths of the sides must satisfy the Pythagorean Relation. Conversely, if the lengths of the three sides satisfy the Pythagorean Relation, the triangle must be a right triangle.

$5^2 + 9^2 \stackrel{?}{=} 10^2$
$25 + 81 \stackrel{?}{=} 100$
$106 \neq 100$

Answer: The triangle is NOT a right triangle.

1. Which of the following represents the lengths of the sides of a right triangle?

   A) 2, 3, 4
   B) 3, 4, 6
   C) 6, 8, 10
   D) 4, 6, 8

2. A rectangle has dimensions 5 cm by 12 cm. How many centimeters long is a diagonal of the rectangle?

   E) 12   F) 13   G) 17   H) 30

3. The two legs of a right triangle have lengths of 5 and 6 units. Between what two integers would the length of the hypotenuse fall?

   A) 5 and 6
   B) 6 and 7
   C) 7 and 8
   D) 8 and 9

4. A right triangle has two sides of lengths 3 and 4. Which of the following could be the length of the third side?

   I. 5   II. $\sqrt{7}$ III. 7

   E) I only
   F) II only
   G) I and II
   H) I and III

5. Pauline walked 4 km due east and then 7 km due north. Which of the following is the most reasonable answer for the distance between Pauline's start and endpoint?

   A) 6.5 km   B) 8.1 km
   C) 9 km   D) 11 km

6. An 8-foot ladder leaning against a wall reaches 6 feet up the wall. How far from the base of the wall is the bottom of the ladder?

   E) 2 ft   F) 5.3 ft   G) 6.2 ft   H) 10 ft

7. Find the value of b in this right triangle.

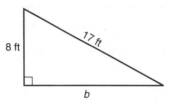

8. Each diagonal of a rectangle has a length of 10 yards. If one dimension of the rectangle is 6 yards, find the perimeter.

9. In circle O, chord $\overline{AB}$ is bisected by segment OM. If $OM = 6$ inches and $AB = 16$ inches, what is the length of a diameter of the circle?

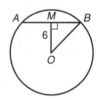

10. Show how you can use the Pythagorean Relation to find the distance from $(0, 0)$ to $(6, 8)$. Use a grid and then write your procedure.

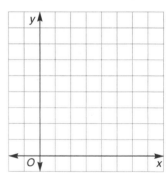

11. Triangle ABC is isosceles with a base of 10 cm and perimeter of 36 cm. Show how you can use the Pythagorean Relation to find the height of the triangle. Give the steps used in your thinking.

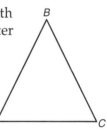

2.19 Trigonometric Ratios

A *trigonometric ratio* is the ratio of the lengths of two sides of a right triangle. Trigonometric ratios can be used to find missing measures within right triangles.

Trig Ratio	Definition
sine of A	$\sin A = \dfrac{\text{leg opposite } \angle A}{\text{hypotenuse}} = \dfrac{a}{c}$
cosine of A	$\cos A = \dfrac{\text{leg adjacent to } \angle A}{\text{hypotenuse}} = \dfrac{b}{c}$
tangent of A	$\tan A = \dfrac{\text{leg opposite } \angle A}{\text{leg adjacent to } \angle A} = \dfrac{a}{b}$

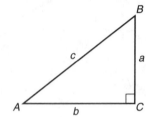

Note: A is the measurement of $\angle A$.

 MODEL PROBLEMS

1. Find $\sin P$, $\cos P$, $\tan P$. Express each ratio as a fraction and a decimal.

Solution: $\sin P = \dfrac{3}{5} = 0.6$

$\cos P = \dfrac{4}{5} = 0.8$

$\tan P = \dfrac{3}{4} = 0.75$

2. Find the value of each expression. Use a scientific calculator to give the value rounded to the nearest ten-thousandth. (*Note:* Make sure the calculator is in degree mode.)

A. $\cos 22°$

B. $\tan 50°$

Solution: $\cos 22 = 0.927183854 = 0.9272$

$\tan 50 = 1.191753593 = 1.1918$

3. A kite is being flown with a 55′ string. If the kite makes a 30° angle with the ground, how high above the ground is the kite? Be sure to show a diagram and the work leading to your solution.

Solution:

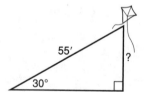

Since you want to know the height of the kite represented by the distance opposite the 30° angle in the given right triangle and you know the adjacent leg, use the trig ratio for sine to find the missing length.

$\sin 30 = \dfrac{x}{55}$

$0.5 = \dfrac{x}{55}$ (use a calculator to find sin 30)

$0.5(55) = x$

$27.5 = x$

Answer: 27.5′ above the ground

1. Find cos A for the given triangle.

   A) 0.3846   B) 0.4167

   C) 0.9231   D) 2.4

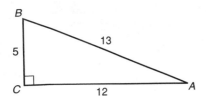

2. Find m$\angle A$ (to the nearest degree) in the right triangle with vertices at $A(6, 0)$, $B(0, 8)$, $C(0, 0)$.

   E) 36°   F) 45°   G) 53°   H) 60°

3. Which of the following would NOT be sufficient information to allow you to complete the task of finding the measures of the three sides and three angles of a right triangle?

   A) The lengths of the two legs

   B) The measures of the two acute angles

   C) The meaure of one acute angle and the length of the hypotenuse

   D) The measure of one acute angle and the length of one leg

4. In right triangle ABC, if sin $A = \dfrac{5}{13}$, find cos A and tan A.

5. A surveyor needs to find how far away she is from a 200-foot cliff. If the angle of inclination she makes with the top of the cliff is 28°, how far (to the nearest foot) is she from the bottom of the cliff?

6. Find the value of x and y. Round to the nearest tenth of a centimeter. Show your process and explain why it is reasonable that the values of x and y are not equal.

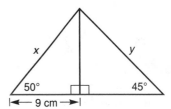

7. An engineer is designing a ramp for wheelchair entry into a building. If the ramp must reach a height of 6 feet and have an angle of elevation of 4°, what should the length of the ramp's base be?

   Draw an illustration to show the situation.

   If the angle of elevation is increased, how will this affect the length of the ramp's base? If the angle is decreased, how will the length be changed?

2.20 Trigonometric Applications

The Law of Cosines

There are several methods for solving problems about triangles that do not contain right angles. If we are given information about two sides and the angle between the two sides, we can use the *Law of Cosines* to find the length of the remaining side. The formula for the Law of Cosines is $c^2 = a^2 + b^2 - 2ab \cos \angle C$, where C is the angle opposite side c, the side whose length is unknown. This formula can be rewritten to express a similar relationship for the lengths of sides to the cosine of angle B or angle A.

 MODEL PROBLEM

In $\triangle ABC$, $a = 11$, $b = 12$, and $m\angle C = 120$. The length of side c, to the nearest integer is

- A) 10
- B) 13
- C) 15
- D) 20

Solution: Sketch $\triangle ABC$ labeling all the given information.

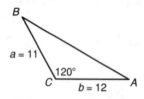

From the diagram, we know that we are looking for the length of the side opposite angle C. Since we know the length of the two other sides of the triangle, we substitute the given values in the formula for the Law of Cosines and solve.

$$c^2 = a^2 + b^2 - 2ab \cos \angle C$$

$$c^2 = 11^2 + 12^2 - 2(11)(12)(\cos 120°)$$

$$c^2 = 121 + 144 - 2(11)(12)\left(-\frac{1}{2}\right)$$

$$c^2 = 121 + 144 + 132$$

$$c^2 = 397$$

$$c = \sqrt{397}$$

$$c \approx 20$$

Answer: D

Sometimes we are asked to find the measure of an angle when given the lengths of the three sides of a triangle. In this case, simply manipulate the Law of Cosines so that the cosine value is isolated.

$$c^2 = a^2 + b^2 - 2ab \cos \angle C$$

$$c^2 - a^2 - b^2 = -2ab \cos \angle C$$

$$\frac{c^2 - a^2 - b^2}{-2ab} = \cos \angle C$$

$$\text{or } \cos \angle C = \frac{a^2 + b^2 - c^2}{2ab}$$

 ## MODEL PROBLEM

In isosceles triangle RED, $RE = ED = 5$ and $RD = 8$. Find the measure of the vertex angle, $\angle E$, to the nearest degree.

Solution:

Let $RE = d = 5$

$ED = r = 5$

$RD = e = 8$

$$\cos \angle E = \frac{d^2 + r^2 - e^2}{2dr}$$

$$= \frac{5^2 + 5^2 - 8^2}{2(5)(5)} = \frac{25 + 25 - 64}{50} = \frac{-14}{50} = -0.28$$

$$\text{m}\angle E = \cos^{-1}(-0.28) \approx 106°$$

Law of Sines

Another method in solving triangles that do not contain a right angle is the **Law of Sines**. The *Law of Sines* can be used to find the measure of a side of a triangle when measures of two angles and a side are known. It can also be used to find the measure of an angle of a triangle when the measure of an angle other than the angle formed by the two given lengths is known. The following are diagrams showing the situations when the Law of Sines is applied.

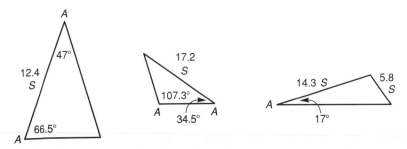

The Law of Sines is $\dfrac{a}{\sin\angle A} = \dfrac{b}{\sin\angle B} = \dfrac{c}{\sin\angle C}$. It states that the sine of an angle is proportional to the side opposite that angle. When using this method, always draw a diagram to be certain you have the correct angle and side relationships. Also remember to use only two of the possible ratios to solve the proportion.

 # MODEL PROBLEMS

1. In $\triangle ABC$, $a = 12$, $\sin\angle A = \dfrac{1}{3}$, and $\sin\angle C = \dfrac{1}{4}$. Find c.

Solution:

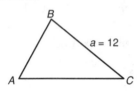

$$\frac{a}{\sin\angle A} = \frac{c}{\sin\angle C}$$

$$\frac{12}{\frac{1}{3}} = \frac{c}{\frac{1}{4}}$$

$$(12)\left(\frac{1}{4}\right) = \frac{1}{3}c$$

$$3 = \frac{1}{3}c$$

$$9 = c$$

2. In $\triangle XYZ$, $XY = 14.3$, $YZ = 5.8$, and $m\angle ZXY = 17$. Find the measure of $\angle YZX$ to the nearest tenth of a degree.

Solution: Because we are given the information about the triangle in a side-side-angle pattern, we must consider the possibility that two different triangles will satisfy the given information. Since $XY > YZ$, the measure $\angle YZX$ must be greater than the measure of $\angle YXZ$. Whether or not it is an obtuse triangle depends on our solution. First, we must find the value of $\sin\angle Z$.

$$\frac{x}{\sin\angle X} = \frac{z}{\sin\angle Z}$$

$$\frac{5.8}{\sin 17°} = \frac{14.3}{\sin\angle Z}$$

$$5.8\sin\angle Z = 14.3\sin 17°$$

$$\sin\angle Z = \frac{14.3\sin 17°}{5.8}$$

$$\sin\angle Z = 0.720847489$$

$$\angle Z = 46.1°$$

However, since the sine function is positive in the first and second quadrants, it is also possible that ∠Z is obtuse, measuring 133.9°. Therefore, it is possible to have two different triangles formed by the information given: one with angles measuring 17°, 46.1°, and an obtuse angle of 116.9°; the second with m∠Z = 133.9, m∠X = 17, and m∠Y = 29.1. This situation is often called the *ambiguous case*, because we do not know the intended measure of ∠Z. So we must give both possible angles. The two different possible triangles are shown below.

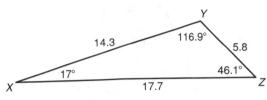

∠Z is acute and ∠Y is obtuse.

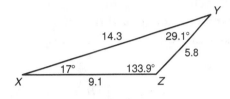

∠Z is obtuse and ∠Y is acute.

When you need to determine how many different triangles are possible when the given information is in side-side-angle pattern, remember the following:

(1) If given ∠A is obtuse and $a \leq c$, then 0 triangles can be formed.
(2) If given ∠A is obtuse and $a > c$, then 1 triangle may be formed.
(3) If given ∠A is acute and $c > a > c \sin \angle A$, then 2 triangles can be formed.
(4) If given ∠A is acute and $a = c \sin \angle A$, then 1 triangle can be formed.
(5) If given ∠A is acute and $a \geq c \geq c \sin \angle A$, then 1 triangle can be formed.
(6) If given ∠A is acute and $a < c \sin \angle A$, 0 triangles can be formed.

PRACTICE

1. An isosceles triangle has equal sides of 12.4 and a vertex angle of 93.4°. What is the length of the third side of the triangle to the nearest tenth?

   A) 4.9   B) 18   C) 18.5   D) 48.9

2. In triangle JAR, m∠JAR = 120, AJ = 5.8 centimeters, and AR = 8.3 centimeters. The length of $\overline{JR}$ to the nearest tenth is which of the following?

   E) 7.4 cm   F) 11.3 cm
   G) 12.3 cm   H) 13.3 cm

3. In △CAT, c = 12 inches, a = 10 inches, and t = 6 inches. What is the measure of the smallest angle of the triangle?

   A) 56.3   B) 38.2   C) 29.9   D) 11.9

4. In △XYZ, x = 9 centimeters, y = 40 centimeters, and z = 41 centimeters. What is the cosine of the largest angle of the triangle?

   E) 0   F) 0.2195   G) 0.7071   H) 0.9756

5. In △FTG, t = 10, g = 14, and f = 20. What is the measure of ∠T to the nearest degree?

   A) 20   B) 22   C) 28   D) 30

6. In △ABC, b = 8.3, c = 6.4, and m∠B = 82.4. The measure of ∠C is

   E) 0.764   F) 49.8   G) 130.2   H) 139.8

7. In △SUN, sin ∠S = 0.6437, sin ∠U = 0.8134, and u = 13.2. The length of s to the nearest tenth is

   A) 10.4   B) 18.6   C) 43.8   D) 67.7

8. If $m = 7$, $n = 10$, and m∠M = 85, how many different triangles MNT can be drawn?

E) 1   F) 2   G) 3   H) 0

9. A ladder that is 10 feet long leans against a wall so that the top of the ladder just reaches the top of the wall. What is the height of the wall, to the nearest tenth of a foot, if the foot of the ladder makes an angle of 72° with the ground?

A) 10.5   B) 9.5   C) 8.5   D) 7.5

10. A wire that is 8.5 meters long runs in a straight line from the top of a telephone pole to a stake in the ground. If the wire makes an angle of 68° with the ground, find to the nearest tenth of a meter the height of the pole.

E) 9.2   F) 7.9   G) 6.2   H) 4.9

11. Donald and Matt bought a piece of marble that they would like to use as the top of a coffee table. Donald is making a triangular base for the table as shown in the diagram below. If the sides of the triangular base are 22 inches, 29 inches, and 32.5 inches, find the measures of the three angles, to the nearest hundredth of a degree, that Donald must construct for the base.

12. Libby and Lise are designing a triangular hopscotch board similar to the one shown in the diagram below. If the equal sides of their board are to be 8.5 feet in length, and the base angles measure 71°, find the length of the base to the nearest tenth of a foot.

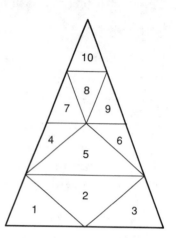

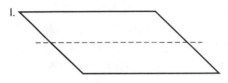

1. In using deductive reasoning to show that *a* equals *c*, which of the following would be the major justification?

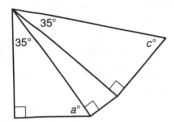

   A) Vertical angles have equal measure.
   B) Corresponding parts of congruent triangles are congruent.
   C) Complements of congruent angles are congruent.
   D) An angle bisector divides an angle into two angles of equal measure.

2. Two vertices of a triangle are $(0, 0)$ and $(6, 0)$. Which of the following points would NOT give you a right scalene triangle?

   E) $(0, -5)$ F) $(6, 4)$
   G) $(-3, 0)$ H) $(6, -4)$

3. Point *A* with coordinates $(8, 15)$ is on a circle with center at the origin. Find the coordinates of point *B* such that *AB* is a diameter of the circle.

   A) $(-15, -8)$ B) $(-8, -15)$
   C) $(8, -15)$ D) $(4, 7.5)$

4. Which of the following shows a line of symmetry for the figure?

I.

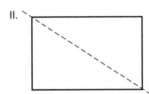

II.

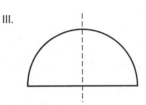

III.

   E) II only   F) III only
   G) II and III   H) I, II, and III

5. A triangle has vertices at $A(-3, 1)$, $B(3, 1)$, and $C(0, -5)$. How many lines of symmetry does the triangle have?

   A) 0   B) 1   C) 2   D) 3

6. If you spin a two-dimensional figure about a vertical axis, a cylinder results. What type of two-dimensional figure did you start with?

E) Right triangle
F) Semicircle
G) Rectangle
H) Trapezoid

7. How many different isosceles triangles can you find that have sides with integral lengths such that the perimeter of the triangle is 20?

A) 3   B) 4   C) 5   D) 6

8. A rectangular swimming pool is 72 feet long and 32.5 feet wide. The pool is surrounded by a concrete walkway that is 3.5 feet wide. What is the area of the walkway?

E) 227.5 square feet   F) 237 square feet
G) 378 square feet   H) 780.5 square feet

9. If the circumference of a circle is divided by the length of a radius, the quotient is:

A) $\frac{1}{2}\pi$ B) π C) 2π D) 2

10. Find the height of a trapezoid with an area of 42.5 square centimeters if one base is 5.2 cm and the other base is 3.3 cm.

E) 4.95 cm   F) 5 cm
G) 10 cm   H) 38.25 cm

11. Which of the conversions below would be done using the following operations?

$$\frac{70 \text{ mi}}{1 \text{ hr}} \times \frac{5,280 \text{ ft}}{1 \text{ mi}} \times \frac{1 \text{ hr}}{60 \text{ min}}$$

A) Miles per hour to miles per minute
B) Feet per minute to miles per hour
C) Miles per hour to feet per minute
D) Miles per hour to feet per second

12. If 1 in. $\approx$ 2.5 cm, then the length of a diagonal of a sheet of paper measuring $8\frac{1}{2}$ in. by 11 in. is closest to:

E) 35 cm F) 35 mm G) 70 cm H) 70 mm

13. Anytown USA has a cylindrical water tank with dimensions as shown. Due to increased demand for water, the council of Anytown wants to build a new cylindrical tank with twice the volume of the original tank. Which of the following options could be used?

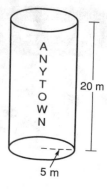

I. Double the height of the tank and maintain the same diameter.
II. Double the diameter of the tank and maintain the same height.
III. Double both the diameter and the height of the tank.

A) I only   B) II only
C) III only   D) I and II

14. Which of the lists below shows the three figures P, Q, and R in order of size from LEAST to GREATEST area?

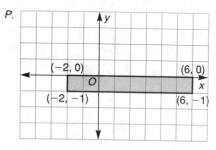

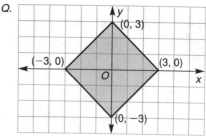

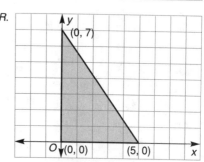

E) P, Q, R   F) Q, P, R
G) R, P, Q   H) P, R, Q

15. The Bagel Express uses an average of 2 lb 8 oz of cream cheese per hour. If the Bagel Express is open 7 hours a day for 7 days per week, about how much cream cheese would be used in 3 weeks?

A) 105 lb   B) 122.5 lb
C) 294 lb   D) 367.5 lb

16. Which of the following is NOT possible for some types of triangles regarding the number of lines of symmetry?

E) A triangle can have no lines of symmetry.
F) A triangle can have exactly one line of symmetry.
G) A triangle can have exactly two lines of symmetry.
H) A triangle can have three lines of symmetry.

17. The volume of a cube is at least 6,000 cubic units but no more than 7,000 cubic units. Determine the range of values (rounded to the nearest hundredth) for the length of a side.

A) 6.00–7.00   B) 12.59–13.26
C) 18.17–19.13   D) 77.46–83.67

18. The points (2, 5) and (2, −5) are the endpoints of a diameter of a circle. Find the area of the circle.

E) 4π square units   F) 5π square units
G) 25π square units   H) 100π square units

19. Which of the following sets of coordinates could represent the vertices of an isosceles trapezoid?

A) {(0, 0), (6, 0), (7, 4), (0, 4)}
B) {(0, 0), (6, 0), (6, 4), (0, 4)}
C) {(−4, 0), (0, 4), (4, 0), (0, −4)}
D) {(−4, 0), (4, 0), (2, 8), (−2, 8)}

20. If the letter **N** is reflected over the y-axis, which of the following represents the image?

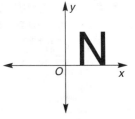

E)   F)

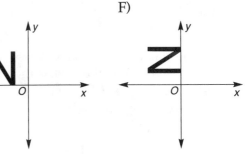

G)   H)

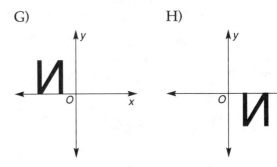

21. If the measure of ∠ECF is 15°, what is the measure of ∠ACD?

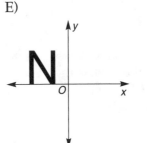

A) 45°   B) 135°   C) 145°   D) 165°

22. ABCD is a square. If you remove a small right triangle at vertices A and C (with right angles at A and C), what type of figure remains?

E) Octagon   F) Hexagon
G) Pentagon   H) Square

23. Draw a three-dimensional figure that has all three of the following characteristics:

A. an odd number of faces
B. an even number of vertices
C. more vertices than faces

24. *ABCD* is a square and the two triangles are equilateral. What is the measure of ∠*EBF*?

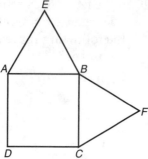

25. Two similar triangles have a ratio of similitude of 2.35 to 1. If the area of the smaller triangle is 8.4 square centimeters, what is the area of the larger triangle?

26. How many revolutions will it take a 24″-diameter bicycle wheel to travel 1 mile? (Give your answer to the nearest whole number.)

27. The diagram shows blocks along First Street and Second Street. If the total frontage on Second Street is 480 feet, find the length of each block along Second Street.

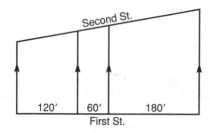

28. The inside of a can of three tennis balls is about 23 cm high and has a diameter of about 7.5 cm. Each ball has an outer circumference of about 23 cm. How much space is left in the can?

29. A piece of wire 106.2 cm long has been bent to form a rectangle. The area enclosed by the rectangle is 623 square centimeters. Find the longer side of the rectangle.

30. A line segment extends from the point (6, 4) to point *P* on the line *y* = 8 such that the slope of the segment is $\frac{1}{4}$. What are the coordinates of point *P*?

31. A wheel rolls along a straight path on the floor. If the diameter of the wheel is 30 centimeters, describe the path followed by the center of the wheel as the wheel rolls along the floor.

32. A pentagon has a perimeter of 50 cm. The shortest side of the pentagon has a length of 3 cm. Find the length of the shortest side of a similar pentagon if the perimeter of the second pentagon is 80 cm.

33. A rectangular solid has a volume of 227.5 cubic inches. If two dimensions are 5 inches and 7 inches, what would the third dimension be?

34. The figure consists of nine small congruent squares. If the area of the figure is 900 square units, find the perimeter of the figure.

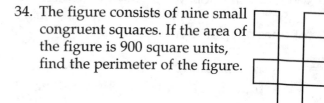

35. A flagpole has cracked 5 feet from the ground and fallen as if hinged. The top of the flagpole hits the ground 12 feet from the base. How tall was the flagpole before it fell?

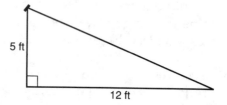

36. Using the grid, determine the area of the shaded figure.

37. Write the contrapositive of the statement "If a donut is a vegetable, then a cookie is a fruit."

38. A tree on level ground casts a shadow 32 feet long. The angle of elevation from the tip of the shadow to the top of the tree is 60°. Find the height of the tree.

39. Provide a convincing argument that the given triangle is a right triangle.

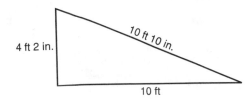

40. Find the area and perimeter of the trapezoid. Show your complete procedure.

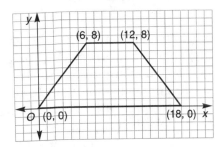

41. Explain why the perimeter of the figure must be greater than 20 units. Also, show how to obtain a good approximation for the perimeter.

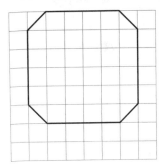

42. A. Explain why a triangle with sides, 5, 10, 12 cannot be a right triangle.
    B. Write an additional set of lengths of sides of a triangle that could NOT serve as the sides of a right triangle.
    C. Write three sets of lengths that could serve as the sides of a right triangle.

43.

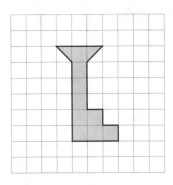

A. On a separate piece of grid paper, draw a rectangle with an area equal to the area of the figure in the grid.

B. On a separate piece of grid paper, draw a triangle with an area equal to the area of the figure in the grid.

44. A. Plot the points (8, 6), (8, 2), (14, 2) on grid paper. Connect them to form a triangle. What type of triangle is formed?
    B. Draw the triangle you get when you apply the rule (0.5x, 0.5y) to the three points given above. How are the two triangles related?
    C. The area of the smaller triangle is what percent of the area of the larger triangle? Explain why.

45. Use the pieces of the tangram to build the rectangle pictured below.

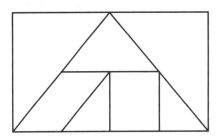

A. Move one piece of the rectangle to change the figure into a parallelogram with no right angles. Sketch your figure.

B. Write a paragraph to explain how the area and perimeter of the original rectangle compare to the area and perimeter of the new parallelogram. Be sure to explain how you know this relationship exists. It is not necessary actually to calculate the area and perimeter of the figures.

46. An octagon is shown on the grid.

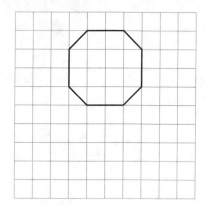

A. Describe any lines of symmetry that are neither horizontal nor vertical.

B. This octagon can be thought of as 4-by-4 square with the corners cut off. The area of the octagon is what percent of the area of the 4-by-4 square? Explain your procedure.

C. Using the blank grid, draw an octagon similar to the original with each side double the length of the original sides.

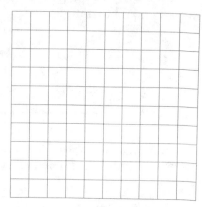

D. Explain what is wrong with the following argument concerning the original octagon and the larger one. Since the sides of the larger octagon are double the original sides, the area of the larger octagon must be double the original area.

CUMULATIVE ASSESSMENT

Chapters 1 and 2

1. Which of the following would represent all the real numbers at least 7 units away from -3 on the number line?

   A) $|x| \geq 7$
   B) $|x + 3| \geq 7$
   C) $|x - 3| \geq 7$
   D) $|x + 7| \geq -3$

2. The following numbers represent volumes of a cube. For which value would the cube NOT have an integral edge?

   E) 125   F) 300   G) 1,000   H) 3,375

3. A college team sweatshirt has a wholesale price of $30.00. The Sports Exchange applies a 20% markup on the wholesale price to obtain the retail price. During a sale, the same sweatshirt is priced at 15% off the retail price. What is the sale price?

   A) $20.40
   B) $30.60
   C) $31.50
   D) $36.00

4. If the area of a rectangle is 10 square units, what is the ratio of the length to the width?

   E) 1 to 10   F) 2 to 5   G) 5 to 2
   H) It cannot be determined from the information given.

5. How many two-digit numbers have all of the following characteristics?

   I. The number is a multiple of 16.
   II. The number is a factor of 144.
   III. The number is divisible by 3.

   A) 0   B) 1   C) 2   D) 3

6. The measures of the angles of a triangle are in the ratio of $3 : 4 : 11$. How many degrees are in the measure of the largest angle of the triangle?

   E) 10   F) 30   G) 55   H) 110

7. A line segment has endpoints at (1, 6) and (4, 6). The segment is translated 4 units to the right and 3 units down, and then reflected over the x-axis. After the reflection, what are the coordinates of the endpoints of the final segment?

A) (5, 3) and (8, 3)
B) (−5, 3) and (−8, 3)
C) (4, −2) and (7, −2)
D) (5, −3) and (8, −3)

8. On a map, 1 centimeter represents 125 kilometers. How many kilometers apart are two cities that are 48 millimeters apart on the map?

E) 60   F) 600   G) 6000   H) 60,000

9. Which of the following does NOT show a 10% increase?

A) $100 \rightarrow 110$
B) $50 \rightarrow 60$
C) $10 \rightarrow 11$
D) $\dfrac{1}{10} \rightarrow \dfrac{11}{100}$

10. If you double the radius of the base of a cylinder and also double the height of the cylinder, what percent increase will there be in the volume of the cylinder?

E) 200%   F) 400%   G) 700%   H) 800%

11. Using the data from this table, which of the following lists the correct order of the surface areas of the three boxes, from LEAST to GREATEST?

Box	Dimensions (in centimeters)
P	$6 \times 6 \times 6$
Q	$4 \times 10 \times 2$
R	$5 \times 8 \times 3$

A) P, Q, R
B) R, Q, P
C) Q, R, P
D) Q, P, R

12. Triangles ABC and ACD are right triangles. Determine the perimeter of quadrilateral ABCD. Give your answer to the nearest tenth of a unit.

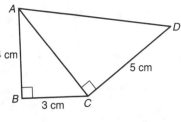

13. If $4^x = 32^y$, write an expression relating x and y.

14. Sketch two additional views from different perspectives for the figure shown.

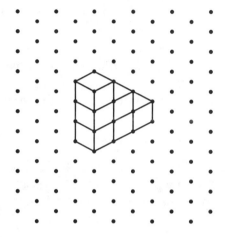

15. Two similar rectangles have areas of 12 square units and 108 square units. If the perimeter of the smaller rectangle is 14 units, what is the perimeter of the larger rectangle?

16. As a back-to-school incentive on Wednesdays, Supply Warehouse plans to give every fifteenth customer a free pen and every twenty-fifth customer a free notebook. On a particular Wednesday, Supply Warehouse had 300 customers.

    A. How many free pens were given away on that Wednesday?
    B. How many free notebooks were given away on that Wednesday?
    C. Did any customers receive a free pen and a free notebook? If so, how many customers?
    D. If pens sell for 79¢ and notebooks sell for $1.19, how much did the Supply Warehouse lose in income by giving away these items?

    Justify your answers.

17. Using the diagram, solve for x. Explain why you need to know that the two segments indicated are parallel in order to do the problem.

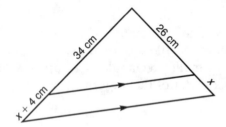

18. An isosceles triangle ABC has vertices at $A(0, 0)$, $B(6, 0)$, and $C(3, -8)$. A median of a triangle joins a vertex to the midpoint of the opposite side. Median AM intersects side BC at point M. Graph the triangle and the median. What are the coordinates at point M?

19. The formula for the volume of a cylinder is $V = \pi r^2 h$. If the height of a cylinder is 10 cm, what is the smallest whole number of centimeters for the length of the radius that would produce a volume of at least 500 cubic centimeters? Explain your procedure.

20. A rhombus has diagonals of length 16 inches and 20 inches.

    A. Draw a reasonable sketch of this rhombus.
    B. In order to find the perimeter of the rhombus, indicate two properties of the diagonals of a rhombus you would need to know. Find the perimeter of the rhombus.
    C. Using trigonometric ratios, find the degree measure of the obtuse angle of this rhombus. Show your work.

21. A square on a coordinate grid has horizontal and vertical sides. The upper left vertex of the square is located at $(-3, 4)$. The perimeter of the square is 32 units.

    A. Draw a sketch of the square and indicate the coordinates of the other three vertices.
    B. What percent of the area of the square is in each quadrant?
    C. Suppose you next translate the square 1 unit to the right. Does this translation change the percent of the area now existing in the third quadrant? Explain.

CHAPTER 3

Data Analysis, Probability, and Statistics

3.1 Probability of Simple Events

The *probability* of an event is the ratio of the number of favorable outcomes to the total number of possible outcomes.

$$\text{probability} = \frac{\text{number of favorable outcomes}}{\text{total number of possible outcomes}}$$

The probability of an event can be expressed as a fraction, decimal, or percent with a value greater than or equal to zero and less than or equal to one. ($0 \le P \le 1$)

If $P(A) = 0$, then it is impossible for A to occur.

If $P(A) = 1$, then it is certain the event will occur.

 MODEL PROBLEM

A standard die is rolled. Find each of the following:

  A. the probability of rolling a 5
  B. the probability of rolling an even number
  C. the probability of rolling a number less than 3
  D. the probability of rolling a number greater than 7
  E. the probability of rolling a number less than 7

Solution: With the sample space consisting of 1, 2, 3, 4, 5, 6, the simple probabilities can be determined by applying the definition of probability.

  A. $P(5) = \dfrac{1}{6}$ (since 5 is the only favorable outcome)

  B. $P(\text{even}) = \dfrac{3}{6}$ (since 2, 4, and 6 are favorable outcomes)

  C. $P(<3) = \dfrac{2}{6}$ (since 1 and 2 are favorable outcomes)

  D. $P(>7) = 0$ (since there are no favorable outcomes)

  E. $P(<7) = \dfrac{6}{6} = 1$ (since all outcomes are favorable)

Odds

Odds are calculated and expressed as ratios: "The odds are 25 to 2 in favor of . . ."
The expression means that if we ran 27 trials, we would expect the event to occur
in 25 of them. We would expect that in 2 of them, the event would not occur. Odds
can also be stated negatively: "The odds are 25 to 2 *against* . . . " This means that
if we ran 27 trials, we would expect the event to *not* occur in 25 of them.

To calculate odds, we find the *ratio of favorable events to unfavorable events*, or vice
versa. (By contrast, probability is the ratio of favorable events to *all* possible
events.) For example, if 80 tickets were sold in a raffle at a school carnival, and you
bought 24 of them, you can calculate your odds of winning as follows:

Favorable events = 24

Unfavorable events = total possible events minus favorable events
$$= 80 - 24 = 56$$

Odds $= 24$ to $56 = \dfrac{24}{56} = \dfrac{3}{7} = 3$ to 7 (or $3:7$)

To calculate your odds of *losing*, find the ratio of unfavorable events to favorable events:

56 to $24 = \dfrac{56}{24} = \dfrac{7}{3} = 7$ to 3 (or $7:3$)

The general formula for odds is as follows:

$$\text{odds in favor} = \frac{\text{number of favorable outcomes}}{\text{number of unfavorable outcomes}}$$

$$\text{odds against} = \frac{\text{number of unfavorable outcomes}}{\text{number of favorable outcomes}}$$

 MODEL PROBLEM

A box contains 9 red balls and 1 white ball.

A. What are the odds in favor of picking red when picking one ball from the box?
B. What are the odds in favor of picking white when picking one ball from the box?

Solution:

A. odds in favor of red $= \dfrac{\text{favorable}}{\text{unfavorable}} = \dfrac{9}{1}$; 9 to 1

B. odds in favor of white $= \dfrac{\text{favorable}}{\text{unfavorable}} = \dfrac{1}{9}$; 1 to 9

Note: While a probability must be a fraction less than or equal to 1, odds can turn out to be greater than 1 $\left(\text{such as } \frac{9}{1} \text{ as in example A}\right)$.

There are two *formulas for the relationship between odds and probability*. If the odds *in favor* of an event are x to y, then its probability is $\frac{x}{x+y}$. For instance, in our example of the raffle tickets, the odds in favor of winning were $3:7$, so the probability of winning is $\frac{3}{3+7} = \frac{3}{10} = .30$ or 30 percent.

If the odds *against* an event are x to y, it probability is $\frac{y}{x+y}$. In our example, the odds against winning were $7:3$, so the probability of winning is $\frac{y}{x+y} = \frac{3}{7+3} = \frac{3}{10} = .30$ or 30 percent.

 # MODEL PROBLEM

A spinner is divided into 5 equal parts, numbered 1, 2, 3, 4, 5. The arrow is spun and the odds that it will stop on a prime number are $3:2$, what is the probability that it will stop on a prime?

Solution:

Apply the formula. Odds in favor of stopping on a prime are 3 to 2, so:

Probability $= \frac{x}{x+y} = \frac{3}{3+2} = \frac{3}{5} = .6$ or 60 percent

Experimental and Theoretical Probabilities

Experimental probability results from conducting an experiment, making observations, or performing a simulation. For example, if you toss a coin 50 times and obtain 30 heads, the experimental probability of obtaining heads would be $\frac{30}{50}$ or $\frac{3}{5}$. Each time you toss the coin 50 times, the experimental probability of heads may vary.

In contrast with experimental probability, *theoretical probability* represents what you would expect from the "theory" or description of the situation. When we say that the probability of obtaining heads on the toss of a coin is $\frac{1}{2}$ or 50%, or the probability of obtaining an ace is $\frac{4}{52}$ or $\frac{1}{13}$, we are giving the theoretical probability.

1.

Girls in Families of Four Children	
Number of Girls	Frequency
0	10
1	15
2	49
3	19
4	7

The above table shows the results of data gathering on the number of girls in 100 families with four children.

    A. Based on the data, what is the experimental probability that exactly two children will be girls?

    B. Explain why your answer would most likely be different if you collected data from another group of 100 families consisting of four children.

Solution:

    A. From the information in the table, the experimental probability is $\frac{49}{100}$.

    B. The probabilities are based on the frequencies. As the data are gathered, it is not likely that you would get the same frequencies.

2. What is the theoretical probability of having exactly two girls in a family of four children?

Solution:

The sample space shows a total of 16 possibilities for combinations of boys and girls in a family with four children.

    BBBB   BGBB   GGGG   GBGG
    BBBG   BGBG   GGGB   GBGB
    BBGB   BGGB   GGBG   GBBG
    BBGG   BGGG   GGBB   GBBB

Since 6 of the sequences above represent exactly two girls (and two boys), the theoretical probability is $\frac{6}{16}$ or $\frac{3}{8}$ or 37.5%.

PRACTICE

1. Two events, A and B, are considered *complementary* if $P(B) = 1 - P(A)$. For example, in tossing a coin, $P(\text{heads}) = \dfrac{1}{2}$ and $P(\text{tails}) = \dfrac{1}{2}$, which is equal to $1 - P(\text{heads})$. Which of the following would NOT represent complementary events?

A) Spinning an odd number on the spinner shown

   Spinning an even number on the spinner shown

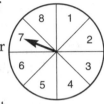

B) Picking a number divisible by 3 from the set of whole numbers between 1 and 30

   Picking a number not divisible by 3 from the set of whole numbers between 1 and 30

C) Obtaining a sum less than 7 when tossing two dice

   Obtaining a sum greater than 7 when tossing two dice

D) Picking a red card from a regular deck of cards

   Picking a black card from a regular deck of cards

2. You flip a fair coin. The first eight flips come up heads. What is the probability that the ninth flip of the coin will be a tail?

   E) $\dfrac{1}{2}$ F) 1   G) $\dfrac{8}{9}$ H) $\dfrac{1}{9}$

3. Which of the following cannot be the answer to a probability question?

   A) 0   B) 30%   C) $\dfrac{11}{10}$ D) $\dfrac{10}{11}$

4. Consider the following events:

   I. Obtaining a sum of 2 in rolling two dice
   II. Obtaining 5 heads when tossing five coins
   III. Obtaining a red with one spin of the spinner shown

   Arrange the events in order from LEAST probable to MOST probable.

   E) III, II, I
   F) I, II, III
   G) I, III, II
   H) II, I, III

5. For the spinner shown, the probability of landing on each color is $\frac{1}{4}$ or 25%.

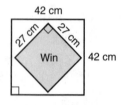

A different spinner has 3 sectors each with a different color (red, green, or yellow). If the ratio $P(\text{red}) : P(\text{green}) : P(\text{yellow})$ is $1:4:7$, draw the resulting spinner. Show your work and use a protractor.

6. A coin-toss game at a carnival has a board as shown. To win, the coin must land in the shaded area. What is the probability of winning the game, expressed to the nearest percent?

7. A dice game is played by two students using a pair of dice.

   Player 1 gets a point if the product of the numbers rolled on the dice is even.

   Player 2 gets a point if the product of the numbers rolled on the dice is odd.

   The player with more points after 20 rounds wins.

   Is the game, as outlined, fair or not? Explain.

8. Mary rolled a die 600 times. The results are shown below.

   odd 252   even 348

   Calculate the experimental probability for rolling odd as shown by the results given. Determine the theoretical probability for rolling an odd number on a die. Compare the experimental and theoretical probabilities. What could Mary have done to see if the experimental results would come closer to the theoretical results?

9. Assume that in the human population, 106 males are born for every 100 females.

   A. On this basis, find the odds that any birth will result in a boy.

   B. On this basis, find the odds that any birth will result in a girl.

   C. Find the probability that any birth will result in a boy.

10. Find the probability of each of the following odds in favor of three events:

    A. $1:1$

    B. $5:3$

    C. $2:1$

3.2 Probability of Compound Events

Compound events consist of two or more events. If the outcome of one event does not affect the outcome of the other event, the events are *independent*.

   For two independent events,

$$P(A \text{ and } B) = P(A) \cdot P(B)$$

   If the outcome of one event affects the outcome of the other event, the events are *dependent*.

   For two dependent events,

$$P(A \text{ and } B) = P(A) \cdot P(B \text{ after } A \text{ occurs})$$

MODEL PROBLEMS

1. Suppose a number cube is rolled twice. What is the probability that an odd number will occur both times?

   Solution: Since the first and second rolls of the number cube are independent of each other, P(rolling two odd numbers) = P(first roll odd) $\cdot$ P(second roll odd)

   outcomes: 1, 2, 3, 4, 5, 6   total 6

   odd numbers: 1, 3, 5   total 3

   $$P(\text{odd}) = \frac{3}{6} = \frac{1}{2}$$

   $$P(\text{rolling two odd numbers}) = \frac{1}{2} \cdot \frac{1}{2} = \frac{1}{4}$$

2. A jar contains 3 red balls, 2 white balls, and 1 green ball. What is the probability of picking two white balls if the first ball is not replaced?

   Solution:

   $$P(\text{first white}) = \frac{2}{6} = \frac{1}{3}$$

   Since the first ball selected was white and not replaced,

   $$P(\text{second white}) = \frac{1}{5}$$

   $$P(\text{two whites}) = \frac{1}{3} \cdot \frac{1}{5} = \frac{1}{15}$$

Probability of *A* or *B*

Sometimes you want to find the probability that either of two events will occur. This calculation depends on whether or not the events are mutually exclusive, that is, events that cannot occur at the same time.

For mutually exclusive events,

$$P(A \text{ or } B) = P(A) + P(B)$$

If the events are not mutually exclusive because it is possible for both to occur at the same time, the probability of *A* or *B* requires you to subtract the $P(A \text{ and } B)$ from the sum of $P(A) + P(B)$, because of the overlapping components of the sample space.

For non–mutually exclusive events,

$$P(A \text{ or } B) = P(A) + P(B) - P(A \text{ and } B)$$

MODEL PROBLEM

For the spinner shown, find the following probabilities:

A. P(a 2 or a 5)
B. P(a multiple of 2 or a multiple of 3)

Solution:

A. Since obtaining a 2 and obtaining a 5 are mutually exclusive, P(a 2 or a 5) $= P(2) + P(5) = \frac{1}{8} + \frac{1}{8} = \frac{2}{8} = \frac{1}{4}$.

B. Since there is an overlapping condition, P(mult. of 2 or mult. of 3) $= P$(mult. of 2) $+ P$(mult. of 3) $- P$(mult. 2 and 3) $= \frac{4}{8} + \frac{2}{8} - \frac{1}{8} = \frac{5}{8}$.

PRACTICE

1. A coin is tossed and a die with numbers 1–6 is rolled. What is P(heads and 3)?

   A) $\frac{1}{12}$ B) $\frac{1}{4}$ C) $\frac{1}{3}$ D) $\frac{2}{3}$

2. Two cards are selected from a deck of cards numbered 1 through 10. Once a card is selected it is not replaced. What is P(two even numbers)?

   E) $\frac{1}{4}$ F) $\frac{2}{9}$ G) $\frac{1}{2}$ H) 1

3. Which of the following is NOT an example of independent events?

   A) Rolling a die and spinning a spinner
   B) Tossing a coin two times
   C) Picking two cards from a deck with replacement of first card
   D) Selecting two marbles one at a time without replacement

4. A club has 25 members, 20 boys and 5 girls. Two members are selected at random to serve as president and vice president. What is the probability that both will be girls?

   E) $\frac{1}{5}$ F) $\frac{1}{25}$ G) $\frac{1}{30}$ H) $\frac{1}{4}$

5. One marble is randomly drawn and then replaced from a jar containing two white marbles and one black marble. A second marble is drawn. What is the probability of drawing a white and then a black?

   A) $\frac{1}{3}$ B) $\frac{2}{9}$ C) $\frac{3}{8}$ D) $\frac{1}{6}$

6. Maria rolls a pair of dice. What is the probability that she obtains a sum that is either a multiple of 3 OR a multiple of 4?

   E) $\frac{5}{9}$ F) $\frac{7}{12}$ G) $\frac{1}{36}$ H) $\frac{7}{36}$

7. Greg rolls a pair of dice. What is the probability that he obtains a sum of 2 OR 12?

8. Jack never pairs his socks after doing laundry. He just throws the socks into the drawer randomly. If the drawer contains 14 white socks and 12 grey socks, what is the probability he will select a pair of grey socks when selecting two socks at random? Give your answer as a decimal rounded to the nearest thousandth.

9. Find the probability of spinning red AND even given the spinners pictured.

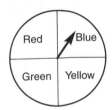 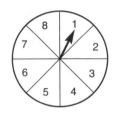

10. A basketball player is given two free throws for a foul committed against him. During the season, he has made 36 out of 50 free throws attempted. Using this experimental probability, find the probability of each event as a percent.

A. Making both free throws
B. Making neither free throw
C. Making one free throw

11. Events A and B are independent. The probability of event A occurring is $\frac{3}{5}$ and the probability of event B not occurring is $\frac{2}{3}$. What is $P(A \text{ and } B)$?

12. Suppose E and F are independent events. The probability that event E will occur is .7 and the probability that event F will occur is .6.

A. Find the probability of E and F both occurring.
B. Explain why the answer should be less than each of the individual probabilities.
C. Suppose E and F are independent events with the probability of E being p and the probability of F being q. If $P(E \text{ and } F) = .36$ and $P(E) \neq P(F)$, find a pair of possible values for p and q.

3.3 The Counting Principle

In finding theoretical probabilities, it is often necessary to have an efficient method for finding the total number of possible outcomes.

AB 79

If special license plates require two letters followed by two digits (with all letters and digits possible), the product $26 \times 26 \times 10 \times 10$ will give the total number of possible license plates. The *counting principle* says that if there are 26 possible letters for the first letter and 26 for the second letter, and 10 choices for the first digit and 10 choices for the second digit, the product will yield the total number of possibilities.

> **The Counting Principle:**
>
> The total number of ways that a multipart event can happen is the *product* of the number of ways that the individual parts can happen.

Factorial Notation

Use of the counting principle often results in the need to indicate products of consecutive descending factors where 1 is the last factor. A notation used for this purpose is called *factorial*.

$$5 \times 4 \times 3 \times 2 \times 1 = 5! \quad \text{read as 5 factorial}$$

Most scientific and graphing calculators contain a factorial key.

Note: 0! is defined as equal to 1.

 MODEL PROBLEMS

1. In how many different ways can five students be seated on a five-seat bench?

Solution: Any of the 5 students may be seated in the first seat. After a student is seated in the first seat, there are 4 choices for the second seat. For each successive seat, the number of choices decreases by 1.

Use the counting principle:

$$\underset{\substack{\text{1st} \\ \text{seat}}}{5} \cdot \underset{\substack{\text{2nd} \\ \text{seat}}}{4} \cdot \underset{\substack{\text{3rd} \\ \text{seat}}}{3} \cdot \underset{\substack{\text{4th} \\ \text{seat}}}{2} \cdot \underset{\substack{\text{5th} \\ \text{seat}}}{1}$$

Answer: = 120 possibilities

2. From the digits 0–9, how many different four-digit numbers are possible if the number must be an odd multiple of 5 with no repeated digits in the number?

Solution: Since the number must be an odd multiple of 5, there is only one choice for the units digit: it must be a 5.

For the digit in the thousands place, you cannot use a 5 or a 0, leaving you with 8 possibilities.

For the digit in the hundreds place, you cannot use a 5 or the digit used in the thousands place. As a result, you have 8 possibilities.

It then follows that you will have 7 possibilities for the digit in the tens place.

Answer: Using the counting principle, you get $8 \cdot 8 \cdot 7 \cdot 1$ or 448 possible numbers.

3. Find the value of $\dfrac{10!}{6!}$.

Solution:

$$10! = 10 \times 9 \times 8 \times 7 \times 6 \times 5 \times 4 \times 3 \times 2 \times 1$$
$$6! = 6 \times 5 \times 4 \times 3 \times 2 \times 1$$

Therefore, as a result of reducing the fraction,

$$\frac{10!}{6!} = 10 \times 9 \times 8 \times 7 = 5{,}040$$

4. How many pizzas can be made using 0, 1, 2, 3, or 4 of the following toppings: pepperoni, onion, mushroom, green pepper?

Solution:

Although it is possible to try to make systematic listing, this process is too time consuming. It is better to apply the counting principle by indicating the number of choices regarding each topping.

$$\underset{\text{pepperoni}}{2} \quad \underset{\text{onion}}{2} \quad \underset{\text{mushroom}}{2} \quad \underset{\text{green pepper}}{2}$$

Using this approach, you are saying that there are 2 possibilities for pepperoni (either it will be on the pie or not), and the same for the other toppings.

Answer: $2 \times 2 \times 2 \times 2 = 2^4 = 16$ total possible pizzas

1. Marcia, Doris, Roberta, and Carmen are running a race. If there are no ties, in how many different ways can they finish the race?

   A) 6   B) 12
   C) 24   D) 36

2. The track team needs to select a four-person team from among Mike, Dan, Steve, Robert, Richard, and John. How many different four-person relay teams can be made from the six runners?

   E) 24   F) 256
   G) 360   H) 720

3. A true/false quiz has 10 questions. How many different sets of answers are possible?

   A) 10!   B) 20   C) 2^{10} D) 100

4. How many different batting orders are possible for a nine-player softball team if the lead-off batter is always Tom Jones; the cleanup hitter (4th in the batting order) is always Sal Rivera; and the pitcher, Sandy Carlton, always bats in the ninth spot?

Lineup	
1. Tom Jones	Left Fielder
2.	
3.	
4. Sal Rivera	Center Fielder
5.	
6.	
7.	
8.	
9. Sandy Carlton	Pitcher

5. Four roads go from town A to town B. Three roads go from town B to town C. In addition, there are two roads that go from A to C without going through B. In how many ways can you go from A to C?

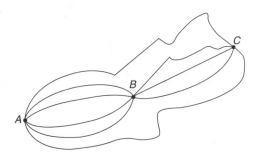

6. If $k \times 8! = 10!$, find the value of k.

7. Observe that $8 \times 7! = 8!$ and $5 \times 4! = 5!$ Write the generalization that follows.

8. Using the digits 5, 6, 7, 8, with repetition of digits possible, how many four-digit numbers can be formed if the number must be greater than 8,000 and also a multiple of 5?

9. Suppose a state's license plates have three digits, then a picture of the state bird, and then three more digits.

   A. If any digit (including zero) can go in any position, how many license plates are possible?

   B. If the state expects to use up all of the license plate numbers within the next year, it needs to have a plan to develop more numbers. If it decides to replace the first three digits with letters of the alphabet, how many license plate numbers are now possible? Show your process.

   C. A member of the state transportation board suggested that one additional digit (for a total of 7 digits) would be better than 6 spaces with the three letters and three digits. Is this suggestion accurate? Explain.

3.4 Relationships Involving Data

A *scatter plot* is a graph used to show a relationship or *correlation* between sets of data. In a scatter plot, we plot the data as ordered pairs, represented by unconnected points. The pattern of the data points shows the correlation, if any, between the two data sets. If most of the data points are clustered together along an imaginary line, the two data sets are correlated.

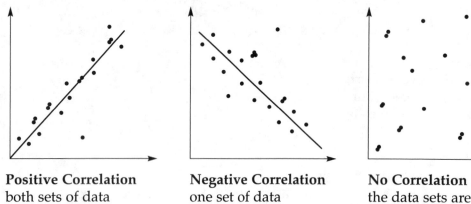

Positive Correlation
both sets of data
increase together

Negative Correlation
one set of data
decreases as the
other set increases

No Correlation
the data sets are
not related

A *line of best fit* or *trend line* can be drawn near where most of the points cluster on a scatter plot. If the line slopes upward, there exists a positive correlation. If the line slopes downward, there exists a negative correlation. Graphing calculators can be used to determine an equation for a line of best fit.

Outliers are points that lie far from the overall linear pattern.

Equation of Line of Best Fit

The scatter plot blow shows the heights and shoe size for a group of males. To determine an equation for the line of best fit, first draw line on the graph so that approximately half of the points are on each side of the line. Notice that the line passes through points (62, 8) and (72, 12). Using these two points, calculate the slope of the line, $\frac{\Delta y}{\Delta x} = \frac{(12 - 8)}{(72 - 62)} = \frac{4}{10} = \frac{2}{5}$.

Comparison of Shoe Sizes

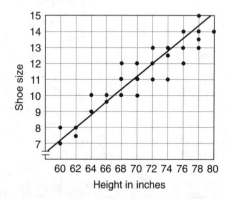

Height in inches

Sub-in the slope into the slope-intercept equation, $y = mx + b$, and solve for the y-intercept, b. The equation for the line of best fit is $y = \frac{2}{5}x - 16.8$.

MODEL PROBLEMS

1. Plot the data given in the table on a graph. Draw the trend line that best fits the data. Does the graph show a positive or negative correlation?

Height (in.)	60	62	63	65	68	69	70	70	72	74	75	75
Weight (lb)	120	122	125	130	132	142	158	147	150	152	160	156

Solution:

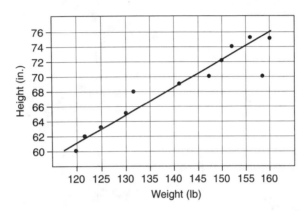

Answer: The trend line slopes upward, showing a positive correlation.

2. Describe the correlation that would exist in each of the following:

A.

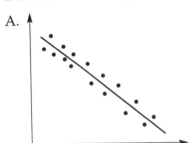

B. Hours worked and earnings

C.

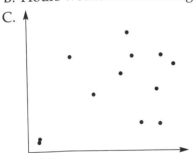

Solution:

A. The scatter plot suggests a line that slopes downward to the right. The two data sets would have a negative correlation.

B. You would expect to earn more if you worked more hours. Therefore, a positive correlation exists.

C. The points are very spread out. There appears to be no correlation.

Regression Models

Regression models are the equations of linear lines or curves that best describe the pattern the scatter plots represent. For linear regression, the equation for the line of best fit is the regression model. Since not all scatter plots that represent sets of data in the real world form linear regression models, other possibilities must be considered. Two other possibilities are exponential and quadratic regression models. Like linear regression, whose equation for a line of best fit is modeled after the form $y = mx + b$, the other two equations are modeled after their general equation. Exponential regression is modeled after the exponential function $y = ab^x$. Likewise, quadratic regression is modeled after the quadratic function of $y = ax^2$.

An example of exponential regression is shown at right.

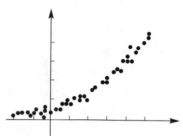

By sketching a curve of best fit onto the scatter plot, it can be observed that the equation of the curve is $y = 2^x$.

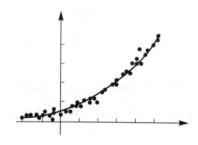

An example of quadratic regression is shown at right.

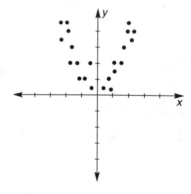

By sketching a curve of best fit onto the scatter plot, it can be observed that the equation of the curve is $y = 2x^2$.

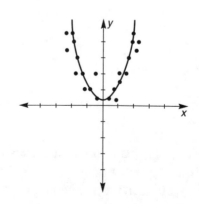

1. For which of the following situations would you expect the scatter plot to show a negative correlation?

   A) The number of students in a high school and the average temperature of the city
   B) The age of a car and the resale value
   C) The price of an item and the amount of tax on the item
   D) The speed of a car and the distance traveled in a fixed time

2. Which scatter plot shows a positive correlation?

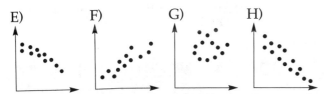

   E)   F)   G)   H)

3. For which of the following situations would you expect the scatter plot to show no correlation?

   A) Miles driven and gallons of gas used
   B) Driving speed and driving time on a 5-mile stretch of highway
   C) Number of pages in a book and number of copies sold
   D) Oven temperature and cooking time for a 12-pound turkey

4. Which of the following could be the equation for the line of best fit for the scatter plot shown?

   E) $y = 4$
   F) $y = -x$
   G) $y = x$
   H) $x + y = 0$

5. Which regression equation best fits the scatter plot below?

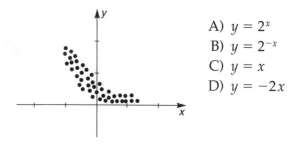

   A) $y = 2^x$
   B) $y = 2^{-x}$
   C) $y = x$
   D) $y = -2x$

6. Display the data in a scatter plot and describe the type of correlation present.

x	10	10.5	11	12	9.5	13	10.5
y	47	35	63	22	55	27	9

7. Two students in a geometry class made a scatter plot to show the relationship between diameter and circumference of circular objects. For each object (such as the top of a coffee can), they plotted the points (diameter on the horizontal axis and circumference on the vertical axis) and drew the line of best fit.

   A. Draw a possible scatter plot to go along with this situation.
   B. What type of correlation did they find? Why does this make sense?
   C. Explain why you would not expect your data to include any outliers.

8. Explain why you would not need to gather data and draw a scatter plot in order to determine the type of correlation between the length of the sides of a square and the perimeter of the square. What type of correlation exists?

9. Using the scatter plot, estimate what the value of new-home sales in the region might have been for 2003. Can you extrapolate a reasonable value for sales in 2005? Explain.

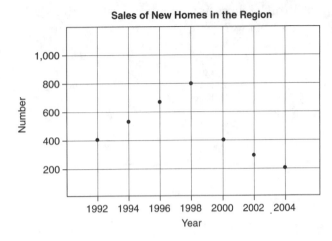

Sales of New Homes in the Region

10. The table below shows the amount of study time students spend before a math test and the test grade.

Study Time (in Hours)	Test Grade (in Percent)
10	90
5	80
4	72
12	94
3	68
6	87

A. Create a scatter plot for the data.
B. Draw a line of best fit.
C. Find the equation of the line of best fit.
D. Using the equation for the line of best fit, predict the grade after 8 hours of study time.

3.5 Direct and Inverse Variation

Direct Variation

Jamal works at a store after school and is paid $5 per hour. He knows that the more hours he works, the more money he makes. The relationship between hours worked and wages paid is described as a *direct variation*, and the wages *vary directly* with the hours worked.

A relationship is a *direct variation* if it can be expressed as:

$$y = kx, \text{ where } k \neq 0$$

The graph of a direct variation is always a straight line passing through the origin, with the slope equal to the constant of variation of y with respect to x. In the direct variation example above, the equation is $y = 5x$, and the slope of the line is 5. The graph of the equation is shown below.

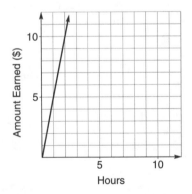

Note: In direct variation ...

    ... the slope is always positive.

    ... if x increases, y increases.

    ... if x decrease, y decreases.

    ... if x is multiplied by a number, y is multiplied by the same number.

    ... if x is divided by a number, y is divided by the same number.

Inverse Variation

A car traveling 50 mph will take 6 hours to go 300 miles. However, a car traveling 60 mph will take only 5 hours to go the same 300 miles. The relationship between rate and time is called an *inverse variation*, and time is said to *vary inversely* with rate.

A relationship is an **inverse variation** if it can be expressed by the equation:

$$y = \frac{k}{x} \quad \text{or} \quad xy = k$$

The graph of an inverse variation always forms a hyperbola, which is a two-part graph that does not cross either axis or the origin. The graph below shows the function $xy = 12$, by plotting the points in the table below.

x	y
-12	-1
-8	-1.5
-6	-2
-2	-6
-1	-12
1	12
2	6
6	2
8	1.5
12	1

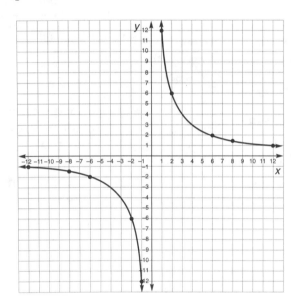

Note: In inverse variation ...

    ... the slope is always negative.

    ... if x increases, y decreases.

    ... if x decreases, y increases.

    ... if x is multiplied by a nonzero number, then y is divided by the same number.

Note: k is called the **constant of variation** for both types of variations.

MODEL PROBLEMS

1. The annual interest on a loan varies directly with the amount borrowed. The interest on a loan of $600 is $27. What is the interest on a loan of $800?

Solution: Since the interest varies directly with the amount borrowed,

$$\frac{600}{27} = k \text{ and } \frac{800}{\text{interest}} = k$$

Therefore: $\dfrac{800}{x} = \dfrac{600}{27}$

$$21,600 = 600x$$

Answer: $x = \$36$

2. For a constant area, the width of a rectangle varies inversely with the length. If the length of one rectangle is 12″ and its width is 3″, how long is a rectangle with the same area and a width of 4″?

Solution: The width varies inversely with the length.

$$\ell w = A$$

$$(12)(3) = A = 36$$

Since the areas are the same, using dimensions of 4 and ℓ for the second rectangle,

$$4\ell = 36$$

Answer: $\ell = 9''$

3. Do the data in each table represent direct or inverse variation? Write an equation to model the data.

A.

x	y
3	15
5	25
6	30
8	40

B.

x	y
1	12
2	6
3	4
4	3
6	2

Solution:

A. As x increases, y increases. The data show direct variation. The equation would be $y = 5x$.

B. As x increases, y decreases. The data show inverse variation. The equation would be $xy = 12$.

PRACTICE

1. Which of the following is NOT an example of a direct variation?

   A) The number of gallons of gasoline purchased and the total cost

   B) If speed is constant, the distance traveled and the time traveled

   C) The value of a used car and the age of the car

   D) The circumference of a circle and the length of the diameter

2. y is directly proportional to x. If $y = 20$ when $x = 16$, find the constant of variation.

   E) 0.8   F) 1.25   G) 32   H) 320

3. For which table do the data NOT represent direct variation?

A)

x	y
−2	−4
−1	−2
0	0
3	6

B)

x	y
0	0
1	10
3	30
6	60
10	100

C)

x	y
0	2
1	3
3	5
10	12

D)

x	y
0	0
2	0.5
4	1
8	2
20	5

4. If y varies inversely with x, what is the missing value in the table?

x	y
1	36
2	18
2.5	?
3	12
4	9

E) 16   F) 15.5   G) 15   H) 14.4

5. x varies inversely as y. If x = 70 when y = 8, find x when y = 28.

6. The perimeter of a square varies directly with the length of a side.

The perimeter is 16 feet when the side measures 4 feet.

What is the perimeter when the side measures 5.25 feet?

7. If it takes 2.5 hours to make a trip traveling at 50 mph, how long would it take to make the same trip at a speed of 40 mph?

8. In a relationship y varies inversely with x. What happens to the value of y if x is doubled?

9. The depth of water in a tub varies directly as the length of time the taps are on. If the taps are left on for 4 minutes, the depth of the water is 24 cm.

   A. Find the depth of the water if the taps are left on for 5 minutes.

   B. Find the length of time the taps were left on if the depth of the water is 42 cm.

   C. Write an equation relating depth to time.

   D. Graph the relation between depth and time.

10. Given the graph shown.

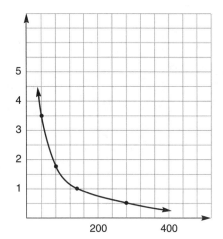

   A. Does the graph illustrate a direct or an inverse variation? Explain.

   B. Give two additional ordered pairs that would appear on the graph if the graph were extended.

   C. Suggest a practical situation represented by the given graph.

3.6 Probability Distributions

Discrete Probability Distribution

A discrete probability distribution lists the values associated with the outcomes of an event and the probabilities associated with the values. The discrete probability distribution for the outcomes in tossing three coins is as follows:

Number of heads	0	1	2	3
Probability	.125	.375	.375	.125

It should be noted that the sum of the probabilities must be 1.

Continuous Probability Distribution

In a continuous probability distribution, the area under portions of a curve corresponds to probabilities. A familiar continuous probability distribution is the *normal distribution* or normal curve.

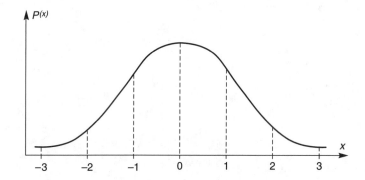

The normal curve distribution is symmetric and bell shaped and has the following properties:

- About 68% of the area (or data) is within 1 standard deviation of the mean.
- About 95% of the area (or data) is within 2 standard deviations of the mean.
- About 99.7% of the area (or data) is within 3 standard deviations of the mean.

The area under the standard normal curve between two data values is closely related to probability. The area under the curve between two values (along the horizontal) is equal to the probability that an outcome (data value) falls between the two limits.

It should be noted that the total area under the curve must be 1.

MODEL PROBLEMS

1. The local Sneaker Pro store needs to make a decision concerning the inventory required of sneakers in men's sizes greater than 14. Assuming that men's sneaker sizes are normally distributed with a mean of 9 and a standard deviation of 1.5, show a graph and explain what decision should be made by the store.

Solution:

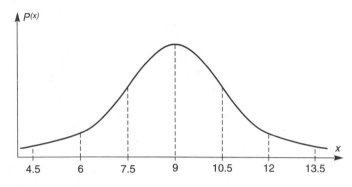

Since you are told that the mean size is 9 and the standard deviation is 1.5, a size of 14 would be more than 3 standard deviations above the mean ($9 + 3 \times 1.5 = 13.5$). As a result, the normal curve properties would say that there is greater than a 99.7% probability that a sneaker size would be 13.5 or smaller. Therefore, the store should not worry about having much of an inventory in sizes greater than 14.

2. The professor of a large class gives 15% each of A's and D's, 30% each of B's and C's, and 10% F's. What is the probability that a student got a B or better?

Solution:

The table shows the probability distribution as stated in the problem.

Grade (X)	A	B	C	D	F
Probability	.15	.30	.30	.15	.10

The probability that the student got a B or better is the sum of the probabilities of an A or a B.

$$P(\text{B or better}) = .30 + .15 = .45$$

1. A number cube has the following faces: 2, 3, 3, 4, 4, 4. Complete the table to show the discrete probabilities for the outcomes of rolling the number cube.

Outcome	2	3	4
Probabilities			

2. Given a normal distribution that has a mean of 10 and a standard deviation of 2, complete the following statements.

   A. Approximately 68% of the data will be between ___ and ___.
   B. Approximately 95% of the data will be between ___ and ___.
   C. Approximately 2.5% of the data will be greater than ___.

3. The graph shows a set of normally distributed test scores. What percentage of the people taking the test scored between 400 and 600?

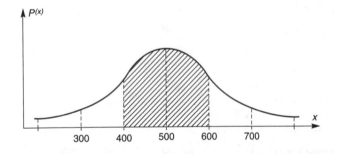

4. What percent of the area under the normal curve shown is shaded if the standard deviation is 150?

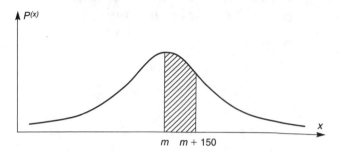

5. A game involves selecting three cards, with replacement, from a deck of 16 cards: ace, 2, 3, and 4 of each suit. Let x represent the number of aces selected. Find the distribution of x. That is, what values can x take, and what are the probabilities for each value?

6. The heights of U.S. males from 18 to 24 years old are approximately normally distributed with a mean of about 70 inches and a standard deviation of about 3 inches.

   A. What is the approximate probability that a randomly selected male in this age group is over 76 inches tall?
   B. Suppose you see a group of 5 males in this age group who are all over 76 inches tall. What is the probability of this happening randomly?

3.7 Populations and Samples

The entire group of objects or people involved in a statistical study is called a *population*. However, it is usually impossible to study a very large group. Hence a subset representative of the population, called a *sample*, is usually used in the study. The process of choosing the sample is called *sampling*. It is important to make sure the sample collected is unbiased and representative of the entire population. A random sample will give everyone or everything the same chance of being selected.

MODEL PROBLEMS

1. The Cake Box surveyed people about the type of frosting they preferred on cakes. Use the results to predict how many of the 952 students at Washington High School would choose whipped cream.

Type of Frosting	Percent
whipped cream	55%
buttercream	40%
no preference	5%

Solution: Since 55% of the sample preferred whipped cream, finding 55% of 952 students allows you to make the prediction.

Answer: 0.55(952) = 523.6 or approximately 524 students

2. A quality tester finds three faulty batteries in a sample of 60 batteries. If there is a 2% margin of error, estimate the interval that contains the number of faulty batteries in a group of 3,000.

Solution: Let x = the number of faulty batteries in the group.

$$\frac{\text{faulty in sample}}{\text{total in sample}} = \frac{3}{60} = \frac{x}{3{,}000} = \frac{\text{faulty in group}}{\text{total in group}}$$

$$3(3{,}000) = 60x$$
$$9{,}000 = 60x$$
$$150 = x$$

Use the margin of error to estimate:

$$2\% \text{ of } 3{,}000 = (0.02)(3{,}000) = 60$$
$$\text{interval is } 150 - 60 \text{ to } 150 + 60$$

Answer: The interval is 90 to 210 batteries in the total group are faulty.

1. A sporting goods company surveyed 800 baseball players to see what type of bat they preferred. Aluminum bats were preferred over wood by 300 players. Which statement is true?

   A) More than $\frac{1}{2}$ of the players surveyed preferred aluminum.

   B) More than 40% of the players surveyed preferred aluminum.

   C) More than 75% of the players surveyed did not prefer aluminum.

   D) More than $\frac{1}{3}$ of the players surveyed preferred aluminum.

2. Which of the following samples is an example of an unbiased survey?

   E) A random sample of 500 teens in the Northeast to determine the favorite music group for teens ages 13–15

   F) A random sample of 500 men over 50 years of age to determine which brand of vitamins men over 50 prefer

   G) A random sample of 250 women aged 18–35 to determine the favorite brand of ice cream of people 18–35

   H) A random sample of 150 zoo visitors to determine if taxpayers feel that federal money should be used to help run the zoo

3. An office supply store surveyed a group of 200 students to determine their preference for backpack colors. Backpacks come in green, black, blue, and red. Based on the survey results the store will determine the color distribution for its order of 1,000 backpacks. If 75 chose black, 25 chose red, 40 chose green, and the rest chose blue, how many green backpacks will the store order?

4. A television rating service found that 945 households out of a sample of 3,340 households watched the Super Bowl. Estimate to the nearest million how many of the 94 million households with a television watched the Super Bowl.

5. Biologists captured 400 deer, tagged them, and released them back into the same region. Later that season, the deer population was sampled to estimate the size of the population that lived in the region. If a sample of 150 deer contained 45 tagged deer, what would be a good estimate for the deer population in the region?

6. A quality tester finds two broken bulbs in every lot of 100. Suppose the margin of error is 3%. Estimate the interval that contains the number of broken bulbs in a lot of 5,000.

3.8 Statistical Measures

A set of data, or values, can be described by using the *mean, median, mode,* or *range.* The mean, the median, and the mode are called *measures of central tendency.*

- The *mean* is the arithmetic *average*. It is found by dividing the sum of the values by the number of values.
- The *median* is the middle value when the values are listed in order. (*Note:* If the set contains an even number of values, the median is the average of the two values in the middle.)
- The *mode* is the value occurring most frequently.
- The *range* is the difference between the largest value and the smallest value.
- The *frequency* of a value is the count of the value—that is, how many times the value appears.

$$\text{data: } 36 \ 36 \ 36 \ 43 \ 43 \ 51 \ 54 \ 58 \ 61$$

$$\text{mean} = 418 \div 9 = 46.4 \quad \text{median} = 43 \quad \text{mode} = 36 \quad \text{range} = 61 - 36 = 25$$

The frequency of 36 is 3, of 43 is 2, and of the other values is 1.

 ## MODEL PROBLEMS

1. Debbie has the following scores on five math tests:

   88 84 80 90 84

   What score must she get on the sixth test in order for her average to fall between 85 and 87?

   Solution: The sum of the six scores must be 6 times the average.

   $$6 \times 85 = 510$$
   $$6 \times 87 = 522$$

   The sum of the first five scores is 426.

   Answer: The sixth score must fall between 84 [510 − 426] and 96 [522 − 426].

2. Give a set of five scores such that the data would have (A) a median of 60, (B) a mode of 52, and (C) a mean of 65.

   Solution:

   A. __ __ 60 __ __
      If the median for five scores is 60, the third score must be 60. **Answer**

   B. 52 52 60 __ __
      Since the mode is 52, the lowest two scores must each be 52. **Answer**

   C. Since the mean is 65, the sum of the five scores must be 5 × 65 = 325. With 164 as the sum of the first three scores, the highest two scores must total 325 − 164 or 161. Hence, the remaining two scores must be any two distinct numbers above 60 that total 161. For example, one solution is: 52, 52, 60, 80, 81. The solution is not unique. **Answer**

1. During a baseball season, the National League home-run champion had the following home-run statistics by month:

April	May	June	July	August	September	October
5	13	7	11	6	8	6

Which month contains the median for the player's home-run statistics?

A) June   B) July
C) August   D) September

2. For each number shown in the box, the units digit is hidden. Which of the following could NOT be the mean of the set?

$$8\triangle \quad 8\triangle \quad 7\triangle \quad 9\triangle \quad 8\triangle$$

E) 85   F) 82   G) 80   H) 71

3. The following data represent morning temperatures for the month of July in Washington, D.C. What are the mean and median of the data?

89 87 85 88 93 93 93 89 90 91 90 89 88 89 87 90
91 92 92 92 90 89 87 85 86 84 84 83 85 86 88

A) Mean 84.3, median 91
B) Mean 82.9, median 90
C) Mean 88.5, median 89
D) Mean 83.9, median 88

4. For the given scores, the mean is 40.

Scores: 20, 30, 40, 50, 60

If the 20 is changed to a 17, which of the following would have to be done in order for the mean to remain at 40?

E) Change the 50 to a 47.
F) Change the 60 to a 57.
G) Change the 50 to a 53.
H) Change the 30 to a 27.

5. For a set of 6 scores, the following can be noted:

> Score #1 is 6 points below the mean.
> Score #2 is 10 points below the mean.
> Score #3 is 4 points below the mean.
> Score #4 is equal to the mean.

Which of the following could be TRUE about the remaining two scores?

A) Scores #5 and #6 are both equal to the mean.
B) Score #5 is 12 points above the mean and Score #6 is 8 points above the mean.
C) Score #5 is 10 points above the mean and Score #6 is 10 points below the mean.
D) Score #5 is 20 points above the mean and Score #6 is 4 points above the mean.

6. Which of the following statements will always be TRUE?

   I. The mode is always close to the median.
   II. The median is sometimes not included in the data.
   III. The mean is always included in the data.

   E) I only
   G) III only
   F) II only
   H) I and II only

7. The list shows the prices for several different concerts:

   $40 $45 $50 $58 $60 $67 $80 $90

   If an additional concert price of $16 is added to the list, which measure of central tendency is affected most?

8. Edgardo had the following test scores in his science class:

   90 73 86 89 97

   What score must he get on the sixth test in order for his average to turn out to be 89?

9. The mean for a set of 5 scores is 60. The mean for a different set of 10 scores is 90. What is the mean for all 15 scores?

10. Give three different values for x so that 80 would be the median.

Score	Number of Students
90	4
85	2
80	3
75	x
70	4

11. Mr. Abbott asked his math students to use the following data to find average test scores.

Mr. Abbott's Classes		
Period	No. of Students	Test Average
1 Algebra	20	80
2 Algebra	20	70
3 Geometry	30	84
5 Geometry	10	80

In computing the average test score for the combined algebra classes, Bill suggested that Mr. Abbott take the average of 80 and 70 to get 75. For the two combined geometry classes, however, using the same approach gives a wrong result of 82. Explain why the first average (75) was correct but the second average (82) was NOT correct. Find the correct average for the two geometry classes. Explain your approach.

3.9 Variance and the Standard Deviation

Variance

The *variance*, v, is the arithmetic average of the squares of the deviation from the mean. The deviation from the mean shows how much each piece of data differs from the mean. The formula for variance is $v = \dfrac{\sum_{i=1}^{n}(x_i - \bar{x})^2}{n}$, where $\bar{x}$ is the mean of all the pieces of data.

MODEL PROBLEM

Jason and Justina have the following test grades:

Jason: 85, 82, 83, 86, 89

Justina: 82, 94, 75, 94, 85

Find the variance for Jason's and Justina's scores.

Solution: Set up two tables with the necessary information to find the variance for Jason's and Justina's scores.

The variance of Jason's scores is:

x_i	$\bar{x}$	$x_i - \bar{x}$	$(x_i - \bar{x})^2$
85	85	0	0
82	85	-3	9
83	85	-2	4
86	85	1	1
89	85	4	16
			$\dfrac{\sum (x_i - \bar{x})^2}{5} = 6$

The variance for Justina's scores is:

x_i	$\bar{x}$	$x_i - \bar{x}$	$(x_i - \bar{x})^2$
82	86	-4	16
94	86	8	64
75	86	-11	121
94	86	8	64
85	86	-1	1
			$\dfrac{\sum (x_i - \bar{x})^2}{5} = 53.2$

Answer: The variance for Jason's scores is 6 and the variance for Justina's scores is 53.2.

Standard Deviation

The variance deals with the square of data, rather than the actual data values themselves. To get a measure that is comparable to the original deviations before they were squared, we can take the square root of the variance, which is called the **standard deviation**. This is a widely used measure of dispersion that indicates the concentration of the data values about the mean. The lowercase sigma, σ, is the symbol for standard deviation. The formula for standard deviation is

$$\sigma = \sqrt{\frac{\sum_{i=1}^{n}(x_i - \bar{x})^2}{n}}$$

Referring to the model problem above, the standard deviation for Jason's scores is $\sqrt{6} \approx 2.449$. The standard deviation for Justina's scores is $\sqrt{53.2} \approx 7.294$.

PRACTICE

1. What is the standard deviation of a set data whose variation is 49?

   A) 2,401
   B) 98
   C) 25
   D) 7

2. If the standard deviation of a set of data is 9, what is the variance?

   E) 81   F) 18   G) 5   H) 3

3. What is the standard deviation for the following set of data?

   8, 12, 14, 20, 25, 27

   A) 6.896
   B) 7.554
   C) 17.667
   D) 47.554

4. After giving a test, Ms. Pankow has decided to raise everyone's score by 5 points. How does this affect the standard deviation?

   E) Increases it by 5 points
   F) Increases it by $\sqrt{5}$ points
   G) No change
   H) The change cannot be determined.

5. What is the standard deviation of the following set of data?

   5, 15, 35, 60, 85

   A) 860.014
   B) 40
   C) 32.787
   D) 29.326

6. If each score in a set of data were doubled, the standard deviation would

   E) be doubled
   F) be halved
   G) not change
   H) The change cannot be determined.

7. Both of the following sets of data have the same mean. Without doing any computation, determine which one has the smaller standard deviation. Explain how you came to your conclusion.

   A: 10, 90, 40, 5, 30, 5
   B: 32, 30, 36, 28, 24, 30

8. The following is a list of a few players on the Philadelphia Eagles and their weights.

Name	Weight (lb)
Chad Lewis	252
Donovan McNabb	240
Todd Pinkston	174
Duce Staley	220
Hollis Thomas	306
Brian Westbrook	200

   A. To the nearest tenth of a pound, what is the mean weight of these members on the Philadelphia Eagles football team?

   B. What is the standard deviation, to the nearest tenth of a pound?

3.10 Data Displays

Data can be organized and displayed by using a variety of different graphs. Tables, charts, matrices, and spreadsheets are also commonly used to display data. The type of graph or device used is determined by the nature of the data and what the data are intended to communicate.

A *circle graph* is used to compare parts of a whole. It is sometimes called a *pie chart*.

Profits From Local Carnival

A *bar graph* compares amounts of quantities.

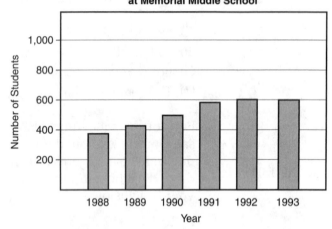

A *pictograph* also compares amounts. A symbol is used to represent a stated amount.

A *tally* or *frequency table* is commonly used to organize information gathered from a census. For example, the results from a class census on how many hours students spend on the Internet each week are 14, 6, 10, 6, 8, 7, 9, 8, 10, 8, 11, 9, 12, 14, 10. The following shows the results organized in a tally or frequency table.

Hours on Internet	Tally	Frequency
6	| |	2
7	|	1
8	| | |	3
9	| |	2
10	| | |	3
11	|	1
12	|	1
14	| |	2
Total Frequency: 15		

A *histogram* is a bar graph used to show frequencies. In a histogram, the bars, which usually represent grouped intervals, are adjacent.

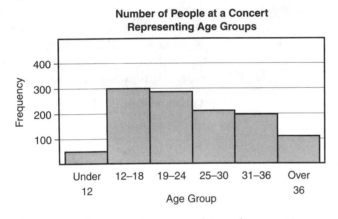

A *line graph* shows continuous change and trends over time.

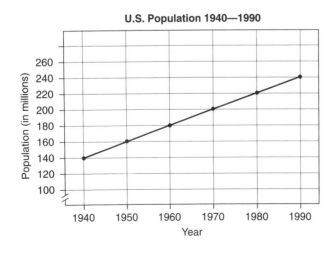

A **line plot** is another way to organize frequency data. A line plot is a picture of the data on a number line corresponding to the range of the data.

Ages of the Haversham Cousins

```
              X         X
         X  X         X      X
    X    X  X         X      X
    X    X  X  X  X  X  X  X
  +--+--+--+--+--+--+--+
  0  2  4  6  8  10  12
```

As is shown in the example above, in a line plot you place an x (or a dot) above the appropriate number to indicate each occurrence.

 MODEL PROBLEMS

1. You need to construct a graph showing the trend in the price of a gallon of gasoline each month over a five-year period of time. Which of the following types of displays would be most appropriate?

A) Circle graph
B) Histogram
C) Line plot
D) Line graph

Solution: Since the situation depicts changing prices over a period of time, the most appropriate display would be the line graph.

A circle graph is not appropriate since you are not looking at parts of a whole.

A histogram is not appropriate since you are not comparing intervals of prices.

A line plot is not appropriate since you are not organizing frequency data.

Answer: D

2. In a circle graph involving a monthly budget, the family in question spends $800 on housing out of a total budget of $2,500. In using a protractor for this sector of the graph, how many degrees (to the nearest tenth of a degree) would correspond to housing?

Solution: Method 1: finding a percent:

$$\frac{\text{housing}}{\text{total}} = \frac{800}{2,500} = 0.32$$

Therefore, we need 32% of 360°, which equals 115.2°.

Method 2: proportion:

$$\frac{800}{2,500} = \frac{x}{360}$$

$$\frac{360(800)}{2,500} = x$$

$$115.2° = x$$

Matrices

A *matrix* (plural: *matrices*) is a rectangular arrangement of numbers corresponding to a real-world situation involving data. In a matrix the numbers are arranged in rows and columns. The 3-by-2 matrix below displays the sales of a particular new car by three dealers in June vs. July.

$$\begin{bmatrix} 20 & 12 \\ 3 & 11 \\ 10 & 7 \end{bmatrix}$$

You can add or subtract matrices containing the same number of rows and columns. You add or subtract matrices by adding or subtracting corresponding values. Graphing calculators may be used to perform matrix operations.

 MODEL PROBLEM

Find $\begin{bmatrix} 8 & 4 & 2 \\ 3 & 0 & 5 \\ 9 & 2 & 1 \end{bmatrix} + \begin{bmatrix} 3 & -4 & 2 \\ 10 & 5 & -4 \\ 1 & 1 & 1 \end{bmatrix}$

Solution: By adding corresponding values, you obtain: $\begin{bmatrix} 11 & 0 & 4 \\ 13 & 5 & 1 \\ 10 & 3 & 2 \end{bmatrix}$

Scalar multiplication of a matrix involves multiplying each element of a matrix by a real number.

$$2\begin{bmatrix} 2 & 7 \\ 5 & 0 \end{bmatrix} = \begin{bmatrix} 4 & 14 \\ 10 & 0 \end{bmatrix}$$

 MODEL PROBLEM

If $k\begin{bmatrix} 4 & 3 & -1 \\ -3 & \frac{1}{2} & 8 \end{bmatrix} = \begin{bmatrix} -4 & -3 & 1 \\ 3 & -\frac{1}{2} & -8 \end{bmatrix}$

what is the value of k?

Solution: Each entry in the matrix on the left was multiplied by a factor to result in the opposite values in the matrix on the right. As a result, $k = -1$.

Two matrices can be multiplied if the rows of the first matrix have the same number of elements as the columns of the second matrix. For example, in matrices A and B shown below, their product matrix, AB, is found by multiplying each entry in A (from left to right) by each corresponding entry in B (from top to bottom) and then adding the results.

$$A = [a \quad b] \text{ and } B = \begin{bmatrix} w \\ x \end{bmatrix}, \text{ then}$$

$$AB = [a \quad b] \times \begin{bmatrix} w \\ x \end{bmatrix} = [aw + bx]$$

MODEL PROBLEM

If $A = \begin{bmatrix} 2 & 3 \\ 5 & 7 \end{bmatrix}$ and $B = \begin{bmatrix} 1 & 6 \\ 4 & 8 \end{bmatrix}$, what is AB?

Solution: $AB = \begin{bmatrix} 2 & 3 \\ 5 & 7 \end{bmatrix} \times \begin{bmatrix} 1 & 6 \\ 4 & 8 \end{bmatrix} = \begin{bmatrix} (2)(1) + (3)(4) & (2)(6) + (3)(8) \\ (5)(1) + (7)(4) & (5)(6) + (7)(8) \end{bmatrix}$

$= \begin{bmatrix} 2 + 12 & 12 + 24 \\ 5 + 28 & 30 + 56 \end{bmatrix} = \begin{bmatrix} 14 & 36 \\ 33 & 86 \end{bmatrix}$

Answer: $AB = \begin{bmatrix} 14 & 36 \\ 33 & 86 \end{bmatrix}$

A *spreadsheet* also organizes data in rows and columns. Typically, spreadsheets are accessed through computers. In working with a spreadsheet, one considers the spreadsheet to be a large rectangular array of boxes or cells, each of which is identified by a unique address. The address consists of a letter to indicate the column in which the cell is located and a number to indicate the row in which the cell is located. A spreadsheet giving dimensions (in inches) for different rectangular solids might look like:

	A	B	C	D
1	length	width	height	volume
2	5	3	10	150
3	20	10	10	2,000
4	10	10	10	1,000

The address A3 indicates the cell being referred to is located in column A, row 3. In the spreadsheet shown, the number 20 is found at that address.

The power of the spreadsheet lies in the fact that each cell can contain a numerical value determined either by direct entry of the value from the keyboard or by a mathematical formula using information obtained from cells anywhere in the spreadsheet under consideration.

For example, the value in D2 was calculated using the formula A2*B2*C2. If the values in any of the cells A2, B2, or C2 were changed, then the value in D2 would also change.

MODEL PROBLEM

The population of two towns has remained stable for many years. Oak Brook has maintained a population of approximately 25,000 and Westville has a population of approximately 40,000. Suddenly, 20% of Oak Brook's population starts moving to Westville each year, while the rest remains in Oak Brook. At the same time, 15% of Westville's population starts moving to Oak Brook each year with the rest of the population staying in Westville. Refer to the spreadsheet given for population figures (rounded to nearest whole number).

A. What is the change in Oak Brook's population over five years?

B. What is the percent of increase in population for Oak Brook over that period?

C. What formula was used to generate the values in A4, B4, C4?

	A	B	C
1	Moving	Population	
2	Year #	Oak Brook Pop.	Westville Pop.
3	0	25,000	40,000
4	1	26,000	39,000
5	2	26,650	38,350
6	3	27,073	37,928
7	4	27,348	37,653
8	5	27,526	37,475

Solution:

A. To determine the change in Oak Brook's population, find the difference between the values in B3 and B8.

$$27,526 - 25,000 = 2,526$$

B. The percent of increase = increase ÷ original population

$$2,526 \div 25,000 = 10\% \text{ approximately}$$

C. The formulas used were:

For A4, add 1 to the prior year: A4 = A3 + 1.

For B4, 80% of Oak Brook's population stayed and 15% of Westville's is added, so B4 = 0.80*B3 + 0.15*C3.

For C4, 85% of Westville's population stayed and 20% of Oak Brook's is added, so C4 = 0.85*C3 + 0.20*B3.

1. Which of the following types of graphs would NOT be an appropriate representation to depict the way a family budgets its September income?

   A) Bar graph
   B) Pictograph
   C) Circle graph
   D) Line graph

2. Using the given pictograph, what percent of the total number of cars sold at Thrifty's in September did Dan sell?

   E) 60%   F) 40%   G) 30%   H) 20%

   Number of Cars Sold at Thrifty's in September

   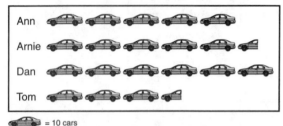

   = 10 cars

3. Use the given circle graph to determine what percent of Tim's exercise program is devoted to running.

   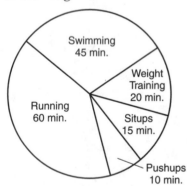

   A) 25%
   B) 40%
   C) 60%
   D) $66\frac{2}{3}$%

4. For which of the following situations would it NOT be appropriate to use a line graph to represent the data?

   E) Show the population of the U.S. from 1900 to 1990
   F) Show the sale of CDs during a five-year period
   G) Show survey results of how students spend one hour of their time
   H) Show the heating time for water at various altitudes

5. Given

   $$A = \begin{bmatrix} 56 & 73 \\ 69 & 84 \end{bmatrix} \quad B = \begin{bmatrix} 29 & 41 \\ 37 & 52 \end{bmatrix}$$

   what is the value of $2A + B$?

   A) $\begin{bmatrix} 85 & 114 \\ 106 & 136 \end{bmatrix}$
   B) $\begin{bmatrix} 114 & 155 \\ 143 & 188 \end{bmatrix}$
   C) $\begin{bmatrix} 141 & 187 \\ 175 & 220 \end{bmatrix}$
   D) $\begin{bmatrix} 170 & 228 \\ 212 & 272 \end{bmatrix}$

6. If $A = \begin{bmatrix} 1 & 3 & 5 \\ 7 & 2 & 3 \end{bmatrix}$ and $B = \begin{bmatrix} 1 & 4 \\ 3 & 7 \\ 4 & 2 \end{bmatrix}$, what is AB?

   E) $\begin{bmatrix} 30 & 35 \\ 25 & 48 \end{bmatrix}$
   F) $\begin{bmatrix} 35 & 30 \\ 48 & 25 \end{bmatrix}$
   G) $\begin{bmatrix} 1 & 7 \\ 3 & 2 \\ 4 & 3 \end{bmatrix}$
   H) $\begin{bmatrix} 1 & 7 \\ 3 & 2 \\ 5 & 3 \end{bmatrix}$

7. Two 4-by-2 matrices have exactly the same values in the corresponding positions. Show what the matrix looks like representing the difference of the two matrices.

8. Assuming that this circle graph applies to the city of Metropolis, which has 42,000 homes, how many homes are NOT heated by natural gas?

   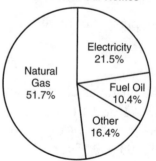

9. The South Side High School annual fundraiser involved the sale of tins of cookies. The freshman class sold 2,586 tins of cookies; the sophomore class, 3,014 tins; the junior class, 3,274 tins; and the senior class, 3,326 tins.

Construct a graph to show how the classes compared in amounts of cookies sold. Explain why you selected that type of graph to represent the data.

10. Test scores in a biology class are as follows: 83, 78, 94, 93, 87, 86, 83, 94, 99, 90, 87, 79, 65, 87, 93, 96, 88, 84, 82, 93, 85.

A. Construct a line plot for the data.

B. State the median score for the data.

11. This graph shows the percentages of pickle buyers who selected various types of pickles.

Pickle Preferences

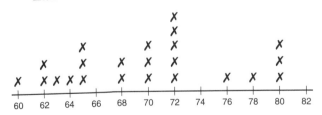

A. Explain why the data cannot be used to construct a circle graph.

B. Explain what is wrong or misleading in the given graph.

12. The line plot displays scores on an 80-point mathematics test.

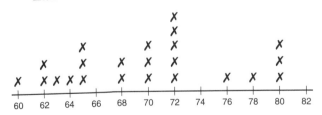

A. Which measure of central tendency (mean, median, or mode) is most easily observed from this line plot? Explain why.

B. What is the median test score? Explain how you find it from this line plot.

C. Suppose the teacher finds six scores that need to be added to the line plot: 72, 76, 76, 78, 80, 80.

  (i) Does the median change? If so, what is the new median?

  (ii) Does the mode change? If so, what is the new mode?

  (iii) In a general way, how does the mean change and why? (Do not actually calculate the mean.)

13. Matrix A represents the number of tickets sold for a performance of a musical play on Saturday. Matrix B represents the number of tickets sold for the performance of the same musical play on Wednesday. The columns represent matinee and evening performances. The rows represent orchestra, mezzanine, and balcony seats.

$$A = \begin{bmatrix} 275 & 295 \\ 143 & 158 \\ 65 & 87 \end{bmatrix} \quad B = \begin{bmatrix} 220 & 251 \\ 133 & 140 \\ 52 & 45 \end{bmatrix}$$

If orchestra seats cost $50, mezzanine seats cost $45, and balcony seats cost $30, how much more did the theater make on the two evening performances compared to the two matinee performances?

14. The spreadsheet shown represents data collected from five students who were asked five questions about changes proposed to the school. A score of 1 indicated a least favorable response, while a score of 5 indicated a most favorable response. To find out the average response for question 4, which cell would you look in?

	A	B	C	D	E	F
1	NAME	Q#1	Q#2	Q#3	Q#4	Q#5
2	Alice	2	1	3	4	5
3	Bill	3	5	2	1	4
4	Dave	4	5	3	2	1
5	Jennifer	2	3	4	1	5
6	Franco	5	2	3	1	4
7						
8	AVERAGE	3.2	3.2	3.1	1.8	3.8

A) E8   B) B8   C) C8   D) D8

3.11 Interpreting Data

To use a graph to interpret data:

- Pay attention to the scale. Check to see if the scale has a broken line between zero and the first interval.
- Know what the numbers mean.
- Read the title and the labels on the axes.
- Check graphs with multiple lines or bars for relationships between points.
- Be able to make predictions about the relation that *goes beyond* what is displayed. This is called ***extrapolation***.

To use a table to interpret data:

- Read the title and labels.
- Know what the numbers mean.
- Be able to estimate values *between* given entries. This is called ***interpolation***.

When interpreting data, be alert for misuses and abuses of statistics. Statistics can be misleading if:

- An inappropriate scale is used to display data.

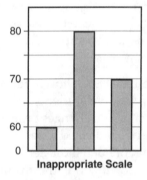
Inappropriate Scale

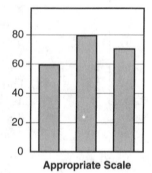
Appropriate Scale

- The wrong measure of central tendency is used to describe the data.
  In a small company of six people, the salaries of individuals are $80,000; $20,000; $25,000; $19,000; $22,500; $23,500. The average salary is about $32,000. Using the average would be inappropriate to describe the set. A better descriptor of the data would be the median, $23,000.

- Insufficient titles or labels are used on the axes or chart.

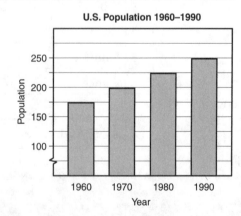

The vertical axis doesn't indicate that the numbers are in millions.

- The graphic has a visual distortion to suggest a disproportionate relation, thus not accurately illustrating the numerical relationship.

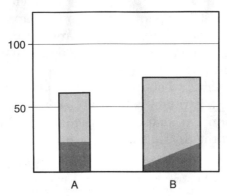

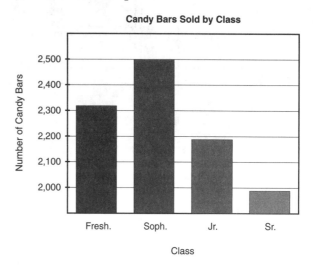

MODEL PROBLEMS

1. The graph displays the average monthly temperatures for two different years. How do the temperatures for Year A compare to those for Year B? Explain.

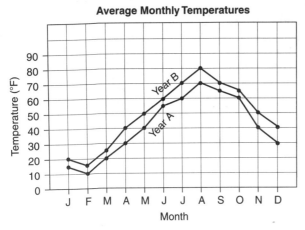

Average Monthly Temperatures

Solution: The graph of the average monthly temperatures for Year B is above the graph for Year A, indicating that the average monthly temperatures for Year B were greater than those for Year A. Since the two graphs never intersect, it is clear that at no time did a month in Year B record a temperature less than or equal to the same month for Year A.

2. What impression is given by the graph? How is this impression created?

Candy Bars Sold by Class

Solution: The graph suggests that the sophomore class sold significantly more candy bars than the senior class. The scale gives the same amount of space to the interval 0–2,000 as to the intervals of one hundred. This is inappropriate.

Analyzing and Interpreting Frequency Distributions

Frequency distributions can be analyzed and interpreted based on spread, clusters, outliers, and the shape of the distribution. The *spread* shows how far apart the data values are. The *clusters* are parts of the graph where the data are grouped around a specific value. The *outliers* are values much lower or much higher than most of the other data. The shape of the distribution can be symmetrical, where two halves are mirror images; skewed right or left; or J-shaped. Distributions that are skewed right have a long tail to the right. Distributions that are skewed left have a long tail to the left. J-shaped distributions are shaped like the letter J. The following graphs show the different shapes of the distribution.

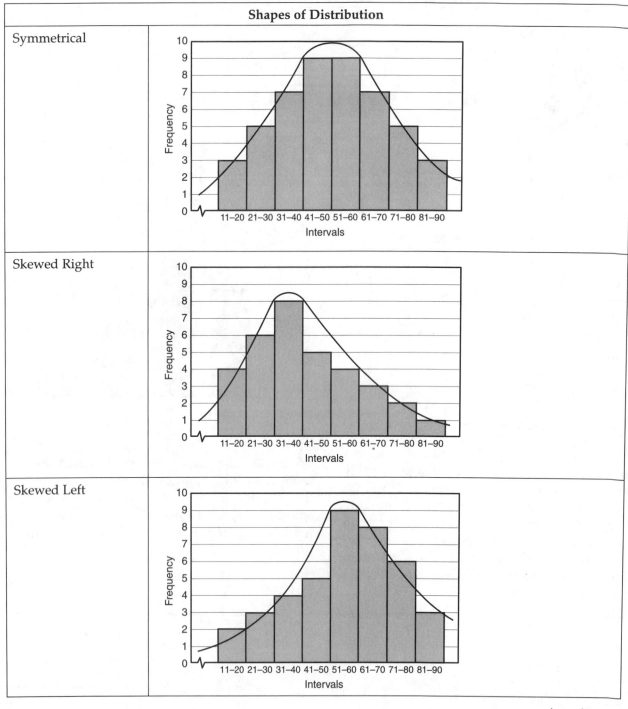

(continued)

Shapes of Distribution (continued)		

J-Shaped

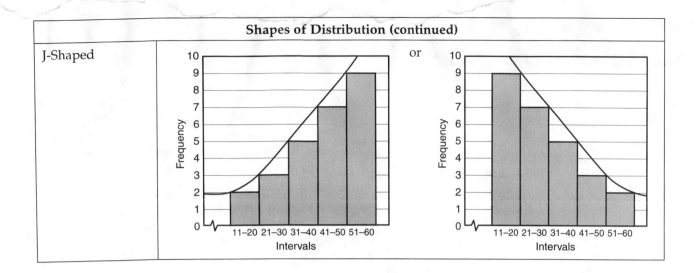

MODEL PROBLEM

Sketch an appropriate histogram for the data below and interpret the distribution.

Intervals	Frequency
1–10	5
11–20	10
21–30	11
31–40	9
41–50	4
51–60	3
61–70	2

Solution:

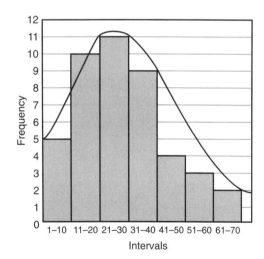

The spread of the graph is between 1 and 70. There are no clusters and outliers. The shape of the curve is skewed right.

1. The following graph shows the average monthly 6:00 A.M. and 6:00 P.M. temperatures (°F) recorded at Newark Airport.

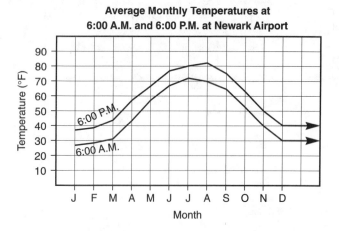

A. How do you know that the graph does NOT show a situation in which the September temperatures at 6:00 A.M. and 6:00 P.M. were the same?

B. According to the graph, was there any month when the average 6:00 A.M. temperature was greater than the average 6:00 P.M. temperature? Explain your response.

2. The circle graphs show how Sally and Michele spend their earnings. How is it possible that Michele can spend a greater dollar amount on recreation than the dollar amount spent by Sally?

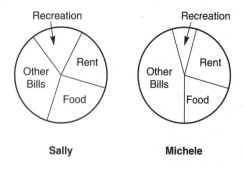

3. The graph shows the volume of sales of cassette tapes and compact discs (CDs) at a local music store over a six-year period. Explain the trend shown separately in Line A and Line B. Discuss the significance of the point of intersection of Line A and Line B.

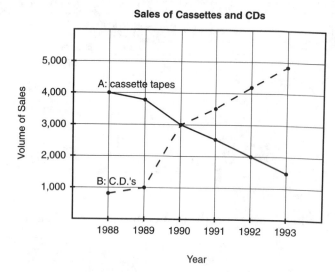

4. The graph is intended to compare morning coffee sales at two convenience stores in the same town. Is the visual message depicted in the graph accurate? Explain your response.

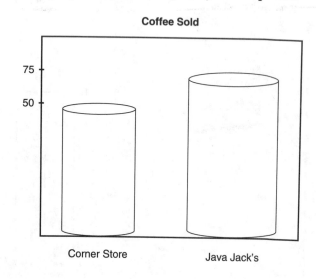

5. Mrs. Mendez is giving a dinner party. She plans to serve a $5\frac{3}{4}$-pound standing rib roast that she plans to cook in a microwave oven. She knows that her guests prefer the meat to be cooked medium. Using the information shown, what is the minimum amount of time (in minutes) needed to cook the roast?

BEEF	Microwave Time			Internal Temperature	
	Step 1 HIGH (100%)	Step 2 MED-HIGH (70%)		At Removal	After Standing
Standing or Rolled Rib	Less than 4 lb: $6\frac{1}{2}$ min	Rare: 9–13 min/lb		120°	140°
	More than 4 lb: $10\frac{1}{2}$ min	Medium: 10–$13\frac{1}{2}$ min/lb		135°	150°
		Well Done: $10\frac{1}{2}$–15 min/lb		150°	160°
Tenderloin	Less than 2 lb: 4 min	Rare: 8–11 min/lb		120°	140°
	More than 2 lb: $6\frac{1}{2}$ min	Medium: 9–13 min/lb		135°	150°
		Well Done: $10\frac{1}{2}$–$14\frac{1}{2}$ min/lb		150°	160°

6. Sketch an appropriate histogram for the data below and interpret the distribution.

Score	55–59	60–64	65–69	70–74	75–79	80–84	85–89	90–94	95–99
Frequency	1	5	13	30	28	12	5	4	2

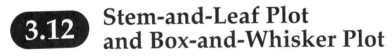

3.12 Stem-and-Leaf Plot and Box-and-Whisker Plot

Stem-and-Leaf Plot

A *stem-and-leaf plot* shows each data item in numerical order. The leaf is always the units digit of the item, while the stem can be the tens digit or tens and hundreds digits of the data.

To Construct a Stem-and-Leaf Plot:

- Find the smallest and largest values of the data.
- Draw a vertical line. To the left of the line, write each consecutive digit from the smallest stem value to the largest stem value.
- Insert the leaves.
- For each stem, reorder the leaves from smallest to largest.
- Include a key.

MODEL PROBLEMS

1. In September, each of the 18 students in a math class reported the number of days he or she worked over the summer break:

   25, 17, 28, 13, 16, 28, 19, 36, 33, 18, 24, 37, 27, 35, 43, 25, 24, 36

   Represent these data in a stem-and-leaf plot, with the values in the *tens* place as the stem and the corresponding values in the *units* place as the leaves.

Solution:

For the data given, the smallest and largest values are 13 and 43 respectively. This means that the smallest tens value is 1 and the largest tens value is 4. The stem-and-leaf plot looks like the following after inserting the leaves.

1	7 3 6 9 8
2	5 8 8 4 7 5 4
3	6 3 7 5 6
4	3

Arrange the leaves for each stem to smallest to largest.

1	3 6 7 8 9
2	4 4 5 5 7 8 8
3	3 5 6 6 7
4	3

The key can show any value, such as 3 | 5 = 35.

From this plot, we find that the most students worked from 24 to 28 days.

2. The following stem-and-leaf plot shows the data from test scores in a geometry class.

9	9 6 6 2 0 0
8	7 7 7 4 3 0 0
7	8 6 6 5 0
6	9 5 5 0
5	9

   A. Find the median for this data.
   B. Find the mode.
   C. The student who received the score of 70 was able to convince the teacher there was an error in the scoring and consequently the score should have been 75. Describe how the stem-and-leaf plot would appear after the error is corrected. How would the change affect the median and the mode?

Solution:

   A. Since the stem-and-leaf plot gives the 23 scores in order from greatest to least, the median is the 12th score, 80.
   B. The mode is the single score that occurs most frequently, 87.
   C. To correct the data, the teacher would change the third line of the steam-and-leaf plot to read:

   7 | 8 6 6 5 5

   The change would have no effect on the median or mode for the data.

Quartiles

Quartiles are values that divide the data set into four equal parts, each containing one-fourth or 25% of the members. For example:

53, 60, 61, 63, 64,   65, 65, 65, 65, 66,   66, 67, 67, 68, 69,   70, 70, 71, 71, 73

| 64.5 | | 66 | | 69.5 |

Median

First quartile   Second quartile   Third quartile

- The *first* or *lower quartile* is the center of the lower half.
- The *second quartile* is the median.
- The *third* or *upper quartile* is the center of the upper half.
- *The interquartile range (IQR)* is the difference between the third quartile and the first quartile. In the example above, interquartile range is $69.5 - 64.5 = 5$.

 MODEL PROBLEM

Find the quartiles and the interquartile range (IQR):

25, 46, 50, 58, 60, 75, 83, 85, 65, 50, 21, 75, 79, 55

Solution:

Step 1. Arrange the members in order:

21, 25, 46, 50, 50, 55, 58, 60, 65, 75, 75, 79, 83, 85

Step 2. Find the median, which is the second quartile.

21, 25, 46, 50, 50, 55, <u>58, 60</u>, 65, 75, 75, 79, 83, 85

Median = $(58 + 60) \div 2 = 59$

Step 3. The first quartile is 50, which is the median of the seven values to the left of 59:

21, 25, 46, <u>50</u>, 50, 55, 58

Step 4. The third quartile is 75, which is the median of the seven values to the right of 59:

60, 65, 75, <u>75</u>, 79, 83, 85

Step 5. To find the interquartile range (IQR), subtract the first quartile from the third:

$75 - 50 = 25$

Answer: The quartiles are 50, 59, and 75. The interquartile range (IQR) is 25.

Box-and-Whisker Plots

A *box-and-whisker plot* is a graph that presents a set of data using the quartiles and the extreme values in the data. The *extreme values* are the highest and lowest values of a set of data. This plot is useful in comparing two or more sets of data. The box-and-whisker plots show the distribution of each data set and its extreme values.

To Construct a Box-and-Whisker Plot:

- Draw a number line that includes the extreme values of the data set.
- Above the number line, mark the quartiles and extreme values using a point.
- Draw a box above the number line, with vertical sides passing through the lower and upper quartiles. Draw a vertical line in the box through the median (second quartile).
- Draw the "whiskers," which are horizontal lines extending from the vertical sides of the rectangle to the extreme values.
- Plot the *outliers*, which are data that fall more than 1.5 times the interquartile range from the quartiles. Do not extend whiskers to any outliers.

 MODEL PROBLEM

Bowling scores of 15 bowlers are listed below:

215 264 189 204 245 226 232 195
240 200 175 210 218 234 212

Express the data in a box-and-whisker plot.

Solution:

Step 1. Arrange the data in ascending order and find the four quartiles.

175, 189, 195, 200, 204, 210, 212, 215, 218, 226, 232, 234, 240, 245, 264

The median is 215.

The lower quartile is 200.

The upper quartile is 234.

The interquartile range (IQR) is 234 − 200 = 34.

Step 2. Draw a number line that contains the extreme values. Plot the values for the median, lower and upper quartiles, and the extreme values above the number line and draw the rectangular box.

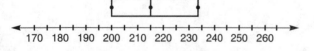

Step 3. Draw the whiskers and plot the outliers. Extend the left whisker from the lower quartile to the lowest value of the data set. Then extend the right whisker from the upper quartile to the highest value of the data set.

The outliers are data more than 1.5(34) = 51 from the quartiles. For left side, 200 − 51 = 149. Since there are no data smaller than 175, there are no low outliers. For the right side, 234 + 51 = 285. Since there are no data larger than 264, there are no high outliers. Therefore, there are no outliers to plot.

Answer:

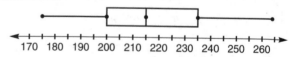

1. The heights of students (in inches) are shown in a stem-and-leaf plot below

4	0 1 3 4 6 6 8
5	2 2 3 4 6 6 6 8 9
6	0 0 1

    5 | 6 = 5 feet 6 inches

    What is the median height of the students?

    A) 4 feet
    B) 5 feet
    C) 5 feet 3 inches
    D) 6 feet 1 inch

2. The key for a stem-and-leaf plot is 3 | 7 = 37. The value 25 would be plotted as:

    E) 5 | 2
    F) 20 | 5
    G) 2 | 5
    H) 25

For questions 3–5, use the following stem-and-leaf plot.

Grades on a Chemistry Test

10	0 0
9	0 2 4 7 7 9
8	1 3 3 6 6 6 8 9
7	0 4 5 8 9
6	2 3 6
5	3

Key: 8 | 3 = 83 percent

3. How many students took the test?

    A) 10
    B) 15
    C) 25
    D) 30

4. What is the mode of the scores?

    E) 100
    F) 97
    G) 86
    H) 78

5. If a failing grade is any grade less than 70 percent, how many students failed the test?

    A) 1
    B) 2
    C) 3
    D) 4

6. Identify the first quartile:

    32, 24, 38, 26, 38, 36, 37, 39, 23, 40, 21, 31

    E) 21
    F) 25
    G) 32
    H) 34

7. The IQR of a data set is 25. The first quartile is 78. Which value could be the median?

    A) 30
    B) 53
    C) 92
    D) 103

8. This is a box-and-whisker plot for 55 test scores.

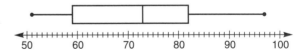

    The lower quartile is

    E) 97
    F) 82
    G) 73
    H) 59

9. Find the IQR for this set of data:

60, 62, 64, 68, 69, 71, 72, 74, 76, 78, 81

A) 76   B) 71
C) 64   D) 12

10. A race car had the following times in seven different races: 182, 158, 159, 150, 162, 180, and 172 miles per hour. What is the upper quartile?

E) 22   F) 158
G) 162   H) 180

11. A. Use a box-and-whisker plot to represent the heights of kindergarten students (in inches).

48, 48, 45, 50, 46, 46, 42, 46, 36, 44, 47, 45, 46, 44, 45

B. In the three previous years, the median height of the kindergarten students had been 48″, and 25% of the classes were taller than 50″. How does this class compare?

12. Test scores from an algebra class are as follows:

83, 78, 94, 93, 87, 86, 83, 94, 99, 90, 87, 79, 65, 87, 93, 96, 88, 84, 82, 93, 85.

A. Construct a stem-and-leaf plot for the data.
B. State the median score for the data.
C. State the range for the data.

3.13   Methods of Counting

Counting of discrete or individual items is a major part of the topic of discrete mathematics.

The counting process often involves making an organized list of the items to be counted. For example, in counting the number of rectangles of any size in the picture shown,

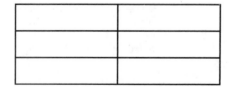

it is necessary to organize to count the number of each different-size rectangle present.

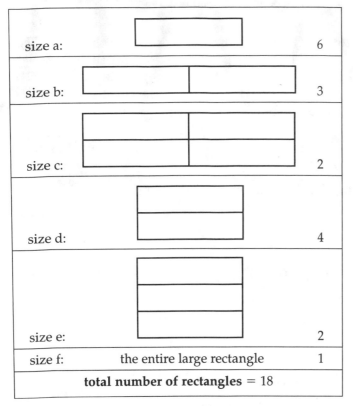

size a:		6
size b:		3
size c:		2
size d:		4
size e:		2
size f:	the entire large rectangle	1
total number of rectangles = 18		

Tree diagrams A graphic called a tree diagram can be used to show all of the possibilities in a counting situation involving a sequence of components, parts, or stages.

 MODEL PROBLEM

A restaurant offers a soup-and-sandwich lunch. There are 2 possible soups (tomato and chicken); for the sandwich, 3 breads (white, rye, wheat) and 4 meats (roast beef, ham, turkey, salami).

How many different lunches are possible?

Solution:

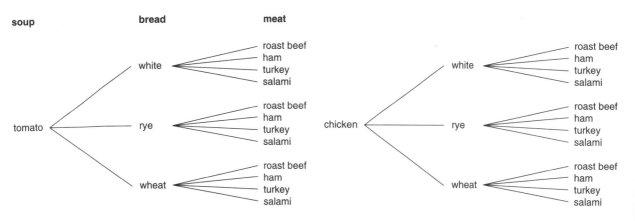

The tree diagram shows 24 final branches. The result (24) is consistent with the use of the counting principle: $2 \times 3 \times 4 = 24$.

Note: To review the counting principle, see page 123.

Permutations

In situations involving counting possibilities, it is necessary to determine if the order of the items matters. A common kind of counting problem is to find the number of arrangements of some or all of a set of objects. Each arrangement is called a *permutation*. The counting principle may be used to calculate the number of permutations. For example, the number of arrangements of four people in line to buy a concert ticket would be:

$$4 \times 3 \times 2 \times 1 = 4! = 24$$

If only two of the individuals were arranged in line, the number of permutations would be $4 \times 3 = 12$.

> Permutations of n objects at a time:
>
> $$_nP_n = n!$$
>
> Permutations of n objects r at a time:
>
> $$_nP_r = \frac{n!}{(n-r)!}$$

 MODEL PROBLEMS

1. Find the value of $_7P_3$.

Solution:

$_7P_3$ (the number of permutations of 7 things taken 3 at a time)

$$\frac{7!}{(7-3)!} = \frac{7!}{4!} = \frac{7 \times 6 \times 5 \times 4 \times 3 \times 2 \times 1}{4 \times 3 \times 2 \times 1} = 7 \times 6 \times 5 = 210$$

2. Using the digits 2, 3, 4, 5, 6, how many three-digit numbers can be formed if repetition of digits is not permitted?

Solution:

Since order does matter (245 and 452 are different numbers), this is a straightforward permutation problem.

$$_5P_3 = \frac{5!}{(5-3!)} = \frac{5!}{2!} = \frac{5 \times 4 \times 3 \times 2 \times 1}{2 \times 1} = 5 \times 4 \times 3 = 60$$

Note: If it is possible to repeat digits, there would be additional numbers possible (such as 445, 333, etc.). With repetition possible, the solution would be:

$$5 \times 5 \times 5 = 5^3 = 125$$

Combinations

Combinations involve selecting from among a given number of people or objects where order does not matter. For example, if you are selecting two girls out of a group of four to be on a committee, a listing would show that there are six committees (or combinations) possible:

Alice (A), Bonita (B), Celine (C), Donna (D)

AB	BC	CD
AC	BD	
AD		

The number of combinations of n things r at a time is always smaller than the corresponding number of permutations. This is due to each combination yielding a number of permutations (two for each combination: for example, AB and BA).

As with permutations, there are formulas for calculating the number of combinations.

Special cases include:

$_nC_n = 1$ (only 1 combination possible in selecting n things n at a time)

$_nC_1 = n$ (n combinations possible in selecting n things 1 at a time)

$_nC_0 = 1$ (1 combination possible in selecting n things 0 at a time)

> Combinations of n things r at a time:
>
> $$_nC_r = \frac{n!}{(n-r)!r!}$$

 MODEL PROBLEMS

1. Find the value of $_{10}C_2$.

Solution:

$_{10}C_2$ (the number of combinations of 10 things 2 at a time)

$$\frac{10!}{8! \times 2!} = \frac{10 \times 9}{2} \quad \text{(after reducing the fraction because numerator and denominator each contain } 8! \text{ as a factor)}$$

$$= \frac{90}{2} = 45$$

2. For a history report, you can choose to write about 3 of the original 13 colonies. How many different combinations exist for the colonies you will be writing about?

Solution:

Since you are making a selection where order does not matter, this is a combinations problem.

$$_{13}C_3 = \frac{13!}{10!3!} = \frac{13 \times 12 \times 11}{3 \times 2 \times 1} = 13 \times 2 \times 11 = 286 \text{ combinations}$$

3. How many pizzas can be made using 0, 1, 2, 3, or 4 of the following toppings: pepperoni, onion, mushroom, green pepper? (*Note:* This is a repeat of a model problem from section 3.3 with a different solution strategy.)

Solution: Make the assumption that a pizza with pepperoni and onion is the same as one with onion and pepperoni; therefore order does not matter and we can use combinations.

$_4C_4 = 1$ (only 1 pizza possible with all toppings)

$_4C_3 = \dfrac{4!}{1!3!} = 4$ $_4C_1 = 4$

$_4C_2 = \dfrac{4!}{2!2!} = 6$ $_4C_0 = 1$

Total number of possible pizzas $= 1 + 4 + 6 + 4 + 1 = 16$

1. Which of the following is a combinations problem or situation?

   A) In how many ways can 5 different books be arranged on a shelf?
   B) How many subsets exist from the set {a, b, c, d}?
   C) How many three-digit numbers are possible using the digits 1, 4, 7, and 9?
   D) A school needs to schedule 4 classes—English, Spanish, math, and science—in the first 4 periods. How many different schedules are possible?

2. Which has the greatest value?

   E) $_8C_6$ F) $_9C_4$ G) $_9P_4$ H) $_8P_6$

3. Which of the following is a true statement?

   I. $_nP_n$ for $n > 1$ must be even
   II. $_nP_{n-1} = {_nP_n}$ for $n > 1$
   III. $_nP_1 = n$

   A) III only   B) I and II
   C) II and III   D) I, II, and III

4. A customer in a computer store can choose one of four monitors, one of two keyboards, and one of four computers. If all the choices are compatible, how many different systems are possible?

   E) 10   F) 16   G) 32   H) 10!

5. How many arrangements are possible of all the letters in ALGEBRA if each arrangement must begin and end with A?

6. If $k(_{10}C_3) = {_{10}P_3}$, what is the value of k?

7. A school committee consists of the Student Council president, 5 other students, the principal, and 3 teachers. In how many ways can a subcommittee be selected if the subcommittee is to consist of the Student Council president, 2 other students from the committee, the principal, and 1 teacher from the committee?

8. A restaurant offers a soup-and-sandwich lunch. There are 3 possible soups, 3 breads possible for the sandwich, and k types of meat available for the sandwich. If the tree diagram constructed yields a total of 45 different lunches possible, find the value of k.

9. How many triangles (of any size) are in the diagram below?

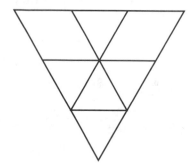

10. From a club with 12 members, a committee of 4 members is needed. The club secretary, a math major, tries to convince everyone that the number of committees of 4 is the same as the number of committees of 8.

    A. Is this correct? Explain.
    B. Using standard notation for combinations, show a generalization of the above.
    C. If $_{15}C_6 = {_{15}C_r}$, $r \neq 6$, what is the value of r?

11. The traveling squad for a college basketball team consists of two centers, five forwards, and four guards. The coach is interested in determining the number of ways she can select a starting team of one center, two forwards, and two guards.

A. Find the number of ways to select one center.

B. In finding the number of ways to select two forwards, are permutations or combinations used? Explain.

C. Find the number of ways to select the two starting forwards.

D. Find the number of ways to select the two starting guards.

E. In using answers to parts A, C, and D, is the number of possible starting teams A + C + D or A × C × D? Explain.

12. If you wanted to determine the number of diagonals in a convex polygon of n sides, you might try to develop a pattern resulting in a formula.

A. For an octagon $ABCDEFGH$, AC, CE, AG are a few of the diagonals. Why are AB, CD, GH (and possibly others) not diagonals?

B. In finding the number of diagonals, explain why you would use combinations and not permutations.

C. For a pentagon $ABCDE$, you can easily count to verify that there are five diagonals. However, when you take the five vertices, two at a time, you get $_5C_2 = 10$. Since this doesn't quite work, what should the formula be for the number of diagonals in a pentagon?

D. See if your formula works when you extend the problem to a hexagon.

E. Using n for the number of sides (or vertices), what would be the general formula?

1. Two dice are rolled. What is the probability that either the sum is 3 or the sum is 8?

A) $\frac{7}{36}$ B) $\frac{1}{6}$ C) $\frac{5}{36}$ D) $\frac{1}{12}$

2. Which of the following is TRUE about the data?

Score	Frequency
80	2
82	4
86	3
90	5

E) The mean is greater than the median.
F) The median is greater than the mean.
G) The mean equals the median.
H) There is no mode for the data.

3. Data that describe a situation in which any value between two given values can theoretically occur are called *continuous data*. Continuous data often result from measurements.

If the data are not continuous, they are called *discrete*. Discrete data come from counting situations.

Which of the following situations illustrates discrete data?

A) Temperatures recorded every half hour at a weather station
B) Lengths of 1,000 bolts of fabric produced in a factory
C) The heights of individuals
D) The number of children in a family

4. This table shows the amounts of candy sold by the classes in Washington High School.

Candy Sale Results	
Freshmen	11,200
Sophomores	9,600
Juniors	11,700
Seniors	7,500

Which graph is the POOREST representation of the data?

E)

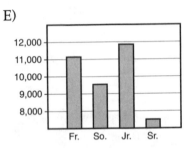

F)

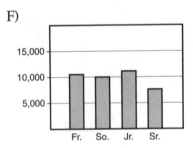

G)

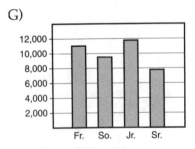

H)

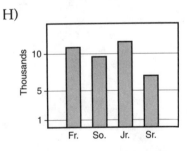

5. Which of the following situations represents events that are *independent*? (That is, the outcome of the first event has no effect on the outcome of the second event.)

   A) Two marbles are selected from a container without replacement.
   B) Two children born in a family are a boy, then a girl.
   C) A ticket is selected for second prize after the first-prize ticket has been removed.
   D) A king is selected from a deck of cards after two kings have already been dealt.

6. A theater did a survey of the ages of people who came to their cabaret. The table summarizes the results. Find the median age of the viewers.

   E) 13–30
   F) 31–48
   G) 49–66
   H) over 66

Ages	Numbers
12 and under	87
13–30	298
31–48	481
49–66	364
over 66	95

7. The rules for a board game call for a player to lose a turn if the player rolls three consecutive doubles on a pair of dice. What is the probability that a player will lose a turn in her first three rolls?

   A) $\frac{1}{6}$ B) $\frac{1}{18}$ C) $\frac{1}{36}$ D) $\frac{1}{216}$

8. A basketball player with a free throw shooting average of 60% is on the line for a one-and-one free throw (the player gets a second shot if the first shot is successful). What is the probability the player will score two points at the free-throw line?

   E) 0.6   F) 0.4   G) 0.36   H) 0.24

9. If y varies directly with x, then when x is doubled y will ___.

   A) not change   B) be halved
   C) increase by 2   D) be doubled

10. Use these data found in the telephone directory to answer the question that follows.

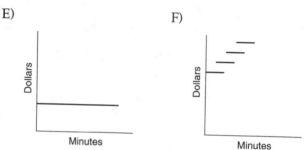

Sample Telephone Day Rates		
From York to	First **Minute**	Each Add'l **Minute**
Marietta	0.33	0.11
Mount Joy	0.17	0.07
Red Lion	0.09	0.03
Gettysburg	0.37	0.11

Which graph is a possible illustration of the charges for calls?

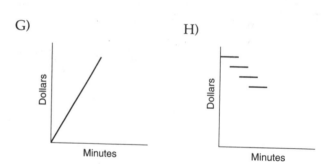

E) F) G) H)

11. In how many different ways can you arrange all of the letters A, B, C, D, E, F, G if each arrangement must begin and end with a vowel and the middle letter must be G?

   A) 7!   B) 5!
   C) $_5P_5 \times 2$ D) $2 \times 4!$

12. The IQR of a data set is 18. The first quartile is 52. Which of the following values could be the median?

   E) 25   F) 34   G) 61   H) 97

13. A contest offers a prize of a trip to London, Paris, or Rome in either spring, summer, or fall.

   How many different choices are possible if a prize consists of one city and one season?

14. If a pair of dice is rolled, what is the probability of getting a sum of 8?

15. The mean of a set of ten scores is 61. What is the sum of the ten scores?

16. Eight scores have a mean of 30. The bottom two scores have a mean of 21. The top two scores have a mean of 50. What is the mean of the four middle scores?

17. The ratio of the central angles of a spinner is $1:2:5:7$. The sections (sectors) of the spinner are marked BOB, ANN, SAM, TAD (in the same order as $1:2:5:7$). If the spinner is spun, what is Probability(BOB)?

18. The probability that a teacher will call a boy to go up to the board is $\frac{11}{25}$. What are the odds against calling a boy up to the board?

19. A test consists of 13 questions. Each student must choose 10 questions and omit 3 questions. How many different groups of questions could be chosen?

20. Brightline Company guarantees that its lightbulbs will last for at least 1,000 hours. If a bulb fails before 1,000 hours of use, the customer can request a refund. The product research division of the company calculated the average life of a bulb to be approximately normally distributed with a mean of 1,020 hours and a standard deviation of 20 hours. What is the approximate percentage of lightbulbs that will not last 1,000 hours?

21. Morse code is a system of communicating information in which ordered sets of dots and dashes represent the letters of the alphabet, numerals, etc. An "e" is represented by a single dot, while a dash followed by two dots represents a "d." How many distinct letters can be represented by arrangements of 1 to 5 symbols, each of which is a dot or a dash?

22. Rectangle $ABCD$ has dimensions as shown below. E is the midpoint of $\overline{DC}$, F is the midpoint of $\overline{EC}$, and G is the midpoint of $\overline{DE}$. If a dart is thrown at random into the rectangle, what is the probability that it lands inside the unshaded region?

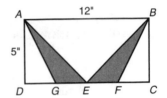

OPEN-ENDED QUESTIONS

23. Give a set of data that has the following measures of central tendency: mode = 9, mean = 12, median = 12. Explain how you constructed the set.

24. The following data represent the heights in inches of students in a kindergarten class. Construct a line plot from the data. State the median, the mode, and the mean for the data.

    48 47 44 46 48 46 42 46 51
    46 50 43 42 45 43 47 49

25. Five students are applying for two student manager positions for the football team. The students include 4 boys and 1 girl. All the students have an equal chance of being selected. Find the probability that the two managers will include:

A. 1 girl
B. 2 boys

26. Construct a bar graph from the information in this table.

Nicole's Fall Fund-Raiser Sales	
Gift Bags	卌 卌 卌 卌 卌 卌 |||
Rolls of Wrap	卌 卌 卌 |||
Bags of Bows	卌 卌 |||
Gift Tabs	卌 卌	

27. A discount clothing store has the following policy. Each week that an item remains on the rack it is discounted by 10% of its current price.

  A. A suit is originally priced at $450. Generate a table to show the price of the suit for the first six weeks it is on the rack.

  B. Write a formula to generalize the sequence produced in part A.

  C. Determine the number of weeks it will take for the suit to be priced less than $100.

28. Given a set of eight elements {a, b, c, d, e, f, g, h}, {c, d, e} is a subset with three members and {c, d, e, f, a} is a subset with five members. Explain why the total number of subsets of three elements is exactly the same as the total number of subsets of five elements.

29. The annual salaries for five major league baseball players are:

  $120,000 $110,000 $140,000
  $120,000 $1,000,000

  A. Find the mean for the salaries.
  B. What is the median salary?
  C. Which of the two measures (mean or median) gives a better indication of the annual salary for the group of baseball players? Explain your response.

30. Jose and Ray were discussing major league baseball players. Jose pointed out that there were 186 players currently with batting averages from .250 to .299. Ray said at least four of the players must have the same average. Is Ray correct? If yes, explain why. If not, explain why not. (Note that batting averages are always rounded to the nearest thousandth.)

31. Two dice are rolled.

  A. Explain why the probability of obtaining a sum less than or equal to 5 is the same as the probability of obtaining a sum greater than or equal to 9.

  B. If the probability of obtaining a sum less than or equal to 6 is the same as the probability of obtaining a sum greater than or equal to k, find the value of k.

  C. If three dice are rolled, what is the probability that the sum obtained is less than or equal to 3?

  D. The answer to part C would be the same as the probability that the sum obtained is greater than or equal to what value?

32. Matrix A represents the enrollment at Washington High School. Matrix B represents the enrollment at Jefferson High School. The columns represent the number of students in grades 9–12 respectively, and the rows represent the number of male and female students.

$$A = \begin{bmatrix} 130 & 128 & 143 & 121 \\ 120 & 131 & 137 & 135 \end{bmatrix}$$

$$B = \begin{bmatrix} 192 & 201 & 193 & 205 \\ 197 & 214 & 201 & 192 \end{bmatrix}$$

  A. What percent the total enrollment of each school is made up of 12th graders?

  B. What percent of each school's total enrollments is male?

33. A school offers baseball, soccer, and basketball to its 120 students. A survey showed that 35 students played baseball, 70 played soccer, 40 played basketball, 20 played both soccer and basketball, 15 played both soccer and baseball, 15 played both basketball and baseball, and 10 played all three sports.

  A. How many students played none of the three sports?

  B. What percent of the students played baseball as their only sport?

  C. How many students played both basketball and baseball but not soccer?

34. Construct a scatter plot using the following information. Is there a correlation? If so, is it positive or negative? What can you conclude about time spent doing homework and time spent watching television?

Time Spent Doing Homework vs. Viewing Television		
Student	Homework (min)	Television Viewing (min)
A	30	60
B	90	45
C	90	0
D	75	90
E	60	120
F	75	30
G	45	60
H	60	0
I	0	180
J	45	30

35. A restaurant offers five entree choices on its dinner menu: turkey, hamburger, chicken, pork chops, and fish. With each entree, the customer may choose one type of potato: french fried, mashed, or baked, and one of two desserts: ice cream or pudding.

   A. Make a tree diagram to show the possible dinner choices.
   B. How many different meals are available assuming the customer selects an entree, a potato, and a dessert?
   C. Suppose the diner has the option of not taking a potato or a dessert. How does that change the number of different meals that are available? Show all work.

36. Refer to the graph given.

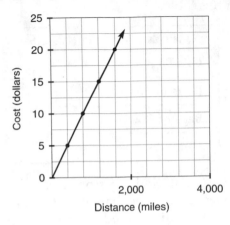

   A. Does the graph illustrate a direct or an inverse variation in the data?
   B. Give two additional ordered pairs that would appear in the graph if it were extended.
   C. Suggest a practical situation that might be represented by this graph.

37. Use the data in the table.

U.S. Population	
Year	Population (in millions)
1890	63
1900	76
1910	92
1920	106
1930	123
1940	132
1950	151
1960	179
1970	203
1980	227
1990	249
2000	281

   A. Draw a line graph of the data given in the table.
   B. *Interpolation* is the process of estimating a value between two known values. Using the graph, interpolate to find the U.S. population in 1975.
   C. Examine the population changes between 1980–1990 and 1990–2000. Predict what the population might be in the year 2010 if this pattern continues. Explain your reasoning.

CUMULATIVE ASSESSMENT

Chapters 1, 2, and 3

1. How many three-digit numbers have all of the following characteristics?

   I. The number is a multiple of 72.
   II. The number is divisible by 5.
   III. The number is less than 500.

   A) 0   B) 1   C) 2   D) 5

2. The measures of two supplementary angles are in the ratio 9 : 1. What is the difference in degree measure between the two angles?

   E) 18   F) 72   G) 144   H) 162

3. Which of the following is NOT equal to the other numbers?

   A) 0.2   B) $\sqrt{\dfrac{1}{25}}$ C) $\dfrac{1}{2} + \dfrac{1}{3}$ D) $\dfrac{0.05}{0.25}$

4. Triangle ABC is isosceles with $\overline{AB} \cong \overline{AC}$.

   $\angle DAB \cong \angle BAC \cong \angle EAC$

   What is the measure of $\angle EAC$?

   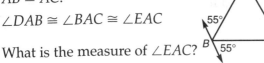

   E) 40   F) 55   G) 70   H) 80

5. A school club consists of only juniors and seniors. If the ratio of juniors to seniors in the club is 3 : 2, which of the following could NOT be the total number of club members?

   A) 16   B) 20   C) 25   D) 30

6. Using four of the five digits 1, 3, 4, 7, 8, how many four-digit numbers can be formed, with no repetition of digits, if the number must be odd?

   E) 625   F) 120   G) 72   H) 36

7. Which of the following does NOT exist?

   A) A rhombus with two angles each measuring 5°
   B) A quadrilateral with one angle measuring 80° and each additional angle measuring 10° more than the previous one
   C) A trapezoid with two right angles
   D) An obtuse isosceles triangle

8. Three dice are rolled. What is the probability of obtaining a sum that is less than or equal to 4?

   E) $\dfrac{1}{216}$ F) $\dfrac{1}{108}$ G) $\dfrac{1}{72}$ H) $\dfrac{1}{54}$

9. This line plot shows test scores for 15 students:

   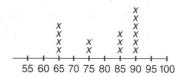

   Which of the following is true about the data?

   A) The mean equals the median.
   B) The median is greater than the mean.
   C) The median is less than the mean.
   D) There is no mode for the data.

10. During a recent month, the exchange rate of Canadian dollars to United States dollars was 1 to 0.81. If you paid $65 in Canadian dollars for a toaster-oven, what would you have paid in United States dollars? (Disregard tax.)

    E) $52.65
    F) $65.81
    G) $80.25
    H) $84.00

11. Which symbol has 90° rotational symmetry?

    A) ⊤   B) □   C) 3   D) ♡

12. About what percent of the big square is shaded?

E) 5%
F) 15%
G) 20%
H) 25%

13. Daniel, David, and Darryl independently answer a question on a test. The probability that Daniel answers correctly is .9. The probability that David answers correctly is .6. The probability that Darryl answers correctly is .8. What is the probability that not one of the three answers the question correctly?

A) .008   B) .432   C) .568   D) .72

14. There are four times as many boys as girls on the newspaper staff of Central High School. If there are 40 staff members in all, how many of them are girls?

E) 8   F) 10   G) 30   H) 32

15. Point *A* is reflected over the *y*-axis and then the image is reflected over the *x*-axis, resulting in the point *A″* with coordinates $(-4, -2)$. What was the *y*-coordinate of the original point *A*?

A) -4 B) -2 C) 0   D) 2

16. Lin bought a sweater at 30% off the original price. The discount saved him $12.60. What was the original price of the sweater?

E) $8.82   F) $21.42
G) $29.40   H) $42.00

17. Which of the following would be a reasonable value for the percent of the figure that is shaded?

A) 75%   B) 40%
C) 20%   D) 10%

18. The population in Culver Heights increased from 1990 to 1993 as shown in the table. What was the average annual percent increase in population over the three-year period?

Years	Population
1990 to 1991	10,000 to 11,000
1991 to 1992	11,000 to 12,000
1992 to 1993	12,000 to 13,000

E) 8.33% F) 9.14% G) 10%   H) 27.42%

19. A square has vertices at $(-3, 0)$, $(0, 3)$, $(3, 0)$, and $(0, -3)$. How many of the following points are in the exterior of the square?

$(-1, 1)$ $(1.5, 1.5)$ $(2, 2)$ $(0, -4)$
$(-2, -2)$ $(-3, 1)$

A) 2   B) 3   C) 4   D) 5

20. Set G consists of the three-digit multiples of 3. Set H consists of the three-digit multiples of 4. Set L consists of the three-digit multiples of 6.

Which of the following statements is true about the three sets of numbers?

E) If a number is in Set G, it is also in Set L.
F) The smallest number contained in all three sets is 144.
G) If a number is in Set L, it is also in Set G.
H) No multiple of 9 is in Set H.

21. A club consists of eight boys and six girls. A committee of five is to be selected so that the committee consists of three boys (one of them must be Roger) and two girls (one of the girls must be Jennifer). How many different committees are possible?

A) 26   B) 48   C) 105   D) 210

22. There are 30 students in a class. The mean grade for that class on a test was computed as 80, but two students' grades were read incorrectly as 90 instead of 50. What will the average grade (rounded to the nearest tenth) be when it is recomputed using the correct scores?

23. Using the digits 5, 6, 7, 8, how many four-digit numbers can be formed if repetition of digits is allowed, except for not allowing four of the same digits?

24. The diagram shows a structure made with nineteen cubes. If each cube has an edge of 1 cm, what is the surface area of the structure (in square centimeters)?

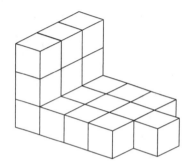

25. Four regular hexagons are similar. Corresponding sides of the four hexagons have lengths in the ratio $1 : 2 : 5 : 10$. If a side of the largest hexagon has a length of 30 centimeters, find the sum of the perimeters (in centimeters) of the other three hexagons.

26. Winter Spring bottled water comes in three sizes:

    6-pack of 0.5-liter bottles at $3.59 per 6-pack

    1-liter bottles at $0.99 each

    1.5-liter bottles at $1.59 each

    If you need 9 liters of bottled water, how much would you save by buying 1.5-liter bottles instead of 6-packs of 0.5-liter bottles?

27. At Joe's Pizzeria, a pizza can be ordered in three sizes and one of three toppings can be ordered. How many different ways can a pizza be ordered?

28. A 12′ ladder is placed against a building so that the ladder makes an angle of 50° with the ground. To the nearest tenth of a foot, at what height does the ladder touch the building?

29. The two spinners shown have eight and four congruent sections. If you spin each spinner once, what is the probability of obtaining the largest possible sum?

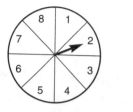
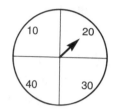

30. ACEF is a square.

    ABC is an isosceles right triangle.

    CDE is an equilateral triangle.

    Find the measure of ∠BCD.

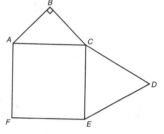

31. A 1-hour driver's test has 100 questions. Mike spends an average of 30 seconds each on the first 60 questions. To finish the test on time, what is the average number of seconds he can spend on each of the remaining questions?

32. A craft store has orders to ship wreaths to four stores: Westwood Garden Center, Creative Gifts, Hands-On Crafts, Gifts for All. The wreaths come in three sizes: small, medium, and large. The given matrix shows the number of wreaths shipped to each store. Columns represent the four stores; rows represent the three sizes small, medium, and large respectively. If the small wreath sells for $18, medium for $24, and large for $40, what is the total amount billed to each store?

$$\begin{bmatrix} 4 & 6 & 0 & 5 \\ 5 & 3 & 3 & 5 \\ 2 & 1 & 6 & 5 \end{bmatrix}$$

33. Use a collection of congruent equilateral triangles. Indicate the minimum number of these equilateral triangles you can place together to form:

    A. a rhombus

    B. an isosceles trapezoid

    C. a regular hexagon

34. An isosceles triangle has vertices at $(0, 6)$, $(k, 0)$, and $(-k, 0)$. Find the value of k such that the slope of the congruent sides of the triangle would be $+6$ and -6.

35. These are tests scores in Mme. Dubin's French class:

    93, 92, 84, 81, 68, 81, 78, 77, 84, 63, 62, 90

    A. Construct a line plot for the data.
    B. State the median score for the data.
    C. What would happen to the median if 1 point were added to each of the test scores? Explain.

36. Find the area and perimeter of the hexagon. Show your complete procedure.

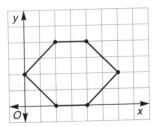

37. A package of gum has a price increase from $0.50 to $0.60. At the old price, a package contained 10 sticks of gum; now a package contains 8 sticks. Determine the percent increase in the cost of a stick of gum. Explain your procedure and thinking.

38. A rectangular garden 60 feet by 80 feet is surrounded by a walk of uniform width, as indicated in the diagram. The area of the walk itself (the shaded region) is 7,200 square feet. Find the width, x, of the walk.

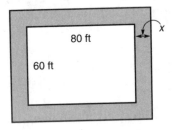

39. Kathryn invests $2,000.00 for six years at 10% interest compounded annually. After the first three years, Elizabeth invests $3,000.00 for three years at 5% interest compounded annually. At the end of the six years, who would have more money? Explain.

40. Given the following four views for a three-dimensional figure, draw the figure on the isometric paper provided. Then give the volume and surface area for the figure drawn.

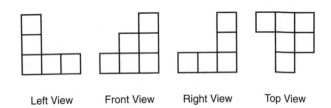

Left View   Front View   Right View   Top View

CHAPTER 4

Patterns, Functions, and Algebra

4.1 Patterns

In a number of applications, problems can be solved by discovering a pattern and using the pattern to draw different conclusions. The pattern might be numerical or visual.

Computational Patterns

Many numerical situations involve patterns.
Examples:

a. repeating decimal

$$\frac{1}{11} = 0.0909$$

b. equivalent fractions

$$\frac{1}{2} = \frac{2}{4} = \frac{3}{6} = \frac{4}{8}$$

c. powers of ten

$10^1 = 10$
$10^2 = 100$
$10^3 = 1,000$
.
.
.
$10^9 = 1,000,000,000$

d. concept of percent

$$1\% = \frac{1}{100}$$

$$10\% = \frac{10}{100}$$

$$50\% = \frac{50}{100}$$

$$100\% = \frac{100}{100}$$

e. multiplication pattern

$9 \times 1 = 9$
$9 \times 2 = 18$
$9 \times 3 = 27$
$9 \times 4 = 36$
$9 \times 5 = 45$
$9 \times 6 = 54$
$9 \times 7 = 63$
$9 \times 8 = 72$
$9 \times 9 = 81$

MODEL PROBLEMS

1. What is the units digit in the number equivalent of 3^{24}?

Solution: Since it is not convenient to compute the value of 3^{24}, you need to see if a pattern exists by examining small powers of 3.

$$\left.\begin{array}{l} 3^1 = \quad 3 \\ 3^2 = \quad 9 \\ 3^3 = \quad 27 \\ 3^4 = \quad 81 \end{array}\right\}$$ For the first four powers of 3, the units digits are different (namely, 3, 9, 7, 1).

$3^5 = 243$
$3^6 = 729$
$3^7 = ..7$
$3^8 = ..1$

Then the units digit begins to repeat. Assume that the pattern for the units digit continues as 3, 9, 7, 1. Note that this pattern is in groups of 4. You may conclude that every power of 3 that is a multiple of 4 will have a units digit of 1.

Answer: Since 3^{24} is a power of 3 that is a multiple of 4, the value of 3^{24} will have a units digit of 1.

2. In the decimal representation for $\dfrac{5}{33}$, what digit would be in the 30th decimal place?

Solution: The decimal representation for $\dfrac{5}{33}$ is 0.15151515. . . . Notice that in the repeating pattern, a 1 is in every odd position and a 5 is in every even position.

Answer: The digit in the 30th decimal place would be a 5.

Visual Patterns

Patterns often occur in diagrams and through visualization.
Example:

Visualizing this pattern shows that the next term is generated by adding a row of squares one greater in length than the bottom row of the previous term.

Visual patterns are often found in flooring, wallpaper, wrapping paper, store displays, and fabric.

> **To extend a visual pattern:**
>
> 1. Explore the pattern concretely, building succeeding terms.
> 2. Convert the visual pattern to a numerical pattern.

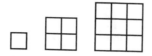

MODEL PROBLEM

How many unit squares are needed to represent the fifth term of the following pattern?

Solution:

METHOD 1: concrete

Notice that the first term is a 1×1 square, the second term is a 2×2 square, and the third term is a 3×3 square. Then build the fourth term (4×4) and the fifth term (5×5).

Answer: Counting the unit squares in the fifth term produces a result of 25 unit squares.

METHOD 2: converting to a numerical pattern

Analyzing the number of unit squares used to build the three given terms produces the numerical pattern 1, 4, 9. Recognizing these numbers as consecutive perfect squares, you realize that the fifth term would have to be the fifth square, or 25.

Answer: 25 unit squares

PRACTICE

1. What is the units digit in 2^{40}?

   A) 2   B) 4   C) 6   D) 8

2. Which one of the following bases does NOT produce the same units digit when raised to any whole-number power?

   E) 10   F) 9   G) 6   H) 5

3. Which of the following would yield a repeating decimal pattern?

   A) $\frac{1}{6}$ B) $\frac{1}{4}$ C) $\frac{3}{16}$ D) $\frac{1}{25}$

4. What digit is in the 45th decimal place in the decimal value of $\frac{7}{11}$?

   E) 1   F) 3   G) 6   H) 7

5. Terrence decides he is going to start saving pennies in a large plastic jar he has found. On Monday, he puts 1 cent into the jar. On Tuesday, he doubles the amount to 2 cents. On each succeeding day, he doubles the number of pennies he put in the day before. How many days will it take Terrence to save at least $20?

   A) 11   B) 12   C) 15   D) 26

6. Which of the following decimals shows a pattern equivalent to the visual pattern below?

   ⊢ T ⊣ ⊥ ⊢ T ⊣ ⊥

   E) 0.12891289 . . .   F) 0.313131 . . .
   G) 0.541541541 . . .   H) 0.7777 . . .

7. Analyze the pattern:

PENCILPENCILPENCIL . . .

If the pattern is continued, what letter will be in the 83rd position?

A) P   B) E
C) I   D) L

8. Juan and Kim started a debating club. It was decided that once a month each member would debate every member of the club. It was also decided to add 1 new member to the club each month. Which of the following patterns could be used to determine the total number of debates in the fifth month the club was operating?

E) 2, 6, 12, 20, 30   F) 1, 4, 9, 16, 25
G) 1, 3, 6, 10, 15   H) 2, 3, 4, 5, 6

9. If the pattern below continues until all letters of the alphabet are shown, how many letters, including repetitions, will precede the last Z?

ABBCCCDDDD

10. How many dots are needed to represent the first five terms, in total, for the given sequence?

11. Given that: $\dfrac{1}{2} + \dfrac{1}{4} = \dfrac{3}{4}$

$$\frac{1}{2} + \frac{1}{4} + \frac{1}{8} = \frac{7}{8}$$

$$\frac{1}{2} + \frac{1}{4} + \frac{1}{8} + \frac{1}{16} = \frac{15}{16}$$

Find: $\dfrac{1}{2} + \dfrac{1}{4} + \dfrac{1}{8} + \dfrac{1}{16} + \dfrac{1}{32}$

12. A local restaurant has small tables that seat 4 people, one on each side. When the restaurant must seat larger groups of people, tables are put together so that they share a common side. When 2 tables are put together, 6 people can be seated. If 5 tables are put together into a long row, how many people can be seated?

13. Jared painted a 4 × 4 × 4 cube green on all 6 faces. When the paint dried, Jared cut the cube into 64 smaller cubes (1 × 1 × 1). If Jared looked at each small cube, how many would have green paint on exactly 2 faces? In completing this problem, discuss cases involving a smaller original cube in order to show a pattern to use to answer the question.

14. Mary notices that on a 2 × 2 checkerboard there are 5 squares of various sizes.

 This 2 × 2 board has four 1 × 1 squares and one 2 × 2 square.

Mary thinks that a 4 × 4 checkerboard would have twice as many squares. Do you agree or disagree with Mary's idea? Explain your reasoning.

15. For the given sequence, determine the total number of squares needed to represent the fifth term.

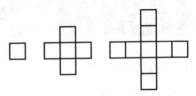

16. If the pattern is continued, how many dots would be in the 20th diagram?

17. In successive stages of the pattern shown, each side of the equilateral triangle has a length equal to 110% of the length in the previous stage. To the nearest hundredth, what would be the perimeter of the triangle in the 6th stage?

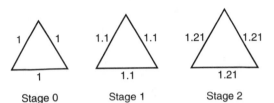

Stage 0   Stage 1   Stage 2

18. Suppose this pattern is continued. On the eighth figure, what percent of the figure is shaded? Explain your thought process.

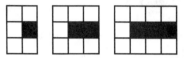

4.2 Sequences and Series

A *sequence* is a list of numbers in a particular order that follows a pattern. A *series* is the sum of the terms of a sequence.

Arithmetic Sequences

An *arithmetic sequence* has a *common difference* between two consecutive terms.

Example: 5,   8,   11,   14,   17, . . .

    3   3   3   3   common difference = 3

The next term is $17 + 3 = 20$.

MODEL PROBLEMS

1. Which of these are arithmetic sequences?

    I. 9, 15, 21, 27, 33, . . .

    II. 18, 10, 2, −6, −14, . . .

    III. 7, 11, 16, 22, 29, . . .

Solution: Check for a common difference.

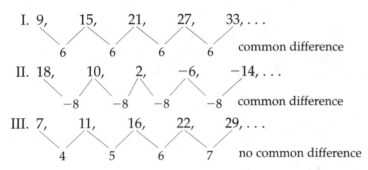

Answer: I and II are arithmetic sequences.

2. Find the 50th term of the arithmetic sequence:

$$3, 7, 11, 15, 19, 23, \ldots$$

Solution: To find a particular term in an arithmetic sequence, use the following formula: $a_n = a_1 + (n − 1)d$, where n = **term number** and d = **the common difference**. To find the 50th term, $n = 50$, $d = 7 − 3 = 4$, and $a_1 = 3$. By substituting into the formula you get:

$$a_n = a_1 + (n − 1)d$$
$$a_{50} = 3 + (50 − 1)4$$
$$a_{50} = 3 + 49 \cdot 4 = 199$$

Answer: The 50th term is 199.

Geometric Sequences

A *geometric sequence* has a *common ratio* between two consecutive terms.
Example: 2, 6, 18, 54, 162, . . .

$$\frac{6}{2} = 3, \frac{18}{6} = 3, \frac{54}{18} = 3, \frac{162}{54} = 3 \quad \text{common ratio} = 3$$

The next term is $162 \times 3 = 486$.

MODEL PROBLEMS

1. Which of these are geometric sequences?

   I. 16, 8, 4, 2, 1, . . .
   II. 10, 20, 80, 640, . . .
   III. 10, 50, 250, 1,250, . . .

Solution: Check for a common ratio.

   I. 16, 8, 4, 2, 1, . . .

$$\frac{8}{16} = \frac{1}{2}, \frac{4}{8} = \frac{1}{2}, \frac{2}{4} = \frac{1}{2} \quad \text{common ratio} = \frac{1}{2}$$

   II. 10, 20, 80, 640, . . .

$$\frac{20}{10} = 2, \frac{80}{20} = 4 \quad \text{no common ratio}$$

   III. 10, 50, 250, 1,250, . . .

$$\frac{50}{10} = 5, \frac{250}{50} = 5, \frac{1,250}{250} = 5 \quad \text{common ratio} = 5$$

Answer: I and III are geometric sequences.

2. Find the 10th term of the geometric sequence:

$$\frac{1}{2}, 1, 2, 4, 8, \ldots$$

Solution: To find a particular term in a geometric sequence you can use the following formula: $a_n = a_1 \cdot r^{n-1}$, **where r is the common ratio and n is the term number.**

For the given problem, $n = 10$, $r = 1 \div \frac{1}{2} = 2$, $a_1 = \frac{1}{2}$.

Using the formula and substituting the appropriate values gives:

$$a_{10} = \frac{1}{2} \cdot 2^{(10-1)} = \frac{1}{2} \cdot 2^9 = 256$$

Answer: The 10th term of the sequence is 256.

Note: 2^9 can be evaluated using the y^x key on a calculator.

Fibonacci Sequence

The *Fibonacci Sequence* is generated by adding the two previous terms to form the next term.

$$
\begin{array}{cccccc}
1, & 1, & 2, & 3, & 5, & 8, \ldots \\
 & & (1+1) & (1+2) & (2+3) & (3+5)
\end{array}
$$

MODEL PROBLEM

In the Fibonacci Sequence 1, 1, 2, 3, 5, 8, . . .

    A. What is the 10th term of the sequence?

    B. What is the sum of the first 10 terms?

Solution:

    A. To determine the 10th term, extend the sequence using the rule "add the two previous terms to form the next term."

Answer: 1, 1, 2, 3, 5, 8, 13, 21, 34, 55

    B. To find the sum, add the 10 given numbers.

$$1 + 1 + 2 + 3 + 5 + 8 + 13 + 21 + 34 + 55 = 143$$

Answer: The sum of the 10 terms is 143.

Arithmetic Series

The sum of the first n terms of an arithmetic sequence is given by the formula:

$$S_n = n\left(\frac{a_1 + a_n}{2}\right) \quad \text{where } a_1 = \text{first term}$$
$$a_n = n\text{th term}$$

> **Arithmetic Sequence Formula:**
>
> The formula can also be written as
> $$S_n = \frac{n}{2}\left[2a_1 + (n - 1)d\right]$$

MODEL PROBLEM

For the arithmetic series $5 + 7 + 9 + \ldots + 99 + 101$, compute the sum.

Solution: Use the formula $S_n = n\left(\dfrac{a_1 + a_n}{2}\right)$ where $a_1 = 5$ and $a_n = 101$.

To find n, use the arithmetic sequence formula.

$$a_n = a_1 + (n - 1)d \quad\quad a_1 = 5, a_n = 101, d = 2$$
$$101 = 5 + (n - 1)2$$
$$96 = 2(n - 1)$$
$$48 = n - 1$$
$$49 = n$$

Therefore, $S_n = 49\left(\dfrac{5 + 101}{2}\right) = 49\left(\dfrac{106}{2}\right) = 49 \cdot 53 = 2{,}597$

Geometric Series

The sum of the first n terms of a geometric sequence is given by the formula:

$$S_n = \frac{a_1(r^n - 1)}{r - 1}$$

where a_1 = first term

n = term number

r = common ratio

> **Geometric Sequence Formula:**
>
> The formula can also be written as
>
> $$S_n = \frac{a_1(1 - r^n)}{1 - r}$$

 MODEL PROBLEM

For the geometric series $3 + 6 + 12 + \ldots$, compute the sum of the first 10 terms.

Solution: Use the formula

$$S_n = \frac{a_1(r^n - 1)}{r - 1}$$

where $a_1 = 3, n = 10, r = 2$

$$S_n = \frac{3(2^{10} - 1)}{2 - 1} = \frac{3(1{,}024 - 1)}{1} = \frac{3(1{,}023)}{1} = 3{,}069$$

Infinite Geometric Series

When the absolute value of the ratio in a geometric sequence is greater than 1, the sequence *diverges* and as a result there is no limit or sum for an infinite number of terms. However, when the absolute value of the ratio is less than 1, the sequence *converges* and there is a limit or sum that can be obtained.

For example: (1) $5 + 15 + 45 + 135 + \ldots$ has no limit or sum for an infinite number of terms since $r = 3$.

$$(2)\ \frac{1}{2} + \frac{1}{4} + \frac{1}{8} + \frac{1}{16} + \ldots \text{ has a limit because } r = \frac{1}{2}.$$

The sum of the infinite series is 1.

The formula for an infinite geometric series where the absolute value of $r < 1$ is $S = \dfrac{a_1}{1 - r}$ where a_1 = first term and r = common ratio.

MODEL PROBLEM

Find the sum: $1 + \dfrac{1}{3} + \dfrac{1}{9} + \dfrac{1}{27} + \ldots$

Solution: $r = \dfrac{1}{3}, a_1 = 1$

$$S = \frac{a_1}{1 - r}$$

$$S = \frac{1}{1 - \dfrac{1}{3}} = \frac{1}{\dfrac{2}{3}} = \frac{3}{2}$$

Answer: $\dfrac{3}{2}$ is the sum or limit for the series.

PRACTICE

1. Which of the following is a geometric sequence?

   A) $6, 7\dfrac{1}{3}, 8\dfrac{2}{3}, 9, \ldots$

   B) $\dfrac{1}{2}, \dfrac{1}{3}, \dfrac{1}{4}, \dfrac{1}{5}, \ldots$

   C) $-10, -100, -1,000, \ldots$

   D) $2, 4, 2, 4, 2, 4, \ldots$

2. Which of the following would give you the 20th term of the arithmetic sequence 6, 13, 20, 27, . . . ?

   E) 20×6 F) $6 + 20 \times 7$

   G) 20×7 H) $6 + 19 \times 7$

3. Which of the following is NOT an arithmetic sequence?

   A) $2, 8, 32, 128, \ldots$ B) $\dfrac{1}{2}, \dfrac{3}{4}, 1, \dfrac{5}{4}, \ldots$

   C) $10, 10, 10, 10, \ldots$ D) $8, 4, 0, -4, \ldots$

4. Which of the following would NOT be a term of this geometric sequence?

   $$3, 6, 12, 24, \ldots$$

   E) 48   F) 64   G) 96   H) 192

5. Which is the next term in the given Fibonacci Sequence?

   $$1, 1, 2, 3, 5, 8, \ldots$$

   A) 11   B) 13   C) 16   D) 40

6. Which of these sequences is a Fibonacci-like sequence?

   E) $1, 4, 5, 9, 14, 23, \ldots$ F) $1, 4, 4, 16, 64, \ldots$
   G) $1, 4, 9, 16, 25, \ldots$ H) $1, 4, 8, 12, 16, \ldots$

7. The sum of the arithmetic series $-27 + -17 + -7 + \ldots + 43$ is:

   A) 32   B) 64   C) 128   D) 280

8. The sum of the first 10 terms of the geometric series $1 + 2 + 4 + 8 + 16 + \ldots$ is:

    E) 128   F) 255   G) 512   H) 1,023

9. The sum of the infinite series $1 + \dfrac{1}{4} + \dfrac{1}{16} + \ldots$ is:

    A) $\dfrac{1}{4}$ B) $\dfrac{3}{4}$ C) $\dfrac{4}{3}$ D) 4

10. For which of the following is it possible to find the sum?

    E) $\dfrac{1}{2} + \dfrac{1}{3} + \dfrac{1}{4} + \dfrac{1}{5} + \dfrac{1}{6} + \ldots$

    F) $\dfrac{1}{2} + \dfrac{1}{2} + \dfrac{1}{2} + \dfrac{1}{2} + \dfrac{1}{2} + \ldots$

    G) $\dfrac{1}{2} - \dfrac{1}{4} + \dfrac{1}{8} - \dfrac{1}{16} + \ldots$

    H) $\dfrac{1}{2} + 1 + 2 + 4 + \ldots$

11. A special sequence is formed by taking twice the sum of the two previous terms to find the third term and all succeeding terms. If the first four terms are 1, 2, 6, 16, find the 8th term.

12. In an arithmetic sequence, the 5th term is 23 and the 7th term is 33. Find the common difference for the sequence.

13. The first four terms of an arithmetic sequence are 2, 8, 14, 20, and 122 is the 21st term. What is the value of the 20th term?

14. In this geometric sequence, what is the common ratio?   81, 27, 9, 3, $\ldots$

15. If the 9th term of an arithmetic sequence is 100 and the 10th term is 111, find the value of the first term.

16. Create an arithmetic sequence of at least six terms for which the common difference is -3. Explain why the sequence you wrote is arithmetic. Also explain why there would be an infinite number of possible sequences fitting the given condition.

17. A tennis ball hit in the air 27 feet rebounds to two-thirds of its previous height after each bounce. Find the total vertical distance (up and down) the ball has traveled when it hits the ground the tenth time.

18. A small business had sales of $50,000 during its first year of operation. If the sales increase by $6,000 per year, what is its total sales in its eleventh year?

19. The number of bacteria in a culture triples every four hours. If 1,000 bacteria are present initially, how many bacteria will be present at the end of 24 hours?

20. A machine's value depreciates annually at a rate of 30% of the value it had at the beginning of that year. If its initial value is $10,000, find its value at the end of the eighth year.

4.3 Representation of Relationships and Patterns

The relationship "The perimeter of a square depends on the length of a side" can be expressed in a variety of ways.

a. Verbal statement: The perimeter of a square is four times the length of a side.

b. Table of values:

Side Length	Perimeter
1	4
2	8
3	12
4	16

c. Set of ordered pairs: {(1, 4), (2, 8), (3, 12), (4, 16)}

d. Equation: $P = 4s$, where s is the length of a side of the square and P is the perimeter.

e. Graph: Plot the table of values to obtain the graph.

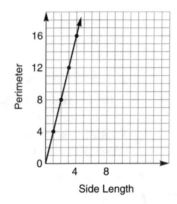

 MODEL PROBLEM

A can of soda costs $0.75. The amount of money you spend on soda is related to the number of cans you purchase. Show the relationship as a table of values containing 5 sets of values and write an equation to summarize the relationship.

Solution:

Table of values

Number of Cans	Cost
1	$0.75
2	$1.50
3	$2.25
4	$3.00
5	$3.75

Equation:

To obtain the cost (C), multiply the number of cans by the cost of one can.

$C = 0.75n$, where n is the number of cans.

1. This table indicates a linear relationship between x and y.

x	1	3	5	7	9
y	1	7	13	?	25

According to this pattern, which number is missing from the table?

A) 15   B) 19   C) 21   D) 23

2. A plumber charges $48 for each hour she works plus an additional service charge of $25. At this rate, how much would the plumber charge for a job that took 4.5 hours?

3. The cost of a long-distance telephone call can be computed based on the following formula:

$T = C + nr$, where T = total cost of the call in dollars

C = charge for the first three minutes in dollars

n = number of additional minutes the call lasts

r = rate per minute for each additional minute in dollars

What is the cost of a 15-minute long-distance call if a person is charged $1.75 for the first three minutes and $0.15 for each additional minute?

4. A local parking lot charges $1.75 for the first hour and $1.25 for each additional hour or part of an hour. Represent the relationship of parking charges to hours parked:

A. in a table of values for 1 to 6 hours.

B. in an equation in which t represents time parked in hours and C the total cost of parking.

C. as a graph with hours parked on the horizontal and total cost on the vertical.

4.4 Relations and Functions

Recall that the formula for the circumference of a circle is $C = \pi d$. The circumference *depends* on the length of the diameter. The length of the diameter is the *independent variable* and the circumference is the *dependent variable*. Another way to express the relationship is to say "circumference is a *function* of diameter." For different values of d, the function can be displayed by a table, a set of ordered pairs, an equation, or a graph.

a. Table

d	1	2	3	4
C	3.14	6.28	9.42	12.56

(d and C in inches)

b. Set of ordered pairs

$\{(1, 3.14), (2, 6.28), (3, 9.42), (4, 12.56), \ldots\}$

c. Equation

$$C = \pi d$$

d. Graph

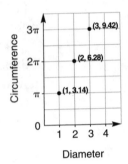

A set of ordered pairs is called a *relation*. The example above shows that circumference and diameter constitute a relation. One can observe that for any specified value for the diameter, there can be only one resulting value for the circumference. A relation with this property is called a *function*.

When a relation is listed as a set of ordered pairs, a function exists when for every *x*-value (first coordinate) there is only one *y*-value (second coordinate).

 # MODEL PROBLEM

Which of the following is NOT a function?

A) (−1, 5), (1, 4), (5, 3), (0, 6)
B) (2, 4), (4, 8), (9, 18)
C) (3, 0), (3, 1), (3, 2), (3, 3)
D) (9, 0), (7, 0), (−5, 0), (13, 0)

Solution: To be a function, a given set of ordered pairs must be such that for every value of *x* there is only one value for *y*. In choice C, 3 is repeated for *x* with four different *y*-values. Hence, C is not a function.

Answer: C

In a function, the values for the independent variable are considered as the input or domain; the values for the dependent variable are considered output or range. For the function $y = 2x$, if the domain is the set of whole numbers, the output or range would be the set of even whole numbers.

$$\nearrow \overset{y = 2x}{} \nwarrow$$

dependent   independent
variable,   variable,
output   input

Consider the following relations displayed as graphs:

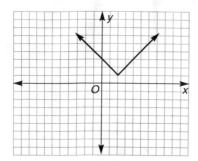
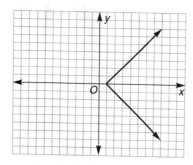

The one on the left is a function, while the one on the right is not. In the graph on the left, one can observe a unique value for y for each value of x considered. In contrast, the graph on the right has two different values for y for given values of x. This distinction can be visualized through a technique known as the vertical line test.

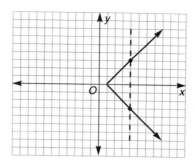

If the vertical line passes through a graph more than once, the graph is not the graph of a function.

There are a few two-dimensional figures whose equations are not functions. For example, the equation of a circle whose center is at the origin is simply $x^2 + y^2 = r^2$, where r represents the length of the radius of the circle. The standard equation of a circle whose center is not the origin, but a point (h, k), is $(x - h)^2 + (y - k)^2 = r^2$, where r again represents the length of the radius.

MODEL PROBLEMS

1. Graph the circle whose equation is $(x - 4)^2 + (y + 3)^2 = 4$.

Solution: The equation $(x - 4)^2 + (y + 3)^2 = 4$ represents a circle with a center at $(4, -3)$ and a radius of length 2. Every point of the circle is 2 units away from the center $(4, -3)$. A vertical line is also drawn through the circle below. As we can see, the vertical line passes through the circle at two points, showing two different y-values for the same x-value. Hence, it is not a function

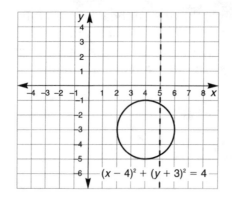

2. Determine the center and length of the radius each of the following circles.

    A. $x^2 + y^2 = 10$
    B. $(x - 1)^2 + (y + 4)^2 = 16$

Solution:
    A. The circle $x^2 + y^2 = 10$ has its center at $(0, 0)$ and a radius of $\sqrt{10}$.
    B. The circle $(x - 1)^2 + (y + 4)^2 = 16$ has its center at $(1, -4)$ and a radius of 4.

Consider the following nonlinear function.

Equation: $y = x^2 + 3$

Table of values: Set of ordered pairs:

$\{(0, 3), (1, 4), (-1, 4), (2, 7), (-2, 7) \ldots\}$

Graph:

x	y
0	3
1	4
-1	4
2	7
-2	7

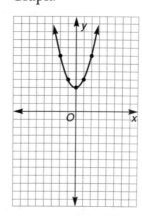

    In this example, y is clearly a function of x. For any given value of x, the value of y is found by adding 3 to the square of x. Since any value can be used for input, the domain of the function is the set of real numbers. Since the square of a real number must be nonnegative, the output values in this function must be 3 or greater. This means that the range is the set of real numbers greater than or equal to 3.

The following table summarizes some different types of functions.

Types of Functions

Linear Function

$y = 2x + 1$
Domain: {all the real x-values}
Range: {all the real y-values}

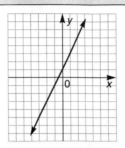

Quadratic Function

$y = x^2$
Domain: {all the real x-values}
Range: {all the real y-values}

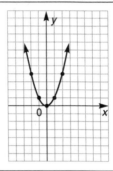

Cubic Function

$y = x^3$
Domain: {all the real x-values}
Range: {all the real y-values}

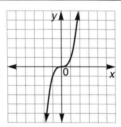

Absolute Value Function

$y = |x|$
Domain: {all the real x-values}
Range: {all the real positve y-values}

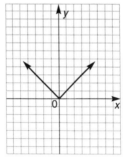

Exponential Function

$y = 2^x$
Domain: {all the real x-values}
Range: {all the real y-values}

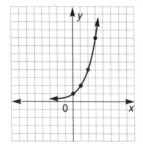

Types of Functions

Logarithmic Function

$y = \log x$
Domain: {all the real positive x-values}
Range: {all the real y-values}

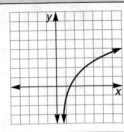

Sine Function

$y = \sin (x)$
Domain: $\{-2\pi \le x \le 2\pi\}$
Range: $\{-1 \le y \le 1\}$

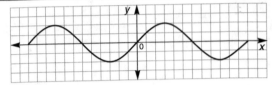

Cosine Function

$y = \cos (x)$
Domain: $\{-2\pi \le x \le 2\pi\}$
Range: $\{-1 \le y \le 1\}$

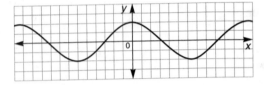

Tangent Function

$y = \tan (x)$
Domain: $\{-2\pi \le x \le 2\pi\}$
Range: $\{-1 \le y \le 1\}$

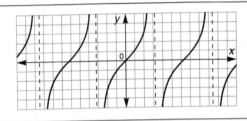

An alternative notation used for functions is referred to as $f(x)$ (read as "f of x" or "f at x").

$$\text{Given } y = x^2 + 3 \qquad f(x) = x^2 + 3$$

For this function, $f(4) = 4^2 + 3 = 19$ and $f(-2) = (-2)^2 + 3 = 7$.

Formulas can often be expressed using function notation. For example, the formula for the perimeter of a square can be expressed as $p(s) = 4s$; perimeter of a square is a function of side length.

PRACTICE

1. Which of the following sets of ordered pairs does NOT represent a function?

   A) {(−2, 2), (2, 2), (−5, 5), (5, 5)}
   B) {(7, 5), (8, 5), (−8, 5), (−7, 5)}
   C) {(2, 3), (2, 4), (2, 5), (2, 6)}
   D) {(1, 1), (2, 8), (3, 27), (4, 64)}

2. If the volume of a cube is a function of the length of an edge, which of the following equations represents the situation?

   E) $V = 3e$ F) $V = e^3$
   G) $V = e + 3$ H) $V = \sqrt[3]{e}$

3. A function is described by the equation $R = 2t + 3$. What value for R is missing from the table?

t	1	2	3	...	10
R	5	7	9	...	?

   A) 11   B) 15   C) 23   D) 26

4. Which of the following equations represents the line containing the points given in the graph?

   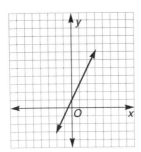

   E) $y = x + 1$ F) $y = x + 2$
   G) $y = 2(x + 1)$ H) $y = 2x + 1$

5. If $f(x) = 3^x - 2^x$, what is the value of $f(-2)$?

   A) $\dfrac{1}{5}$ B) $\dfrac{5}{36}$ C) $\dfrac{-5}{36}$ D) -2

6. Which of the following tables would be a reasonable representation for the relationship between the price (P) of an item and the sales tax (T) for that item?

   E)

P	T
2.00	0.12
6.00	0.12
15.50	0.12
85.00	0.12

   F)

P	T
2.00	0.48
6.00	0.36
15.50	0.24
85.00	0.12

   G)

P	T
2.00	0.12
6.00	0.36
15.50	0.93
85.00	5.10

   H)

P	T
2.00	0.12
6.00	0.14
15.50	0.24
85.00	0.12

7. This graph illustrates a constant function:

   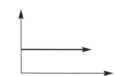

   Which of the following is a situation that can be modeled by a constant function?

   A) The number of cars at a parkway tollbooth during the day
   B) The ratio of the circumferences of various circles to the lengths of their diameters
   C) Your heart rate during a 20-minute exercise period
   D) The value of a car over a 10-year period

8. The given table is generated from which of the following rules?

x	−2	−1	0	1	2
$f(x)$	−2	−3	−4	−5	−6

   E) $f(x) = 2x + 2$ F) $f(x) = -4 - x$
   G) $f(x) = x + 4$ H) $f(x) = -3x$

9. What is the range of the function $y = x^2 + 1$ when the domain is $\{0, 2, 4\}$?

A) $\{1, 3, 5\}$ B) $\{1, 5, 9\}$
C) $\{1, 9, 25\}$ D) $\{1, 5, 17\}$

10. If $f(x) = 2^x$, what is the value of $f(10) - f(6)$?

E) 4 F) 64 G) 512 H) 960

11. Carol purchases an appliance on an installment plan. She pays $50 a month until the appliance is paid off. Which of the following graphs matches the relationship between months and the unpaid balance?

A) B)

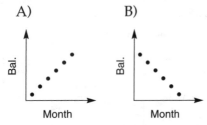

C) D)

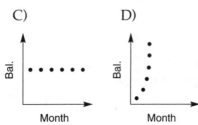

12. The functions $y = 3x$ and $y = 3^x$ represent very different relationships. If you take $x = 4$ from the domain of each, how many times larger is the range value for $y = 3^x$ than for $y = 3x$?

E) They are equal. F) 6.75

G) $\dfrac{4}{27}$ H) 5.33

13. The given graph shows the linear function $y = 2x + k$ ($k > 0$).

Based on the graph, which of the following must be true about the solution to the equation $2x + k = 0$ ($k > 0$)?

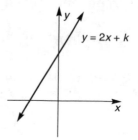

A) There is no solution.
B) The solution is approximately $x = 3$.
C) There is one negative real number solution.
D) There are two solutions, one positive and one negative.

14. If $f(x) = |x - 4|$, find the value of $f(8) - f(-8)$.

E) -8 F) -4 G) 0 H) 4

15. A periodic function is a function whose graph shows a continuously repeating pattern. For example:

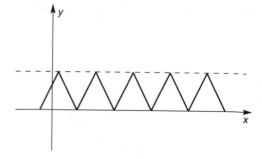

Which of the following is an example of a periodic function?

I.

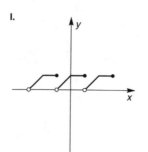

II.

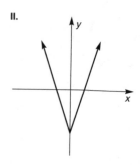

A) I only B) II only
C) I and II D) Neither

16. Karen and Samantha were looking at the table showing selected Pennsylvania towns and cities with their zip codes.

Town or City	Zip Code
Hamburg	19526
Berne	19526
Clinton	15026
Cuddy	15031
McKeesport	15130
McKeesport	15131
McKeesport	15132

The two girls agreed that the relationship of town or city to zip code was not an example of a function. Karen said the Hamburg and Berne example was the reason. However, Samantha said that it was the McKeesport example that resulted in it not being a function. Who is correct? Explain your position.

17. The graph below displays a function: $y = f(x)$.
    A. What is the value of $f(1)$?
    B. What is the value of $f(6.73)$?
    C. What two values satisfy $f(x) = 4$?

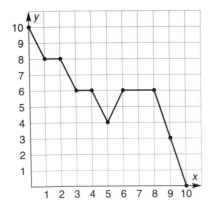

18. Consider the exponential functions $y = 4^x$ and $y = 5^x$.
    A. The graphs of these functions intersect at exactly one point. What are the coordinates of the point?
    B. In the first quadrant, which graph is closer to the y-axis? Explain or show an illustration.
    C. Explain what happens to the graphs as they cross the axis and enter the second quadrant.
    D. Explain why these graphs do not cross into quadrant III or IV.

4.5 Slope

Slope of a Line

Consider the linear function $y = 2x + 3$. By looking at a table of values, one can see that as the x-value increases by 1, the y-value always increases by 2. This means that there is a constant rate of change for the function. The rate of change is called the *slope*. This can also be shown through the graph of the line associated with the function.

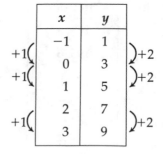

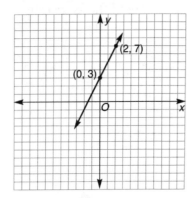

If the coordinates of two points on the line are known, the slope can be found using the formula.

$$\text{slope} = \frac{\text{rise}}{\text{run}} = \frac{\text{change in } y}{\text{change in } x} = \frac{y_2 - y_1}{x_2 - x_1} = \frac{7 - 3}{2 - 0} = \frac{4}{2} = 2$$

Lines with different types of slopes:

If a line is parallel to the x-axis, the line has no steepness. Its slope is zero.

If a line is parallel to the y-axis, the line has an undefined slope.

If a line rises from left to right, its slope is positive.

If a line falls from left to right, its slope is negative.

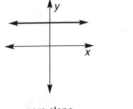

zero slope

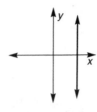

undefined slope

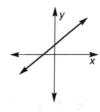

positive slope

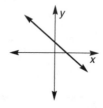

negative slope

MODEL PROBLEM

A line passing through the points $(-3, 5)$ and $(5, y)$ has a slope of $\frac{1}{4}$. Find the value of y.

Solution:

$$\text{slope} = \frac{y_2 - y_1}{x_2 - x_1}$$

$$\frac{1}{4} = \frac{y - 5}{5 - (-3)}$$

$$\frac{1}{4} = \frac{y - 5}{8}$$

$$4y - 20 = 8$$
$$4y = 28$$
$$y = 7$$

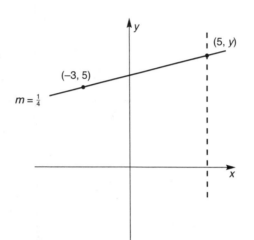

Slope-Intercept Form of the Equation of a Line

For the family of parallel lines shown, the lines have the same slope. However, note that each line crosses the y-axis at a different point. This point is known as the y-intercept. For the linear function, $y = 2x + 3$, when x is equal to zero, the value of y becomes 3. Hence, the ordered pair $(0, 3)$ becomes the y-intercept for the line.

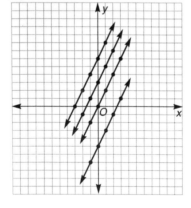

Slope-Intercept Form:	
$y = 2x + 3$	$y = mx + b$
↑ ↑	↑ ↑
slope y-intercept	slope y-intercept

Equation	Slope	y-intercept	Illustration
$y = -3x - 1$	$m = -3$	$b = -1$	
$y = \dfrac{3}{4}x$	$m = \dfrac{3}{4}$	$b = 0$	
$y = 5$	$m = 0$	$b = 5$	

MODEL PROBLEMS

1. Change the equation $3y - 5x = 15$ into slope-intercept form and graph the resulting line.

Solution: $3y - 5x = 15$

$$3y = 5x + 15$$

$$y = \frac{5}{3}x + 5$$

Since the equation is now in slope-intercept form, $m = \frac{5}{3}$ and $b = 5$.

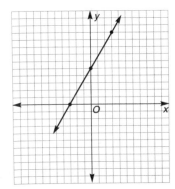

2. Find the equation of the line passing through the points $(-2, 5)$ and $(6, 1)$.

Solution: In order to use slope-intercept form, first find the slope.

$$m = \frac{y_2 - y_1}{x_2 - x_1} = \frac{5 - 1}{-2 - 6} = \frac{4}{-8} = -\frac{1}{2}$$

The equation would be $y = -\frac{1}{2}x + b$. It is now necessary to find the value of b. Knowing that either given point satisfies the equation, one can substitute in the coordinates of either point in order to find b.

$$y = mx + b$$

$$y = -\frac{1}{2}x + b$$

Using $(6, 1)$ $\quad 1 = \left(-\frac{1}{2}\right)6 + b$

$$1 = -3 + b$$

$$4 = b \text{ and the final equation is}$$

$$y = -\frac{1}{2}x + 4$$

3. A small company makes a new type of container. A mathematician employed by the company claims that the total cost (in dollars) of producing n containers is given by the formula

$$C = 2n + 600$$

Graph this cost function and explain the significance of the slope and the y-intercept.

Solution: The y-intercept, $(0, 600)$, shows that the cost is $600 before any containers are produced. The slope, 2, indicates that the cost of producing each new container is $2.

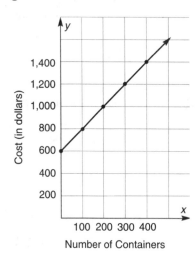

Nonlinear functions

x	$y = 3x + 1$
1	4
2	7
3	10
4	13
5	16

x	$y = x^2$
1	1
2	4
3	9
4	16
5	25

x	$y = 2^x$
1	2
2	4
3	8
4	16
5	32

In contrast with the linear function on the left ($y = 3x + 1$), the other two are examples of nonlinear functions. In these examples, you do not obtain a constant rate of change.

$$y = x^2$$

From (1, 1) to (2, 4) the rate of change is $\dfrac{4 - 1}{2 - 1} = \dfrac{3}{1} = 3$

From (2, 4) to (3, 9) the rate of change is $\dfrac{9 - 4}{3 - 2} = \dfrac{5}{1} = 5$

$$y = 2^x$$

From (1, 2) to (2, 4) the rate of change is $\dfrac{4 - 2}{2 - 1} = \dfrac{2}{1} = 2$

From (2, 4) to (3, 8) the rate of change is $\dfrac{8 - 4}{3 - 2} = \dfrac{4}{1} = 4$

PRACTICE

1. Which of the following is true about rates of change?

   A) Rates of change are always constant.
   B) A horizontal line has a rate of change of zero.
   C) Two perpendicular lines have the same rate of change.
   D) The line $y = 8x$ has the same rate of change as $y = -8x$.

2. Find the equation of the line containing the points $(-1, -3)$ and $(0, 5)$.

   E) $y = 8x$ F) $y = -8x + 5$

   G) $y = 8x + 5$ H) $y = \dfrac{1}{8}x + 5$

3. How many of the following lines have a slope of 2?

   $$y = x + 2 \qquad y = 2x \qquad 2y = x$$
   $$4y - 8x = 11 \qquad 8x - 4 = 7$$

   A) 1   B) 2   C) 3   D) 4

4. Write the equation, in slope-intercept form, for the line passing through (8, 0) perpendicular to the line $y = 2x$.

   E) $y = -\dfrac{1}{2}x + 8$ F) $y = -\dfrac{1}{2}x + 4$

   G) $y = -2x + 4$ H) $y = -2x + 8$

5. Isosceles triangle *ABC* has vertices at *A*(−6, 0), *B*(6, 0), and *C*(0, 10). Point *M* is the midpoint of *BC*. What is the equation, in slope-intercept form, of the line containing segment *AM*?

6. Brittany has a potted kudzu vine that is 10 inches long. As long as she waters it, it grows two inches each day.

   A. Explain why this situation is an example of linear change.

   B. Write an equation, in slope-intercept form, to represent the situation.

   C. Draw the resulting graph.

   D. If Brittany keeps watering the vine, when will it be 30 inches long? Show where this answer is on the graph.

7. In a linear function there is a constant rate of change.

   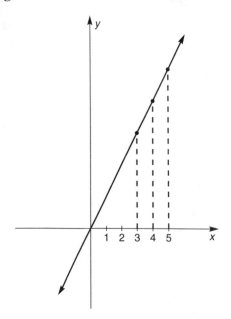

   For example, in the graph shown, $f(5) - f(4) = f(4) - f(3)$. Show that this does not hold for each of the following nonlinear functions. Include a graph with your explanation.

   A. $y = x^2$

   B. $y = 2^x$

4.6 Transformations of Functions

Many functions have graphs that result from performing simple transformations of other functions.

Original Function	Transformation	New Function
$y = f(x)$ 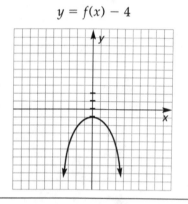	vertical shift 3 units upward (a translation)	$y = f(x) + 3$ 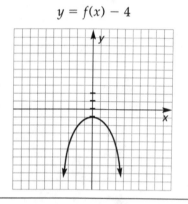
$y = f(x)$	vertical shift 4 units downward (a translation)	$y = f(x) - 4$
$y = f(x)$	horizontal shift 3 units to right (a translation)	$y = f(x - 3)$
$y = f(x)$	reflection in the x-axis	$y = -f(x)$

Original Function	Transformation	New Function
$y = f(x)$	reflection in the y-axis	$y = f(-x)$
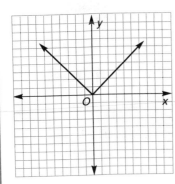		

 MODEL PROBLEM

Starting with the function shown at the left, draw the graph resulting from translating the original function 3 units to the right and 2 units down.

Solution:

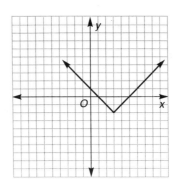

Family of Functions

Vertical and horizontal shifts generate a family of functions. For example, in looking at a graph of parallel lines, one can consider each line as the result of a translation on any of the other lines.

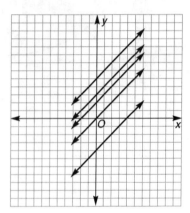

In this illustration, the line $y = x - 4$ results from translating (or shifting) $y = x + 2$ down 6 units; the line $y = x + 5$ results from translating the line $y = x + 2$ left 3 units.

The following illustrations show a family of absolute value functions and a family of quadratic functions.

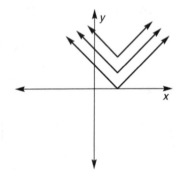

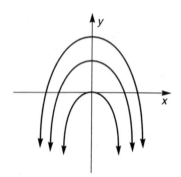

Dilations

The function $y = x^2$ is graphed as a standard parabola. If you change the coefficient of x^2 from 1 to some other number, the resulting parabola is a dilation of the original.

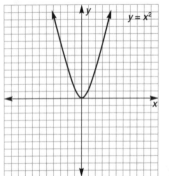

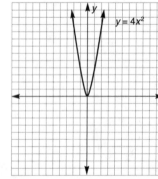

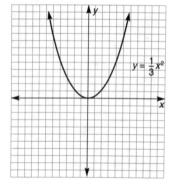

As you can see from the graphs, the parabola is wider than $y = x^2$ when the absolute value of the coefficient is less than 1, and narrower when the absolute value of the coefficient is greater than 1.

1. The graph of the function $f(x)$ is given below.

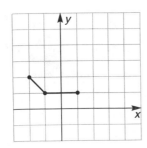

Which graph would represent $-f(x)$?

A)

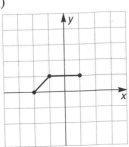

B)

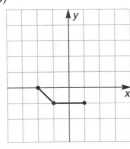

C)

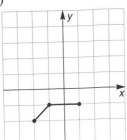

D)

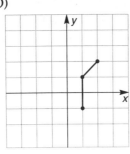

2. The graph of a function, $f(x)$, is given below.

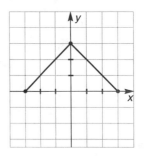

Which graph results from a translation 3 units to the left and 1 unit down?

E)

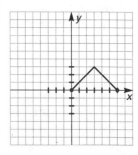

F)

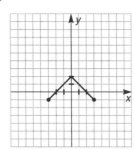

G)

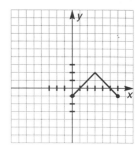

H)

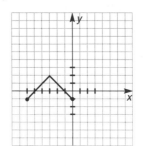

3. Explain how each graph would differ from the graph of $f(x) = |x|$.

A. $g(x) = |x| + 7$

B. $g(x) = -|x| - 2$

C. $g(x) = |x + 3| + 3$

4. Name a point on the graph of $y_1 = -f(x) + 4$ if $(5, 9)$ is a point on the graph of $y_2 = f(x)$.

4.7 Trigonometric Functions

Basic Trigonometric Graphs

Just as other functions have graphs that represent them, so do trigonometric functions. We set the x-axis for the graph of trigonometric functions differently from all other functions. We use values of θ in radian measure for the x-axis. Trigonometric functions are most commonly graphed in a domain values of $-2\pi \le x \le 2\pi$. It is always helpful to find the amplitude, frequency, and period when sketching the graphs for sine and cosine by hand.

In the standard form of a trigonometric equation for sine and cosine curves, $y = a \sin bx$ or $y = a \cos bx$, the $|a|$ represents the *amplitude* of the equation. The amplitude corresponds to the maximum value of the equation. The amplitude is used to determine the range of a trigonometric function. For example, the range of a trigonometric function in form $y = a \sin bx$ is $-|a| \le y \le |a|$. The *frequency*, the number of whole curves in 2π, is represented by b in the standard form of a trigonometric equation.

The *period* of a trigonometric function is the length of the interval needed to see one full curve. The formula for period 2π divided by the frequency of the function, that is, period $= \dfrac{2\pi}{|b|}$.

The table and graph for $y = \sin x$ are shown below. The amplitude and frequency for the graph are both 1 and the period is $\dfrac{2\pi}{1} = 1$.

x	0	$\dfrac{\pi}{2}$	π	$\dfrac{3\pi}{2}$	2π
$\sin x$	0	1	0	-1	0

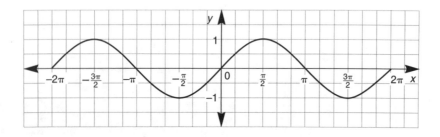

The table and graph for $y = \cos x$ are shown below. The amplitude and frequency for the graph is 1 and the period is $\frac{2\pi}{1} = 1$.

x	0	$\frac{\pi}{2}$	π	$\frac{3\pi}{2}$	2π
$\cos x$	1	0	-1	0	1

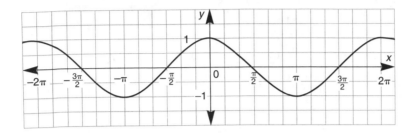

The tangent graph is very different from the sine and cosine graphs. As we have seen above, the graphs for sine and cosine are continuous. The tangent graph, on the other hand, is undefined at $x = \frac{\pi}{2}$ and again at $\frac{3\pi}{2}$. It is also undefined at any other odd multiples of $\frac{\pi}{2}$. As x approaches $\frac{\pi}{2}$ and any other of its odd multiples, the values of tan x increase toward infinity. We use a dashed vertical line to represent the asymptotes at these values of x. The following is a table of values of $y = \tan x$ for $0 \leq x \leq 2\pi$.

x	0	$\frac{\pi}{6}$	$\frac{\pi}{4}$	$\frac{\pi}{3}$	$\frac{\pi}{2}$	$\frac{2\pi}{3}$	$\frac{3\pi}{4}$	$\frac{5\pi}{6}$
$\tan x$	0	$\frac{\sqrt{3}}{3} \approx 0.58$	1	$\sqrt{3} \approx 1.7$	U	$-\sqrt{3} \approx -1.7$	-1	$\frac{-\sqrt{3}}{3} \approx -0.58$
x	π	$\frac{7\pi}{6}$	$\frac{5\pi}{4}$	$\frac{4\pi}{3}$	$\frac{3\pi}{2}$	$\frac{5\pi}{3}$	$\frac{7\pi}{4}$	$\frac{11\pi}{6}$	2π
$\tan x$	0	$\frac{\sqrt{3}}{3} \approx 0.58$	1	$\sqrt{3} \approx 1.7$	U	$-\sqrt{3} \approx -1.7$	-1	$\frac{-\sqrt{3}}{3} \approx -0.58$	0

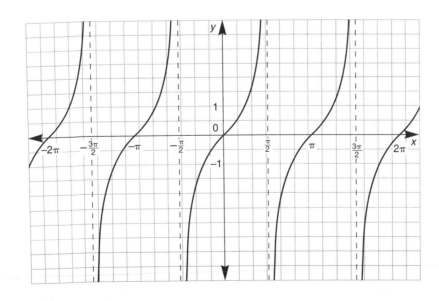

1. In the graph below, what is amplitude of the equation?

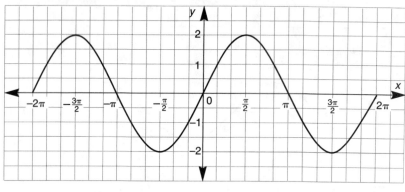

A) 1   B) 2   C) 3   D) 2π

Solution: Since the maximum value of the graph is 2 and the amplitude corresponds to the maximum value of a trigonometric equation, the amplitude is 2.

Answer: B

2. Given the equation $y = 3\cos 2x$, which of the following is the period of the function?

E) π F) 2π G) 3   H) $\dfrac{2\pi}{3}$

Solution: The formula for the period of a trigonometric equation is $\dfrac{2\pi}{|b|}$. In this equation, frequency, which is b, is 2. Therefore the period $= \dfrac{2\pi}{2} = \pi$.

Answer: F

Degrees and Radians

In addition to degrees as a unit to measure angles, radians is a common unit of measure. A *radian* is the measure of an angle that, when drawn as a central angle of a circle, intercepts an arc whose length is equal to the lengths of a radius of the circle.

In the circle below, θ represents the measure of the central angle, in radians, s is the length of the intercepted arc, and r is the length of the radius. We can see that there is a relationship between the central angle to the intercepted arc and the radius.

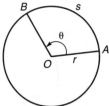

This relationship can be expressed by the formula $\theta = \dfrac{s}{r}$.

MODEL PROBLEM

If $s = 12$ and $r = 4$, then θ is equal to

A) 1 radian
B) 2 radians
C) 3 radians
D) 4 radians

Solution: Substitute the given information into the formula $\theta = \frac{s}{r}$.

$$\theta = \frac{12}{4}$$

$$\theta = 3$$

Answer: C

Converting From Degrees to Radians

We know that the measure of the central angle formed by a complete rotation is $360°$. We can use the formula $\theta = \frac{s}{r}$, to find the measure of the same central angle in radians.

Since s represents the length of the intercepted arc, we can substitute the circumference of a circle in for s. Therefore,

$$\theta = \frac{2\pi r}{r} = 2\pi$$

From this relationship, we see that 2π radians $= 360°$. Then dividing both sides by 2, π radians $= 180°$.

Notice that since π radians $= 180°$, then $90° = \frac{\pi}{2}$ radians, $60° = \frac{\pi}{3}$ radians and so on. From the pattern, we can convert from degrees to radians by **multiplying the measure of angle by $\frac{\pi \text{ radians}}{180°}$**.

MODEL PROBLEM

Express $40°$ in radians.

Solution:

Multiply $40°$ by $\frac{\pi \text{ radians}}{180°}$.

$$40° \cdot \frac{\pi \text{ radians}}{180°} = \frac{2\pi}{9} \text{ radians}$$

Answer: $\frac{2}{9}\pi$

Converting From Radians to Degrees

Since we know that π radians $= 180°$ we can find out how much 1 radian is equal to. Dividing both sides of the equation by π, 1 radian $= \dfrac{180°}{\pi \text{ radians}}$. From this we can see that 2 radians $= 2\left(\dfrac{180°}{\pi \text{ radians}}\right)$, which is equivalent to $2\pi = 360°$. We can also see that $3\pi = 540°$, $4\pi = 720°$, and so on.

When converting from radians to degrees, **multiply the measure of the angle by** $\dfrac{180°}{\pi \text{ radians}}$.

 MODEL PROBLEM

Express $\dfrac{2}{3}\pi$ in degrees.

Solution: Multiply $\dfrac{2}{3}\pi$ by $\dfrac{180°}{\pi}$.

$$\frac{2\pi}{3} \cdot \frac{180°}{\pi} = 120°$$

Answer: $120°$

PRACTICE

1. The graph of which equation has an amplitude of 3 and a period of π?

   A) $y = 3\sin x$

   B) $y = 3\sin 2x$

   C) $y = \dfrac{1}{3}\sin 2x$

   D) $y = -3\sin x$

2. What is the amplitude of the graph of the equation below?

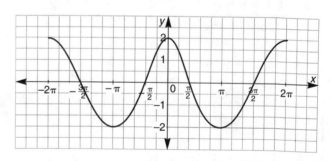

   E) 1

   F) 2

   G) π

   H) 2π

3. $f(x) = 3 \sin \frac{1}{2} x$ reaches its maximum value when x, expressed in radians, equals:

A) 3

B) $\dfrac{\pi}{2}$

C) π

D) $\dfrac{3\pi}{2}$

4. The period of the function $y = 2 \sin 3x$ is:

E) π

F) 2π

G) 3

H) $\dfrac{2\pi}{3}$

5. $120°$ expressed in radians is:

A) $\dfrac{3}{2}\pi$

B) $\dfrac{3}{4}\pi$

C) $\dfrac{2}{3}\pi$

D) $\dfrac{1}{3}\pi$

6. In a circle, a central angle of $\dfrac{1}{2}$ radian intercepts an arc of 30 millimeters. What is the length of a radius of the circle?

E) 15 millimeters

F) 60 millimeters

G) 90 millimeters

H) 100 millimeters

7. As the pendulum of a clock swings through an angle of 30°, the tip of the pendulum travels along an arc whose length is 4π inches. What is the length of the pendulum?

A) 6 inches

B) 6π inches

C) 24 inches

D) 24π inches

8. What is the degree measure of $\dfrac{7\pi}{3}$ radians?

E) 180°

F) 270°

G) 360°

H) 420°

9. On a clock, the length of the pendulum is 30 centimeters. A swing of the pendulum determines an angle of 144°. Find, in centimeters, the distance traveled by the tip of the pendulum during this swing.

4.8 Expressions and Open Sentences

A *variable* is a letter used to represent a number. The value of a variable can change. A *term* is a number, a variable, or the product or quotient of a number and a variable. A *variable expression* is made up of one or more terms.

Variable Expressions
$6a$
$x + 4$
a^2b

Constant Terms
7
4π
$\sqrt{2}$

The value of an expression involving a variable depends upon the value used for the variable.

When evaluating an expression, be sure to follow the established algebraic *order of operations*.

- Perform any operation(s) inside grouping symbols.
- Simplify any terms with exponents.
- Multiply and divide in order from left to right.
- Add and subtract in order from left to right.

MODEL PROBLEMS

1. If ☐ represents x^2, ☐ represents x, and ☐ represents 1, write the expression represented by:

☐☐☐☐☐☐☐☐☐

Solution:

Since ☐ $= x^2$, ☐ $= x$, and ☐ $= 1$, the expression is $3x^2 + 2x + 4$.

2. Evaluate $3a^2 + 4ab - b^2$ for $a = 2$ and $b = -1$.

Solution:

$$3(2)^2 + 4(2)(-1) - (-1)^2$$
$$3 \cdot 4 + \quad (-8) \quad - 1$$
$$12 - \quad 8 \quad - 1$$
$$4 \quad - 1 = 3$$

In a term that contains a variable, the numerical factor is called the *coefficient*.

coefficient ⌐ ⌐ exponent
$$3x^2$$
base

If terms have exactly the same variables raised to the same powers, they are called *like terms*.

Like Terms
$5x^2$ and $\frac{1}{2}x^2$
$5a^2b$ and $6a^2b$

Not Like Terms
$3x^2$ and $3x^3$
$5ab$ and $6ac$

If an expression contains like terms, the terms can be combined to simplify the expression.

To combine like terms:

- Add (or subtract) the coefficients.
- Carry along the like base and exponent.

 MODEL PROBLEM

Simplify $5x^2 + 8y + 2x^2 - 5y$.

Solution: Combine like terms.

$$
\begin{array}{c}
\overset{3y}{\overbrace{}} \\
5x^2 + 8y + 2x^2 - 5y \\
\underbrace{} \\
7x^2
\end{array}
$$

$5x^2 + 8y + 2x^2 - 5y = 7x^2 + 3y$

Verbal statements can be written as variable expressions.

To translate from a verbal statement to a variable expression:

- Identify the variable(s) to be used.
- Using the key words, determine the operation(s) involved.
- Form the expression, using symbols of grouping as needed.

MODEL PROBLEM

Write a variable expression for each of the verbal statements:

    A. The product of two consecutive integers
    B. 10 less than twice a number

Solution:

    A. $n(n + 1)$
    B. $2n - 10$

Variable expressions can be used to translate word problems into equations or inequalities, which are also called open sentences.

To translate a word sentence into an open sentence:

- Write a variable expression to represent each word phrase.
- Determine the appropriate relationship symbol to be used ($=, \neq, <, >, \leq, \geq$).

Word Phrase	Symbol
is equal to	$=$
is not equal to	$\neq$
is greater than	$>$
is less than	$<$
is at least	$\geq$
is greater than or equal to	$\geq$
is at most	$\leq$
is less than or equal to	$\leq$

MODEL PROBLEM

Translate each verbal sentence into an open sentence.

    A. What number doubled gives a result of 18?
    B. Three times one more than a number gives a result of at least 26.

Solution:

    A. $2x = 18$
    B. $3(n + 1) \geq 26$

1. Evaluate a^2b^3 when $a = 2$ and $b = -1$.

   A) 4 B) -4 C) -32 D) -64

2. Evaluate $5 + x(x + 2)$ when $x = 8$.

   E) 71 F) 85 G) 122 H) 130

3. If $n + 7$ is an even number, the next larger even number is:

   A) $n + 5$ B) $n + 9$
   C) $10n + 7$ D) $2n + 14$

4. Which of the following cannot be simplified?

   E) $2a^2 + 5a^2$
   F) $3a^2 - 3a$
   G) $5a - 11a$
   H) $16a^3 - 6a^3$

5. Which expression must be added to $2x - 4$ to produce a sum of 0?

   A) 0   B) $x + 2$
   C) $2x + 4$ D) $-2x + 4$

6. The perimeter of the parallelogram is $6a + 8b$. Find the length of each of the other two sides.

   E) $2a + 3b$
   F) $2b + 3a$
   G) $4a + 6b$ $a + b$ $a + b$
   H) $3a + 4b$

7. Write an open sentence to represent the statement.

   If 7 is subtracted from 4 times a certain number, the difference is 25.

   A) $7 - 4n = 25$ B) $4(n - 7) = 25$
   C) $4(7 - n) = 25$ D) $4n - 7 = 25$

8. Write an open sentence to represent the statement.

   5 less than twice a number is 3 more than the number.

   E) $2n - 5 = 3n$ F) $2n - 5 = n + 3$
   G) $5 - 2n = n + 3$ H) $5 - 2n = 3n$

9. Write an equation to show that segment y is 5 units longer than 3 times the length of segment x.

   A) $y = 15x$ $\overline{}$
             x
   B) $y = 3x + 5$
   C) $x = 3y + 5$ $\overline{}$
   D) $y = 3x - 5$ y

10. Find the value of A in the formula $A = \dfrac{1}{2}bh$ if $b = h = 5$.

11. A rectangle has dimensions $2x$ by $x + 3$. Write an expression for the perimeter of the rectangle. Combine any like terms.

12. Write the open sentence represented by the following situation. The congruent sides of an isosceles triangle have lengths that are each 5 inches greater than the length of the base. The perimeter is at most 31 inches.

13. Pat thinks that if $y = 5$, the expression $-y^2$ and the expression $(-y)^2$ will result in the same value. Write an explanation to agree or disagree.

14. Is the expression for twice the sum of a number and 10 the same as the expression for the sum of twice a number and 10? Explain.

15. Write the equation modeled by the following diagram.

4.9 Linear Equations and Inequalities

An equation represents that two expressions are equal to each other.
  An equation is similar to a balanced scale.
  To determine the unknown weight in a balance:

- Remove (cancel) identical items from both sides of the scale.
- Determine a relationship among the remaining items.
- Substitute the value for the known quantity.
- Determine the weight of the unknown quantity.

 MODEL PROBLEMS

Given the balances as shown, find the weight of one cube if each ball weighs 1 pound and the cubes are all the same weight.

1.

Solution:

- Remove two cubes and one ball from each side of the scale.
- One cube is balanced by three balls.
- Each ball weighs 1 pound.
- One cube weighs 3 pounds. **Answer**

2.

Solution:

- Remove three cubes and two balls from each side of the scale.
- Three cubes are balanced by six balls.
- Each ball weighs 1 pound.
- Three cubes weigh 6 pounds, and one cube weighs 2 pounds. **Answer**

The more traditional method of solving an equation involves use of mathematical properties.
  To solve an equation:

- Remove parentheses by multiplication. (Apply the Distributive Property.)
- Combine like terms in each member of the equation. Use addition or subtraction as indicated.
- Collect the terms containing the variable on one side and the number terms on the other side. Using the opposite operation of the one indicated (the inverse operation) will move a term from one side of the equation to the other.
- Rewrite the variable term with a coefficient of 1. Use the opposite operation of the division or multiplication indicated.

MODEL PROBLEMS

1. Solve for x: $6x = 2(x + 1) + 10$

Solution:

$$6x = 2(x + 1) + 10$$

$$6x = 2x + 2 + 10 \qquad \text{Remove parentheses.}$$

$$6x = 2x + 12 \qquad \text{Combine like terms.}$$

$$6x - 2x = 2x - 2x + 12 \qquad \text{Collect the variable terms on one side.}$$

$$4x = 12$$

$$\frac{4x}{4} = \frac{12}{4} \qquad \text{Rewrite the variable term with a coefficient of 1. Divide.}$$

$$x = 3$$

2. Solve for y: $-5y + 7 = -2(y - 5)$

Solution:

$$-5y + 7 = -2(y - 5)$$

$$-5y + 7 = -2y + 10 \qquad \text{Remove parentheses. No need to combine like terms. Collect the variable terms on one side}$$

$$-5y + 2y + 7 = -2y + 2y + 10$$

$$-3y + 7 = 10$$

$$-3y + 7 - 7 = 10 - 7 \qquad \text{and the number terms on the other side.}$$

$$-3y = 3$$

$$\frac{-3y}{-3} = \frac{3}{-3} \qquad \text{Rewrite the variable term with a coefficient of 1. Divide.}$$

$$y = -1$$

Solutions to some equations can be found by using a table or a graph.

Consider the equation $6(x + 1) = 15$. If you graph $6(x + 1) = y$ and locate the point on the graph where $y = 15$, the corresponding x-value of the ordered pair containing $y = 15$ would represent the solution to the equation.

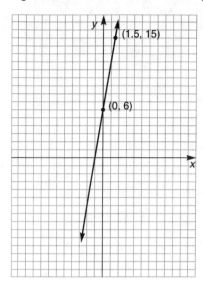

Another approach involves using a table of values. Look at the table given for $6(x + 1) = y$.

x	y
0	6
1	12
2	18

To solve $6(x + 1) = 15$, observe that 15 is midway between 12 and 18. Therefore the value of x that satisfies the equation must be midway between 1 and 2, or 1.5.

 MODEL PROBLEM

Use a table to find the solution for the linear equation $3x + 4 = 6$.

Solution: Consider $3x + 4 = 6$ as $3x + 4 = y$ and generate a table of values.

x	y
0	4
1	7
2	10

Notice that $y = 6$ falls between 4 and 7. In fact it is $\frac{2}{3}$ of the way between 4 and 7. Therefore the corresponding x-value must be $\frac{2}{3}$ of the way between 0 and 1, or $\frac{2}{3}$.

Answer: $x = \frac{2}{3}$

Inequalities

An inequality consists of two or more terms or expressions connected by an inequality sign.

The solution to an inequality is given as a solution set and can be represented on a number line.

The process of solving an inequality is very similar to the process of solving an equation. The major difference is if you are multiplying or dividing the inequality by a *negative number*, you must reverse the order of the inequality sign.

Note: A closed circle indicates the value is included in the solution set. An open circle indicates the value is excluded from the solution set.

 MODEL PROBLEMS

1. Graph the inequality on the number line: $-2 < x \le 4$

Solution: The inequality is read "x is between -2 and 4 with -2 excluded and 4 included." On the number line the graph would be:

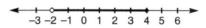
$$-3\ -2\ -1\ \ 0\ \ 1\ \ 2\ \ 3\ \ 4\ \ 5\ \ 6$$

2. Solve for x: $-4x + 4 \le -16$

Solution:

$$-4x + 4 \le -16$$
$$-4x + 4 - 4 \le -16 - 4 \quad \text{Add } -4.$$
$$-4x \le -20$$
$$\frac{-4x}{-4} \ge \frac{-20}{-4} \quad \begin{array}{l}\text{Divide by } -4; \text{ reverse} \\ \text{inequality sign.}\end{array}$$
$$x \ge 5$$

$$0\ \ 1\ \ 2\ \ 3\ \ 4\ \ 5\ \ 6\ \ 7$$

3. Write an inequality to describe the following situation and solve: Seven less than twice a number is greater than -3. Find the number.

Solution:

$$2x - 7 > -3$$
$$2x > 4$$
$$x > 2$$

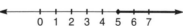
$$0\ \ 1\ \ 2\ \ 3\ \ 4$$

PRACTICE

1. Within the set of integers, which of the following represents the solution of the inequality?

$$3x + 1 < 8$$

A) $\{\ldots, -3, -2, -1, 0, 1, 2\}$
B) $\{\ldots, -3, -2, -1, 0, 1, 2, 3\}$
C) $\{\ldots, -3, -2, -1, 0, 1, 2, 3, 4, 5, 6, 7\}$
D) $\left\{\ldots, -3, -2, -1, 0, 1, 2, 2\frac{1}{3}\right\}$

2. Which of the following transformations is NOT correct?

E) $3x + 1 < 8 \quad \rightarrow 3x < 7$
F) $5x - 4 > 0 \quad \rightarrow 5x > 4$
G) $3(x + 1) < -5 \rightarrow 3x < -8$
H) $3x - 7 < 0 \quad \rightarrow 3x > 7$

3. Which equation has NO integral solution?

A) $3x = 9$ B) $16x = 32$
C) $3x = 2$ D) $17x = 51$

4. Solve for c: $\dfrac{c}{6} + 14 = 38$

E) 4   F) 144   G) 214   H) 312

5. Which number line shows the graph of $-3 \le x < 4$?

A)
```
←──┼─●─●─●─●─●─●─●─●─┼──→
   -3 -2 -1 0 1 2 3 4 5
```

B)
```
←──┼─○─●─●─●─●─●─●─○─┼──→
   -3 -2 -1 0 1 2 3 4 5
```

C)
```
←──┼─○─●─●─●─●─●─●─●─┼──→
   -3 -2 -1 0 1 2 3 4 5
```

D)
```
←──┼─●─●─●─●─●─●─●─○─┼──→
   -3 -2 -1 0 1 2 3 4 5
```

6. Solve for x: $-5x + 3 \ge 28$

7. Write an inequality to describe the following situation and solve:

Nine more than half a number is at most -8.

8. Solve for x: $2(x + 1) - 4 = x + 3$

9. How do you know that the solution to the equation $3x = 251$ is NOT an integral value?

10. Given the balance shown, find the weight of each identical cube if each ball weighs 1 pound.

11. Solve for r.

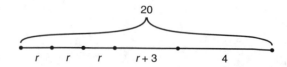

12. The temperature at High Point is 28°C and is dropping at the rate of 1.5° per hour. The temperature at Belmare is about 18°C and rising to 2° per hour.

A. Write an expression representing the temperature at each place after x hours.

B. Write an equation to represent that both cities are at the same temperature.

C. Solve the equation to find out how many hours (to the nearest tenth) it will take for the two cities to be at the same temperature.

4.10 Solving Systems of Linear Equations

A *system of linear equations* is formed by two or more linear equations with the same variables. Systems of linear equations are sometimes referred to as *simultaneous equations*. Any pair of values (x, y) that make all the equations true are called *solutions*. For example, the pair $(3, 6)$ means $x = 3$ and $y = 6$. $(3, 6)$ is a solution to the system of equations $y = 2x$ and $y = x + 3$.

The following table lists the three types of linear systems based on the number of solutions. Any system of linear equations will fall into one of these three types of systems.

Inconsistent System	Consistent System	Dependent System
No solutions	One solution	An infinite number of solutions
Equations $x + y = 3$ and $x + y = 6$ have no solutions. It is impossible to have the sum of the same numbers equal to both 3 and 6.	Equations $x + y = 7$ and $x - y = 5$ have one solution, that is $(6, 1)$.	Equations $x + y = 6$ and $2x + 2y = 12$ form a dependent system. Each term in the second equation is two times each term of the first equation.

There are two methods for algebraically solving systems of equations: the *addition-subtraction method* and the *substitution method*. Remember that the solution to a system of equations is not just one solution; rather, there is a value for *each variable*.

Addition-Subtraction Method

- If necessary, rewrite the equations to the *standard form* of a linear equation, $ax + by = c$.
- Decide which variable you want to eliminate.
- If necessary, multiply one or both equations by constants, so that the coefficients of the variable you want to eliminate have opposite signs.
- Align like terms by setting up the equations in columns.
- Add the columns to get a single equation in one variable.
- Solve the single equation.
- Substitute the resulting value into *either of the original* equations.
- Solve the resulting equation.
- Check the solution by substituting both values into *both original equations*.

Solve the system of equations: $x - 2y = 1$ and $x + y = 13$

Solution: The coefficients of x are the same.

Write the first equation.

$x - 2y = 1$

Multiply each term by -1.

$(-1)x + (-1)(-2y) = (-1)1$

Simplify.

$-x + 2y = -1$

Set up the equations in columns and add.

$$\begin{array}{r} -x + 2y = -1 \\ \underline{x + y = 13} \\ 3y = 12 \end{array}$$

Solve.

$y = 4$

Replace y in either equation.

$x + y = 13$
$x + 4 = 13$
$x = 9$

Check by substituting 4 for y and 9 for x in both original equations.

$x - 2y = 1$	$x + y = 13$
$9 - 2(4) = 1$	$9 + 4 = 13 \checkmark$
$9 - 8 = 1 \checkmark$	

Answer: $(x, y) = (9, 4)$

Substitution Method

- Solve one of the equations for one of the variables.
- Substitute the resulting algebraic expression in the second equation.
- Solve the second equation for the second variable.
- Substitute the resulting value into either original equation.
- Solve for the first variable.
- Check by substituting both values into both original equations.

MODEL PROBLEM

Solve the system of equations: $3x - 2y = 3$ and $y = 2x + 1$

Solution: Since the solutions are the same for each equation, $y = 2x + 1$ is true in both equations.

Write the first equation.	$3x - 2y = 3$
Substitute $2x + 1$ for y.	$3x - 2(2x + 1) = 3$
Distribute the -2.	$3x - 4x - 2 = 3$
Combine like terms.	$-x - 2 = 3$
Add x to both sides.	$-2 = x + 3$
Subtract 3 from both sides.	$-5 = x$

Substitute -5 for x into either equation.

$y = 2(-5) + 1$

$y = -10 + 1$

$y = -9$

Check by substituting -5 for x and -9 for y into both original equations.

$$3x - 2y = 3 \qquad\qquad y = 2x + 1$$
$$3(-5) - 2(-9) = 3 \qquad -9 = 2(-5) + 1 \checkmark$$
$$-15 + 18 = 3 \checkmark$$

Answer: $(x, y) = (-5, -9)$

PRACTICE

1. What is the solution for the following systems of equations?

$$2x + y = 7$$
$$3x - y = 3$$

   A) (4, 1)   B) (2, −1)

   C) (2, 3)   D) (3, 2)

2. A circus act has 3 times as many tigers as acrobats. George notices that all together, there are 56 legs in the circus ring. How many tigers are in the show?

   E) 4 tigers   F) 9 tigers

   G) 12 tigers   H) 14 tigers

3. The sum of two numbers is 78. The difference of the same two numbers is 18. The solution for the system of linear equations is:

   A) (30, 48)   B) (−30, −48)

   C) (48, 30)   D) (−48, −30)

4. What type of linear system is the following system of linear equations?

$$x + y = 8$$
$$-3x - 3y = -24$$

   E) Inconsistent   F) Dependent

   G) Consistent   H) Codependent

5. Daniel ordered a hamburger and soda. His cost was $5.25. Maria ordered two hamburgers. Her cost was $7.50. How much will it cost to purchase 15 cups of sodas?

4.11 Graphing Systems of Linear Equations and Inequalities

Solving Systems of Linear Equations Graphically

Recall that there are two methods for solving systems of linear equations algebraically: the addition-subtraction method and the substitution method. Systems of linear equations can also be solved by graphing the lines on the same coordinate plane and finding the point of intersection.

Solving Systems of Linear Equations Graphically

- Draw the graph of each equation on the same coordinate plane.
- The coordinates of the point of intersection of the graphs are the solution for the system of linear equations.
- Check the solution in both original equations.

 MODEL PROBLEM

The perimeter of a rectangular vegetable patch is 12 feet, and the length is twice the width. Find the dimensions of the vegetable patch by solving the systems of equations graphically.

Solution: Let x represent the width and y represent the length of the patch.

The formula for the perimeter of a rectangle is $2l + 2w$. In this case the perimeter is represented by the equation $2x + 2y = 12$, or $x + y = 6$.

The length is twice the width, which translates algebraically to $y = 2x$.

The two equations form a system of linear equations:

$x + y = 6$
$y = 2x$

Graph the two equations on the same coordinate plane.

Locate the point of intersection, which is (2, 4).

Check the solution (2, 4) in both original equations:

$x + y = 6$	$y = 2x$
$2 + 4 = 6$	$4 = 2(2)$
$6 = 6$ ✓	$4 = 4$ ✓

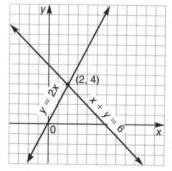

Answer: (2, 4)

The three types of systems of equations—consistent, inconsistent, or dependent—can be illustrated in the coordinate plane.

Consistent Equations

- The lines have different slopes and y-intercepts.
- The lines intersect at exactly one point.

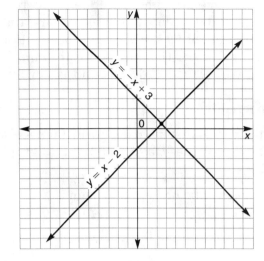

Inconsistent Equations

- The lines have the same slope but different y-intercepts.
- There are no points of intersection; the lines are parallel.

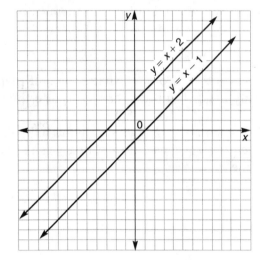

Dependent Equations

- The lines have the same slope and y-intercept.
- The lines are identical and share all points in common.

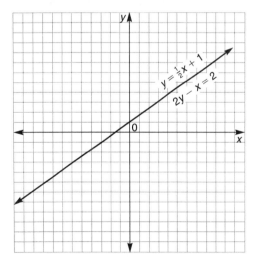

Solving Linear Inequalities Graphically

The coordinate plane divided into two regions by a line is called *half planes*. When the equation of the line is written in slope-intercept form, the half plane *above* the line is the graph of the inequality $y > mx + b$ and the half plane *below* the line is the graph of the inequality $y < mx + b$. If the solution set includes a half plane, the entire region is shaded. The line itself is the **boundary line**. It is drawn as a solid line when it is part of the solution set and as a broken line when it is not.

To Graph a Linear Inequality

- Express the inequality in slope-intercept form (if necessary) and graph its boundary line. A table of values maybe used also to graph the boundary line for the inequality.

    The boundary line will be broken if the sign is $>$ or $<$.
    The boundary line will be solid if the sign is $\geq$ or $\leq$.

- There are two methods for shading the half plane of the inequality.

    METHOD 1: Choose two points from the coordinate plane, one from either side of the boundary line, and substitute them into the inequality. Shade the half-plane that contains the point that makes the inequality true.

    METHOD 2: Solve the inequality for y or for x.

    If the inequality begins with $y >$ or $y \geq$, shade the half plane *above* the boundary line. If the inequality begins with $y <$ or $y \leq$, shade the half plane *below* the boundary line.

    If the inequality begins with $x >$ or $x \geq$, shade the half plane to the *left* of the boundary line. If the inequality begins with $x <$ or $x \leq$, shade the half plane to the *right* of the boundary line.

 MODEL PROBLEM

Graph $y \geq x + 2$ and check.

Solution:

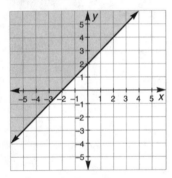

Check $(-3, 4)$ by substituting.

$$y \geq x + 2$$
$$4 \geq -3 + 2$$
$$4 \geq -1 \checkmark$$

Check $(0, 0)$ from outside the solution set.

$$y \geq x + 2$$
$$0 \geq 0 + 2$$
$$0 < 2 \text{ (not in solution set)} \checkmark$$

Systems of Linear Inequalities

The *feasible region* is the shaded region of the plane containing all the points that are common solutions of all the given inequalities.

To Find the Solution Set of a System of Linear Inequalities

- Solve each given inequality for y.
- Graph the boundary lines for each inequality.
- Shade the correct region for each graph.
- Label the common region, where all the graphs of the inequalities overlap, with a capital letter S for *solution*.
- If the inequalities do not overlap, then there is no solution.

 MODEL PROBLEM

Find the feasible set for the following system of inequalities:

$$y > 2x + 1$$
$$x + y \leq 0$$

Solution:

Graph the boundary line for $y > 2x + 1$ as a broken line and shade the half plane above the line. Graph the boundary line for $x + y \leq 0$ as a solid line and shade the half plane below the line. The common region is where the two shadings overlap. Mark the region S.

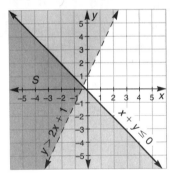

1. The solution for the systems of linear equations $y = 5$ and $y = 4x - 3$ is:

   A) (5, 17) B) (2, 5)
   C) (0, 5)   D) (3, 8)

2. The lines $y = 2x + 2$ and $y = 3x - 1$ intersect at:

   E) (3, 8)   F) (1, 4)
   G) (−1, −4) H) (−3, −8)

3. The system of equations represented by the graph below is:

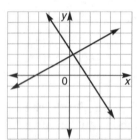

   A) Consistent   B) Inconsistent
   C) Dependent   D) Codependent

4. Which equation best describes the shaded area of the graph shown below?

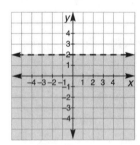

   E) $y \leq 2$ F) $y \geq 2$
   G) $y < 2$ H) $y > 2$

5. Which graph shows $y \geq 2x - 1$?

   A)
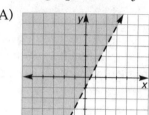

   B)
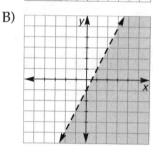

   C)
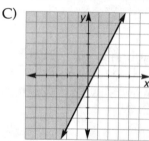

   D)
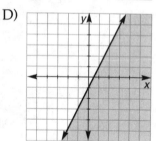

6. Which set of inequalities describes the shaded area of the graph?

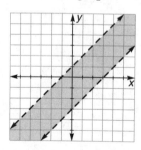

   E) $y > x - 1$ and $y < x + 3$
   F) $y < x + 1$ and $y > x - 3$
   G) $y > x + 1$ and $y < x + 3$
   H) $y < x + 1$ and $y < x - 3$

For problems 7 and 8, solve each system of equations graphically and check. Label each system as consistent, inconsistent, or dependent.

7. $x + y = 4$
   $-3x + y = -8$

8. $2x + 3y = 7$
   $y - x = 4$

For problems 9 and 10, graph each system of inequalities and label the solution set S.

9. $y \geq -x$
   $8x + 2y < 4$

10. $x + y \geq -3$
    $6x + 2y < 4$

ASSESSMENT CHAPTER 4

1. Which of the following is NOT a geometric sequence?

   A) $1, 1, 1, 1, 1, \ldots$
   B) $10, 100, 1,000, 10,000, \ldots$
   C) $6, 4, 2, 0, -2, \ldots$
   D) $6, 3, 1.5, 0.75, \ldots$

2. Which of the following diagrams does NOT represent a function?

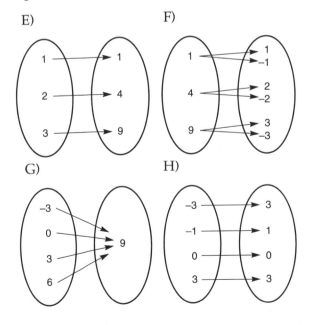

3. What digit is in the 20th decimal place in the decimal value of $\frac{35}{101}$?

   A) 3   B) 4   C) 5   D) 6

4. What is the units digit in 12^{15}?

   E) 2   F) 4   G) 6   H) 8

5. Given the pattern TEXASTEXASTEXAS . . . , what letter is in the 99th position?

   A) A   B) T   C) X   D) S

6. Which graph corresponds to $x - y = 5$?

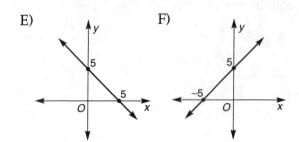

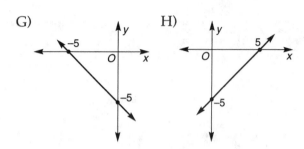

7. The table illustrates the function $y = -2x - 2$. What value do you get for y when $x = -6$?

x	y
0	-2
1	-4
2	-6

A) 14   B) 10   C) -10 D) -14

8. Which of the following equations expresses the area of a square as a function of the perimeter?

E) $A = \dfrac{p^2}{16}$ F) $A = 4p$

G) $A = p^2$ H) $A = \dfrac{1}{4}p^2$

9. A sequence is generated by the rule $3n^2 - 4$, where n represents the number of the term in the sequence. What is the difference in the values of the 25th and 26th terms in the sequence?

A) 6   B) 153   C) 159   D) 459

10. Which of the following is a translation for "6 less than 3 times a number"?

E) $6 < 3n$ F) $3n > 6$
G) $3n - 6$ H) $3(n - 6)$

11. A function uses the following rules:

A. Input any number greater than or equal to zero, and the function yields the same value that was input.

B. Input any negative number, and the function yields the opposite of that number.

Which of the following graphs matches the description of the function?

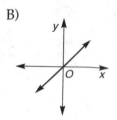

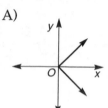

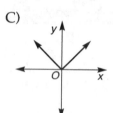

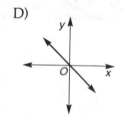

12. In which of the inequalities would you need to reverse the inequality symbol when solving?

E) $-5x > -35$ F) $6y \le 20$

G) $x + 16 \ge -14$ H) $\dfrac{1}{5}x \le 6$

13. If the horizontal axis is used for time and the vertical axis is used for price, which graph shows the sharpest increase in price over a period of time?

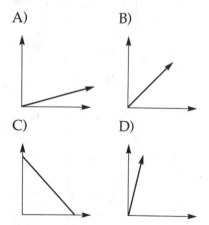

14. What is the difference between the 15th terms of Sequence A and Sequence B?

Sequence A: 2, 4, 8, 16, . . .
Sequence B: $-2, 4, -8, 16, . . .$

E) 0   F) 16,384
G) 32,768   H) 65,536

15. The number of mold cells on a piece of bread doubles every 12 minutes. If there are 35 mold cells on the bread now, about how many cells will there be 2 hours from now?

A) 420   B) 840   C) 2,458   D) 35,840

16. Suppose you start with $39.65 in your bank. Each day you put in $1.35 more than you put in on the previous day. That is, on day 1 you put in $1.35, on day 2 you put in $1.35 + $1.35 or $2.70, on day 3, $4.05, and so on. How much money will you have in the bank on the 12th day?

E) $55.85   F) $128.75
G) $144.95   H) $492

17. At We-Carry, shipping charges are $4.25 for the first 3 pounds and 75¢ for each additional pound. At that rate, how much did a package weigh if the charges were $11?

A) 6 pounds   B) 9 pounds
C) 12 pounds   D) 15 pounds

18. Which of the following lines has a negative slope?

E)   F)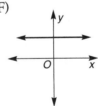

G) 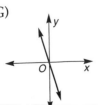   H)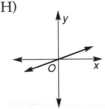

19. Which of the following points is NOT on the graph of $3x + y = 15$?

A) $(5, 0)$ B) $(-5, 0)$ C) $(3, 6)$ D) $(6, -3)$

20. Which of the following equations represents the line containing the points given in the graph?

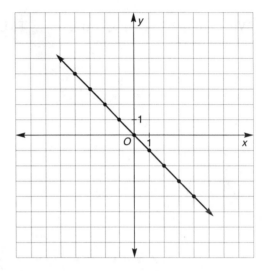

E) $y = x$ F) $y + x = 0$
G) $x - y = 0$ H) $y = x - 1$

21. Heather spends the equivalent of d days, h hours, and m minutes on a task. Into what expression does this translate for the total number of MINUTES on the task?

A) $d + h + m$
B) $24 \cdot 60d + 60h + m$
C) $7d + 24h + 60m$
D) $24d + 60h + m$

22. Which transformation is NOT correct?

E) $6x > 18$ $\rightarrow$ $x > 3$
F) $-7x + 4 < 0$ $\rightarrow -7x < -4$
G) $-5x < 20$ $\rightarrow$ $x < -4$
H) $\frac{x}{4} > 10$ $\rightarrow$ $x > 40$

23. Solve for x: $4(x + 2) - 2(x - 3) = 20$

A) $x = 10.5$ B) $x = 9$
C) $x = 7.5$ D) $x = 3$

24. Evaluate $3 - 5c^3$ when $c = 2$.

E) -27 F) -37 G) -120 H) -997

25. Describe the following systems of linear equation.

$$y = x - 1$$
$$-2x + y + 4 = 0$$

A) Consistent   B) Inconsistent

C) Dependent   D) Codependent

26. Which of the following equations is TRUE for all values that could replace x?

E) $3(x - 2) = 3x - 6$

F) $15 - x = x - 15$

G) $\dfrac{x}{6} = \dfrac{6}{x}$

H) $7(x - 5) = 7x - 5$

27. Note the following pattern:

 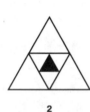 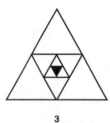

    1   2   3

If the pattern is extended, what percent of the 5th diagram would be shaded?

A) Less than 1%   B) 4%

C) 40%   D) 400%

28. Find the sum of the infinite geometric series

$$1 + \frac{1}{3} + \frac{1}{9} + \frac{1}{27} + \ldots$$

E) $\dfrac{1}{3}$ F) $\dfrac{2}{3}$ G) $\dfrac{3}{2}$ H) 3

29. For the arithmetic series $1 + 4 + 7 + 10 + \ldots + 97 + 100$, the sum is:

A) 150   B) 606   C) 1,700   D) 1,717

30. If $y = f(x) = x^3$, which of the following is NOT true?

E) $f(x)$ is a function.

F) $\left| f(-4) \right| = \left| f(4) \right|$

G) $f(x)$ is a periodic function.

H) $f(x)$ does not have a constant slope.

31. Which of the following does NOT result from a translation of $y = x^2$?

A) $y = 7x^2$ B) $y = x^2 + 4$

C) $y = (x - 2)^2$ D) $y = (x + 3)^2$

32. Evaluate $a^b + b^a$ when $a = 5$ and $b = 2$.

33. Pictured are nine congruent squares. If the total area is 144 square units, solve for x.

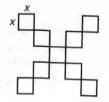

34. Solve for r.

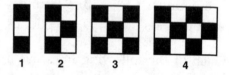

35. A display of Frisbees has been hung on a wall in the shape of a triangle.

There is 1 Frisbee in the top row, 2 Frisbees in the second row, 3 in the third, and so on, with each row containing 1 more Frisbee than the row above.

The display contains 12 rows.

How many Frisbees are used in the entire display?

36. Consider the following pattern:

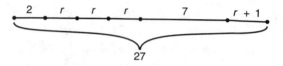

   1   2   3   4

If the pattern is continued, how many small squares would be shaded in the 9th diagram?

37. A special sequence is formed by taking 5 more than the sum of the two previous terms to find the third term and all succeeding terms. If the first four terms of the sequence are 1, 2, 8, 15, ..., find the 10th term.

38. The first four terms of an arithmetic sequence are 3, 7, 11, 15, and 123 is the 31st term. What is the value of the 30th term?

39. A. Plot the ordered pairs (8, 0), (7, 1), (6, 2), (5, 3).
    B. Sketch the graph suggested by the ordered pairs.
    C. Describe the pattern in words.
    D. What equation describes the pattern?

40. Starlite Pizzeria has regular expenses of $500 per week. In addition, their cost is $3 on average for each pizza made. They charge $8 for a pizza (this is the average price regardless of topping).

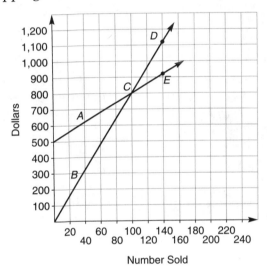

Using the given graph:

A. Identify the line that represents expenses and the line that represents revenue (income).
B. Explain the significance of point *C*.
C. What is the significance of the value of *D* less the value of *E*?

41. Miguel has read five novels this summer. His goal is to read two more by the end of each month.
    A. Write an equation in slope-intercept form to represent the situation.
    B. Draw the graph that illustrates the relationship.
    C. If Miguel continues this process, how many novels will he have read at the end of two years? Show your work.

42. Use a pattern to find this product:

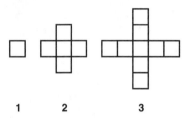

$$\left(1 - \frac{1}{2}\right)\left(1 - \frac{1}{3}\right)\left(1 - \frac{1}{4}\right)\left(1 - \frac{1}{5}\right)\cdots\left(1 - \frac{1}{50}\right)$$

State the product and show how your pattern allowed you to find the product without doing the actual computation.

43. Consider the pattern shown.

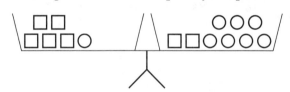

A. If the pattern is extended, how many small squares will there be in the 20th picture?
B Explain why the number of small squares will always be 1 more than a multiple of 4.

44. The boxes are of equal weight. Each ball weighs 1 kg. The scales are in balance. Find the weight of one box. Explain your process.

45. Jack and Bob are twins. Jack is trying to save money at a weekly rate to have the same amount of money as Bob. Bob has $310 saved but needs to withdraw $20 per week to help meet his expenses. Jack has $100 to start and adds $10 per week to the amount.

A. Write an expression that represents the amount of money Jack will have after *x* weeks.
B. Write an expression that represents the amount of money Bob will have after *x* weeks.
C. At this rate, how many weeks will it take until Jack and Bob have the same amount of money?

1. The distance on the number line between a number x and -5 is 7 units. Find all the possible values for x.

   A) $-12, 2$ B) $12, -2$
   C) -12 D) -2

2. Find the value of x:

   $$\frac{9}{x} = \frac{63}{112}$$

   E) 7   F) 9   G) 16   H) 58

3. Every 4 days, 180 cars come through the assembly line. At this rate, how many cars come through in 7 days?

   A) 45   B) 315   C) 720   D) 1,260

4. The school board projects a 2.5% increase in enrollment for next year. If the present enrollment is 8,657, what is the projected enrollment?

   E) 10,822   F) 8,874
   G) 8,682   H) 8,660

5. The diameter and height of a right circular cylinder are equal. If the volume of the cylinder is 2, what is the height of the cylinder?

   A) 1.37   B) 1.08   C) 0.86   D) 0.85

6. Which pair of points determines a line parallel to a line with slope $\frac{2}{3}$?

   E) $(1, 4), (2, 5)$ F) $(4, 5), (6, 8)$
   G) $(3, 2), (0, 0)$ H) $(-3, 2), (0, 0)$

7. The angles of a triangle are in the ratio of $1 : 2 : 6$. What kind of triangle results?

   A) Acute   B) Right
   C) Obtuse   D) Isosceles

8. How many ways can seven different books be arranged on a bookshelf?

   E) 7^2 F) $7!$ G) $7\frac{1}{2}$ H) 7^7

9. Suppose that the time needed to do a job varies inversely with the number of people working on the job. If it takes 8 hours for 3 people to load a moving van, how long would it take for 4 people?

   A) 4   B) 6   C) 7   D) $10\frac{2}{3}$

10. A set of data is normally distributed with a mean of 24 and a standard deviation of 7. What percent of the data values lies between 17 and 31?

    E) 34.1%   F) 47.7%
    G) 68.2%   H) 95.4%

11. What kind of line has no y-intercept?

    A) A line with a slope of 1
    B) A line with a slope of -1
    C) A horizontal line
    D) A vertical line (other than the y-axis)

12. Select the inequality that describes the situation. Luis has $22. He works for 5 days, receiving the same pay for each day. Then he will have no more than $100.

    E) $5x + 22 \geq 100$ F) $5(x + 22) \leq 100$
    G) $22 - 5x \leq 100$ H) $5x + 22 \leq 100$

13. A ball is dropped from a building 80 feet tall. If on each bounce the ball rebounds to 80% of the height of the previous bounce, how far does it travel by the time it hits the ground for the eighth time?

14. The perimeter of an equilateral triangle depends on the length of a side. Represent the function as an equation.

15. What digit is in the 52nd decimal place in the decimal value for $\frac{3}{11}$?

16. A palindrome is a number that reads the same from left-to-right and from right-to-left. For example, 737 and 8,228 are palindromes.

   A. How many palindromes are there between 2,000 and 5,000? Explain an efficient procedure for arriving at the answer.

   B. What fraction of these palindromes are multiples of 3?

   C. What is the first palindrome greater than 10,000 that also is a multiple of 3?

17. Of the students at a high school, 60% are bused to school. Of those who are bused, 80% favor a rule mandating the use of seat belts on the school bus. Of those who are not bused, 90% favor this rule.

   A. Draw a tree diagram to illustrate this problem.

   B. What is the percent of the students who favor this rule?

   C. If a randomly selected student favors the rule, what is the probability that the student rides the bus?

18. If the sum of four consecutive even integers is less than 250, what is the greatest possible value for one of these even integers? Explain your procedure.

CHAPTER 5

Fundamentals of Calculus

5.1 Maximum and Minimum Values of a Function

A function, $f(x)$, is said to have a **maximum** value at point c if and only if, when evaluated, the value of $f(c)$ is greater than or equal to $f(x)$. In general, the maximum value of a function is shown graphically in a coordinate plane as a *peak* on the curve. The following graph is an example of a maximum point of the function $f(x)$ at point c.

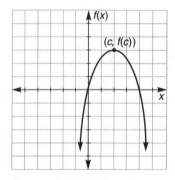

A function, $f(x)$, is said to have a **minimum** value at point a if and only if, when evaluated, the value of $f(a)$ is less than or equal to $f(x)$. In general, the minimum value of a function is shown graphically in a coordinate plane as a *valley* on the curve. The following graph is an example of a minimum point of the function $f(x)$ at point a.

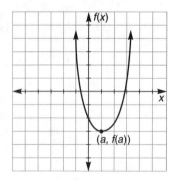

Finding the maximum and minimum values of functions is an important real-world application. For example, these values can help manufacturers minimize their costs and calculate the maximum acceleration of a space shuttle.

There are various methods for solving maximum and minimum problems: algebraic, deductive, graphic, trial and error, and calculus. The model problem on the next page is solved by using all five of these methods.

MODEL PROBLEM

In a football game, a field goal is kicked. The height, in feet, of the football is given by function $h = 100t - 25t^2$, where t is the time in seconds.

   A. At what time does the football reach the maximum height?

   B. What is the maximum height reached by the football?

   C. At what time does the football hit the ground?

Solution:

Algebraic Method

   A. Since the function is a downward-facing parabola, the maximum point occurs on the axis of symmetry. Use the formula $x = \dfrac{-b}{2a}$ to calculate the x-value.

$$x = \frac{-100}{-50} = 2 \ \text{ or } \ t = 2.$$

   B. Since we found that the football will reach its maximum height at $t = 2$ seconds, simply substitute 2 for t into the function and calculate the maximum height.

$h = 100t - 25t^2$

$h = 100(2) - 25(2)^2$

$h = 200 - 100$

$h = 100$

   C. The time the football hits the ground is when the height is zero.

Set the function equal to zero and solve.

$100t - 25t^2 = 0$

$25t(4 - t) = 0$

$25t = 0 \qquad\qquad 4 - t = 0$

$t = 0 \qquad\qquad\quad 4 = t$

Deductive Method

   A. Set the function equal to zero and solve.

$100t - 25t^2 = 0$

$25t(4 - t) = 0$

$25t = 0 \qquad\qquad 4 - t = 0$

$t = 0 \qquad\qquad\quad 4 = t$

Since the function is a downward-facing parabola, the maximum occurs at the axis of symmetry, that is, halfway between 0 and 4, which is 2 seconds.

   B. If the maximum occurs 2 seconds after the football is kicked, the height can be found by substituting 2 into the height equation.

$h = 100t - 25t^2$

$h = 100(2) - 25(2)^2$

$h = 200 - 100$

$h = 100$

   C. By factoring the equation in part A, $t = 0$ and $t = 4$. Since the football is kicked at $t = 0$, it hits the ground at $t = 4$.

(continued on next page)

MODEL PROBLEM

Graphic Method

Graph the function $h = 100t - 25t^2$ by plotting points, as shown below.

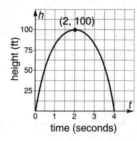

The maximum height is the largest y-value at its respective x-value. The maximum height occurs at $(2, 100)$. The two points at which the graph crosses the x-axis are when the football is on the ground. Since the football is kicked at $t = 0$, the football hits the ground at $t = 4$.

Trial-and-Error Method

Make a table of t values calculating when the maximum height occurs and when the football hits the ground.

t (sec)	$100t - 25t^2$	h (ft)
0	$100(0) - 25(0)^2 =$ $0 - 0 = 0$	0
1	$100(1) - 25(1)^2 =$ $100 - 25 = 75$	75
2	$100(2) - 25(2)^2 =$ $200 - 25(4) =$ $200 - 100 = 100$	100
3	$100(3) - 25(3)^2 =$ $300 - 25(9) =$ $300 - 225 = 75$	75
4	$100(4) - 25(4)^2 =$ $400 - 25(16) =$ $400 - 400 = 0$	0

Note: There are no negative t values because time is never negative.

(continued on next page)

 **MODEL PROBLEM**

Calculus Method

A. Find the critical value(s) of the function by finding the roots of the first derivative.

$h = 100t - 25t^2$

$h' = 100 - 50t$

$100 - 50t = 0$

$100 = 50t$

$2 = t$

> **Power Rule:**
>
> Use the Power Rule to find the derivative of a function.
> If $f(x) = x^n$, then $f'(x) = nx^{n-1}$.

To determine if a maximum value exist at $t = 2$ seconds, either test values of t that are greater than or less than 2 or evaluate the second derivative at $t = 2$.

To determine if a function has a maximum or minimum value at a critical point through testing intervals, there are two key points to remember:

1. A function has a *maximum* at a critical value, c, when the function is increasing for values less than c and is decreasing for values greater than c.
2. A function has a *minimum* at a critical value, c, when the function is decreasing for values less than c, and is increasing for values greater than c.

To determine if a function has a maximum or minimum value by using the second derivative test there are two key points to remember. If the value of the second derivative evaluated at the critical value is

1. negative, then the function has a maximum at the critical value.
2. positive, then the function has a minimum at the critical value.

Testing interval:

Substitute the values of t that are less than and greater than 2 into the original function. For $t = 0$; $h = 0$ and for $t = 1$; $h = 75$. For $t = 3$; $h = 75$ and for $t = 4$; $h = 0$. From these calculations, the function is increasing when evaluated at values that are less than 2 and is decreasing when evaluated at values that are greater than 2. Therefore, a maximum value exists at $t = 2$ seconds.

Second derivative test:

First take the second derivative of the function, then substitute $t = 2$ into the equation.

$h' = 100 - 50t$

$h'' = -50$

Since the second derivative is negative for every value of t, there is a maximum value at $t = 2$.

> **Second Derivative:**
>
> The second derivative is the derivative of the first derivative of a function.

(continued on next page)

B. Since we found in part A that the maximum height occurs at $t = 2$ seconds simply just substitute 2 into the height function.

$h = 100(2) - 25(2)^2$

$h = 200 - 25(4)$

$h = 200 - 100$

$h = 100$ feet

C. To find when the football hits the ground, set the function equal to zero and solve.

$100t - 25t^2 = 0$

$25t(4 - t) = 0$

$25t = 0 \qquad\qquad 4 - t = 0$

$t = 0 \qquad\qquad\quad 4 = t$

Answer:

A. The football reaches its maximum height at $t = 2$ seconds.

B. The maximum height the football reaches is 100 feet.

C. The football is kicked at $t = 0$, therefore, it hits the ground when $t = 4$. That is, 4 seconds after it is kicked.

PRACTICE

1. The function $f(x) = -x^2 - 2x$ has maximum value of:

   A) -8 B) -3 C) 1   D) 8

2. Which of the following functions has a minimum value of 8?

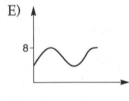

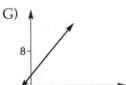

3. An arrow is shot into the air at an angle. Its height, in feet, during the flight is found by the function $h(t) = 40 + 120t - 4t^2$, where $h(t)$ is the height in seconds. What is the maximum height of the arrow?

   A) 15 feet   B) 40 feet

   C) 120 feet   D) 940 feet

4. The graph of the function shown below has a maximum value when $t =$

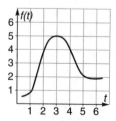

   E) 1   F) 3   G) 5   H) 6

5. A small manufacturer of toys finds the profit he will make in one year using the function $P(t) = -6t^2 + 204t + 300$, where t is the number cases of toys he sells. What is the manufacturer's maximum profit?

A) $17.00
B) $300.00
C) $2,084.00
D) $3,000

6. The maximum area of a rectangle whose perimeter is 80 feet is:

E) 40
F) 80
G) 160
H) 800

7. Ms. Kuztown has 200 feet of wire fencing with which to enclose a vegetable garden. What are the dimensions and the area of the largest rectangular garden which she can fence off with this wire, whose perimeter is 100 feet.

8. In a circus act, a performer is shot out of a canon. The height, in feet, he travels is given by the function $H(t) = 120 + 48t - 6t^2$ and t is the time in seconds.

A. What is the maximum height reached by the circus performer?
B. At what time, t, does he reach the maximum height?
C. At what time, t, does he land safely on the net?

5.2 Exponential Growth and Decay

Exponential growth and decay involves a quantity growing or decaying at a constant percentage over time. *Exponential growth* focuses on populations growing in size, while negative exponential growth, commonly known as *exponential decay*, focuses on the decrease in the price of a product or a steady decrease in a population.

In general, exponential functions are in the form $f(x) = ab^x$, where $a \neq 0$, $b > 0$, and $b \neq 1$, and x represents a specific period of time such as months, years, or decades. In an exponential function, since $f(0) = ab^0 = a(1) = a$, a is called the *initial value* and b is called the *growth factor*. If $b > 1$, the model is increasing or growing; if $0 < b < 1$, the model is decreasing or decaying.

The most common form of an exponential function is $y = 2^x$. The graph of this function is shown below.

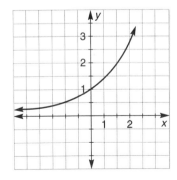

Note: Given an exponential function in the form $y = ab^x$, the y-intercept is always $(0, a)$.

MODEL PROBLEMS

1. Justin has begun his own business designing and printing custom greeting cards. The number of customers has grown steadily, as illustrated in the graph below.

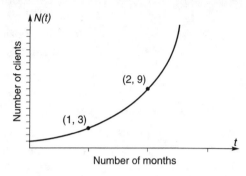

A. How many customers did Justin have initially?

B. Write an exponential equation for $N(t)$, the number of customers Justin has t months after he began his business.

C. Based on your equation from part B, how many customers will Justin have 4 months after he began his business?

Solution:

A. By looking at the graph, at time 0, Justin has 1 customer.

B. There are three points that we know are on the line on the graph: (0, 1), (1, 3), and (2, 9). We can see that the graph is an exponential function. Observe that each of the three known values for $N(t)$ is always a power of 3; that is, $N(0) = 3^0$, $N(1) = 3^1$, and $N(2) = 3^2$. So, our equation is $N(t) = 3^t$.

   We can also determine the formula algebraically. The formula for an exponential function is $N(t) = ab^t$, where a is the initial value. Since our initial value is 1, we know that our formula is $N(t) = 1 \cdot b^t = b^t$. Substituting the values for t that we already know into $N(t)$, gives us $3 = b^1$. Thus $b = 3$ and our equation is $N(t) = 3^t$.

C. Substitute 4 for t in the above formula: $N(4) = 3^4 = 81$. Justin will have 81 customers 4 months after he began his business.

2. A piece of machinery that costs \$8,000 depreciates during each year by an amount equal to $\frac{1}{10}$ of its value at the beginning of the year. To the nearest dollar, how much will it be worth at the end of the 5th year?

Solution: Since the machinery loses $\frac{1}{10}$ or 0.1 of its value each year, that means it is worth only $\frac{9}{10}$ or 0.9 of its value each year. Thus, $a = 8,000$, $b = 0.9$, and the exponent is 5. By substitution, $8,000(0.9)^5 = 8,000(0.59049) = \$4,723.92$.

Answer: \$4,724 (to the nearest dollar)

PRACTICE

1. In the 2002–2003 school year, the average cost for one year at a four-year private college was $17,300, which was an increase of 7.2% from the previous year. If this trend were to continue, the equation $C(x) = 17{,}300(1.072)^x$ could be used to model the cost of a college education x years from 2002. To the nearest dollar, how much will a college education cost in 2006?

   A) $17,300 B) $22,847
   C) $26,255 D) $260,255

2. The current population of a large herd of 6,000 buffalo increases at a rate of 20% each year. If this trend continues every year, what will the population of the herd be 2 years from now?

   E) 6,000 F) 7,200
   G) 8,640 H) 10,368

3. The equation $h = 5(0.8)^x$ shows the relationship between the number of bounces x of a ball and the height h in feet of the bounce. What is the height of the ball, to the nearest foot, after the fourth bounce?

   A) 2 feet B) 3 feet
   C) 4 feet D) 5 feet

4. The Bank of Brescia offers Kristin a CD rate of 3.6% compounded annually (interest given once each year). If Kristin deposits $5,000 into this CD account, what is the total money available (to the nearest dollar) at the end of 6 years?

   E) $5,000 F) $5,360
   G) $6,182 H) $7,000

5. Elisabeth cut a piece of paper in half. She put the two pieces together and then cut them in half again. She then put the four pieces of paper together and cut them in half again. If she continues to do this over and over again, the number of pieces obtained after each cut could be represented by the graph below.

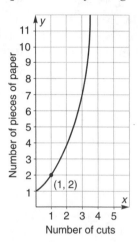

Which of the following equations could be used to represent the graph?

   A) $y = 2x$ B) $y = 2x + 1$
   C) $y = 2^x$ D) $y = 2^{x-1}$

6. A beach ball loses 5% of its air every day. If the beach ball originally contained 4,000 cubic centimeters of air, how many cubic centimeters of air does it hold after 8 days? Give the answer to the nearest integer.

7. Sarah invested $500 in the bank at 6% interest compounded annually.

   A. Write the equation, $A(x)$, that will help Sarah calculate how much money is in her account at the end of each year.

   B. How much money will be in Sarah's account at the end of 4 years?

5.3 Estimating Area Under a Curve

A common method for estimating the area of a closed curve is to inscribe polygons into the figure and find the sum of the areas of the polygons. To estimate the area under the curve between a given interval $a \leq x \leq b$, the same concept is applied. Rectangles or trapezoids are commonly inscribed under the curve and the sum of their areas is found to estimate the area under the curve.

Rectangle Method

To estimate the area under a curve, we can draw rectangles starting from the left side or the right side of the curve. For example, we can use rectangles to estimate shade region, S, the area under the parabola $y = x^2$ from 0 to 1.

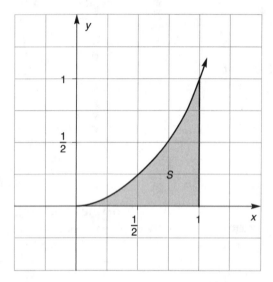

We can estimate that the area of S is somewhere between 0 and 1 since S is contained in a square with side length 1. However, we can obtain a much more accurate estimation by dividing S into four equally wide strips S_1, S_2, S_3, and S_4 by drawing the vertical lines $x = \dfrac{1}{4}$, $x = \dfrac{1}{2}$, and $x = \dfrac{3}{4}$ as shown in the figure below.

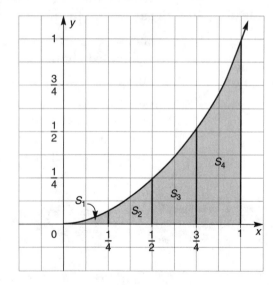

We can approximate each strip by forming a rectangle whose width can be found by the formula $\Delta x = \dfrac{b - a}{n}$, where a and b are the endpoints of the interval and n is the number of subintervals. In this example, the width $\Delta x = \dfrac{1 - 0}{4} = \dfrac{1}{4}$. The height is the same length as the right edge of the strip. As shown below, the heights of these rectangles are the values of the function $f(x) = x^2$ evaluated at the right endpoints of the subintervals $\left[0, \dfrac{1}{4}\right], \left[\dfrac{1}{4}, \dfrac{1}{2}\right], \left[\dfrac{1}{2}, \dfrac{3}{4}\right],$ and $\left[\dfrac{3}{4}, 1\right],$ that is, $\left(\dfrac{1}{4}\right)^2, \left(\dfrac{1}{2}\right)^2, \left(\dfrac{3}{4}\right)^2,$ and 1^2.

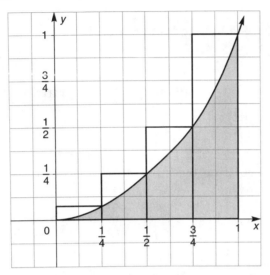

Since we know that each rectangle has a width of $\dfrac{1}{4}$ and their respective heights are $\dfrac{1}{16}, \dfrac{1}{4}, \dfrac{9}{16},$ and 1, we can take sum of the areas of the rectangles to estimate the area of S. Let R represent the area.

$$R = \frac{1}{4} \cdot \frac{1}{16} + \frac{1}{4} \cdot \frac{1}{4} + \frac{1}{4} \cdot \frac{9}{16} + \frac{1}{4} \cdot 1 = \frac{15}{32} = 0.46875$$

The area of the shaded region S can also be estimated by rectangles whose height is the same length as the left edge of the strip and the width is $\dfrac{1}{4}$, as shown in the figure below.

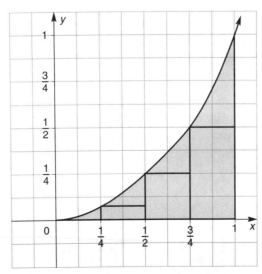

The leftmost rectangle is not visible because its height is 0. Let L represent the area. Use the sum of the areas of these rectangles to estimate the area of S.

$$L = \frac{1}{4} \cdot 0^2 + \frac{1}{4} \cdot \left(\frac{1}{4}\right)^2 + \frac{1}{4} \cdot \left(\frac{1}{2}\right)^2 + \frac{1}{4} \cdot \left(\frac{3}{4}\right)^2 = \frac{7}{32} = 0.21875.$$

From both of our calculations, we see that the area of S is greater than L but less than R that is $0.21875 < S < 0.46875$.

Trapezoid Method

Referring back to the example above, trapezoids can be inscribed instead of rectangles, as shown in the figure below.

Recall that the area of a trapezoid is $\frac{1}{2}(b_1 + b_2)h$. The height of each trapezoid can be found by using the formula $\Delta x = \frac{b - a}{n}$, which is equal to $\frac{1 - 0}{4} = \frac{1}{4}$. The length of each base is the value of the function $f(x) = x^2$ evaluated at each endpoint of the subintervals, $\left[0, \frac{1}{4}\right]$, $\left[\frac{1}{4}, \frac{1}{2}\right]$, $\left[\frac{1}{2}, \frac{3}{4}\right]$, and $\left[\frac{3}{4}, 1\right]$.

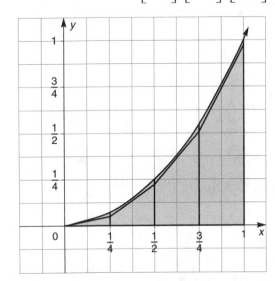

The area of S can be approximated by calculating the sum of the areas of the trapezoids.

$$T_1 = \frac{1}{2}\left(0^2 + \frac{1^2}{4}\right)\frac{1}{4} = 0.0078125$$

$$T_2 = \frac{1}{2}\left(\frac{1^2}{4} + \frac{1^2}{2}\right)\frac{1}{4} = 0.0390625$$

$$T_3 = \frac{1}{2}\left(\frac{1^2}{2} + \frac{3^2}{4}\right)\frac{1}{4} = 0.1015625$$

$$T_4 = \frac{1}{2}\left(\frac{3^2}{4} + 1^2\right)\frac{1}{4} = 0.1953125$$

The approximate area of S is $T_1 + T_2 + T_3 + T_4 = 0.0078125 + 0.0390625 + 0.101625 + 0.1953125 = 0.34375$.

If we compare the diagrams for the rectangle method and the trapezoid method, we can see that the trapezoid method provides a more accurate approximation of the area of the shaded region S. In the rectangle method, either some parts of the shaded region are not calculated or the region above the curve is also calculated into the approximation, therefore leading to a less accurate approximation. However, when trapezoids are inscribed under the curve, most of the shaded region is included.

Note: In both the rectangle and trapezoid methods, the more subintervals the region under a curve is divided into, the more accurate is the approximation for the its area.

MODEL PROBLEM

Find the area under the curve $f(x) = \sqrt{x}$ from $x = 2$ to $x = 4$ and four subintervals using
- A. the rectangle method with rectangles drawn from the left side of each subinterval.
- B. the rectangle method with rectangles drawn from the right side of each subinterval.
- C. the trapezoid method.

Solution

Calculate $\Delta x = \dfrac{b - a}{n} = \dfrac{4 - 2}{4} = \dfrac{1}{2}$.

A. Sketch the curve and the rectangles formed by the left endpoints of each subinterval.

Approximate the area under the curve by taking the sum of the areas of the rectangles.

$$A \approx \frac{1}{2}(\sqrt{2}) + \frac{1}{2}(\sqrt{2.5}) + \frac{1}{2}(\sqrt{3}) + \frac{1}{2}(\sqrt{3.5})$$

$$A \approx 3.2991$$

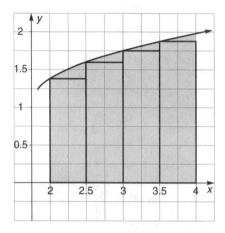

B. Sketch the curve and the rectangles formed by the right endpoints of each subinterval.

$$A \approx \frac{1}{2}(\sqrt{2.5}) + \frac{1}{2}(\sqrt{3}) + \frac{1}{2}(\sqrt{3.5}) + \frac{1}{2}(\sqrt{4})$$

$$A \approx 3.5929$$

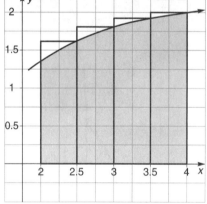

C. Sketch the curve and the trapezoids.

Since the formula for the area of a trapezoid is $\dfrac{1}{2}(b_1 + b_2)h$ and the height of each trapezoid is represented by Δx, which is $\dfrac{1}{2}$, the area of each trapezoid can be found by the formula $\dfrac{1}{4}(b_1 + b_2)$.

$$A \approx \frac{1}{4}(\sqrt{2} + \sqrt{2.5}) + \frac{1}{4}(\sqrt{2.5} + \sqrt{3}) +$$
$$\frac{1}{4}(\sqrt{3} + \sqrt{3.5}) + \frac{1}{4}(\sqrt{3.5} + \sqrt{4})$$

$$A \approx 3.4281$$

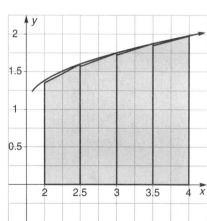

1. Which of the following methods most accurately approximates the area under the curve of $y = 3x^2$?

A)

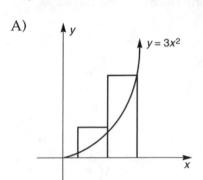

B)

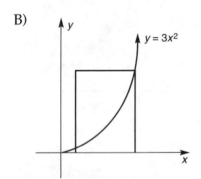

C)

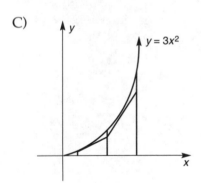

D)

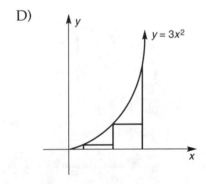

2. The most accurate estimation of the area under the curve shown below is

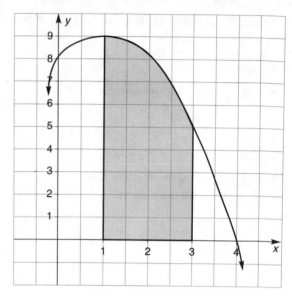

E) 15.75

F) 15.50

G) 15.25

H) 15.00

3. The area under the parabola $y = 6 - x^2$ between $x = 0$ and $x = 2$ and with 4 subintervals using the rectangles formed by the left endpoints of the subintervals is approximately:

A) 8.25

B) 9.38

C) 10.25

D) 10.75

4. The area under the parabola $y = x^2$ between $1 \le x \le 3$ and with 4 subintervals using the rectangles formed by the right endpoints of the subintervals is approximately:

E) 6.75

F) 8.67

G) 10.75

H) 11.25

5. Using the trapezoid method, approximate the area under the cubic function $y = x^3$ for $x = 2$ to $x = 6$ with 8 subintervals.

6. Estimate the area under the parabola $y = x^4 - 2$ between $x = 0$ and $x = 1$ with 4 intervals using

A. the trapezoid method.

B. rectangles formed by the left endpoints of the subintervals.

7. Approximate the area of the shaded region below using the trapezoid method.

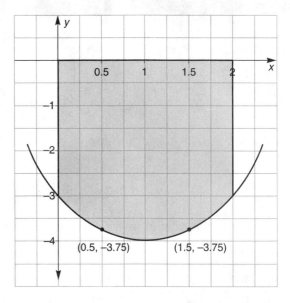

(0.5, −3.75)   (1.5, −3.75)

1. The function $x^4 + 2x^3 + x^2$ has a minimum value at $x =$

   A) -2 B) -1 C) 1 D) 2

2. What is the minimum value of the function $x^2 - 2x + 3$?

   E) 0 F) 1 G) 2 H) 3

3. Where is the maximum value of the function $-x^2 + 2x - 3$?

   A) $x = -2$ B) $x = -1$
   C) $x = 1$ D) $x = 2$

4. What is the maximum value of $f(x) = x^3$ in the interval $-1 < x < 3$?

   E) 0 F) 1 G) 8 H) 27

5. Albert has invested $1,000 in a video game company. The value of his investment can be modeled by the function $V(t) = 1,000(0.70)^t$, where t is the time, in years, since Albert made his investment. How much will Albert's investment be worth after 10 years?

   A) $50.00   B) $28.25
   C) $20.00   D) $4.75

6. The population of Acme, PA, can be modeled by the equation $P(t) = 2,300(0.85)^t$, where $t = 0$ represents the year 2000. What will the population of Acme be in 2006?

   E) 1,627   F) 1,000
   G) 1,021   H) 868

7. A car's value depreciates every year. Assume that your family bought a new car in February 2002 for $13,500 and that it depreciates at approximately 10% per year. An equation that will model the value of the car, $V(t)$, where t is the number years since 2002, is

   A) $V(t) = 13,500(0.90)^t$
   B) $V(t) = 13,500(1.90)^t$
   C) $V(t) = 13,500(0.10)^t$
   D) $V(t) = 13,500(1.10)^t$

8. According to the U.S. Census Bureau, there were approximately 7 million households with access to a computer in 1984. Computer usage in the United States from 1984 through 1997 grew at a rate of approximately 14% per year. Which of the following equations could be used to model the number of households (in millions) with computers, beginning in the year 1984?

   E) $N(t) = 7(0.14)^t$
   F) $N(t) = 7(1.14)^t$
   G) $N(t) = 7.14^t$
   H) $N(t) = 14(0.07)^t$

9. The area under the curve $f(x) = -(x - 1)^2 + 1$ on the interval $x = 0$ to $x = 2$ with four subintervals using the rectangles formed by the left endpoints of the subintervals is approximately

   A) 0.75   B) 1   C) 1.25   D) 2

10. The area under the curve $f(x) = x^4$ on the interval $x = 1$ to $x = 2$ with four equal subinterval using rectangles formed by the right endpoints of the subintervals is approximately

    E) 4.47   F) 6.20   G) 8.22   H) 16

11. The rate of growth of a population of bacteria is proportional to the population in a culture dish. At time $t = 0$ there are 1,000 bacteria and at time $t = 4$ there are 10,000 bacteria present.

   A. Write the equation that can be used to find the bacteria at any time t.

   B. How many bacteria will be present in the dish at $t = 7$?

12. Given the function $F(x) = 15(0.75)^x$, where $F(x)$ is the number of fish in Jack's fish tank and x is the number of days since Jack set up the tank.

   A. How many fish did Jack have to start?

   B. What is happening to Jack's fish? Explain.

13. During a recent snowfall, several students monitored the accumulation of snow on the flat roof of their school. The table records the data they collected for the 12-hour period of snowfall.

Number of Hours	Rate of Snowfall (in./hour)
0	0
2	1.5
3	2.1
4.5	2.4
6.5	2.8
8	2.2
10.5	1.8
12	1.6

Using the trapezoid method, approximate the total depth of snow at the end of 12 hours.

14. The cost in thousands of dollars to construct a building of n floors is calculated by the function $C(n) = 100n^2 - 600n + 1,500$.

   A. What is the minimum cost for constructing the building?

   B. How many floors does the building have at the minimum cost?

Section 1

Directions: You are **not** allowed to use a calculator for questions 1 through 5.

1. If $r = -2$ and $t = -5$, find the value of $r^4 - t$.

   A) -21 B) -11
   C) 11 D) 21

2. Every 5 days, 175 stoves come through the assembly line. At this rate, how many stoves come through in 7 days?

   E) 45   F) 245
   G) 315   H) 725

3. $\dfrac{0.0912}{0.3} =$

   A) 0.0304   B) 0.0340
   C) 0.3040   D) 3.0401

4. Which of the following is **not** equal to the other three?

   E) 1.5×10^1 F) $\dfrac{15}{10}$
   G) 150%   H) $\sqrt{2.25}$

5. Regina earns $8.00 an hour for the first 40 hours a week she works. She earns time and a half for any hours over 40 she works during the week and double time for hours worked on the weekend. Her time card for one week is shown below. How much did Regina earn?

Mon.	Tues.	Wed.	Thurs.	Fri.	Sat.
$8\frac{1}{2}$	9	9	$8\frac{1}{2}$	$7\frac{1}{2}$	3

   A) $341.25   B) $361.88
   C) $375.00   D) $386.00

Directions: You may use a calculator for the remainder of the questions on this test.

6. What is the distance between the points $(2, -4)$ and $(6, -9)$ in the xy-plane?

   E) $\sqrt{185}$
   F) $\sqrt{89}$
   G) $\sqrt{41}$
   H) 0

7. The number of Central High School students who gave to the United Fund this year was 342. This figure is 110% of what it was the previous year. This means that:

   A) 10 more Central High School students gave to the United Fund.
   B) The number of Central High School students giving to the United Fund decreased from last year to this year.
   C) Central High School raised more money for the United Fund this year than it did last year.
   D) The number of Central High School students giving to the United Fund increased from last year to this year.

8. Which point on the number line below could represent the product of the numbers represented by *W* and *X*?

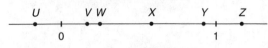

E) *U*
F) *V*
G) *Y*
H) *Z*

9. If triangular region *ABC* below is rotated 360° about side $\overline{BC}$, which of the following three-dimensional solids is formed?

A) Pyramid
B) Ball
C) Cylinder
D) Cone

10. Which of the following points lies on the graph of $3x - y = 6$?

E) $(-1, -3)$
F) $(0, 6)$
G) $(1, -3)$
H) $(1, 3)$

11. Start with the set of whole numbers between 10 and 40, including 10 and 40.

10 11 12 13 14 15 16 17 18 19
20 21 22 23 24 25 26 27 28 29
30 31 32 33 34 35 36 37 38 39 40

Remove all prime numbers.
Remove all perfect squares.
Remove all factors of 72.
Remove all multiples of 9.
Remove all numbers in the following sequence 1, 1, 2, 3, 4, 5, 8, . . .

How many numbers remain?

A) 11   B) 12   C) 13   D) 14

12. Which of the following sets of coordinates could represent the vertices of a quadrilateral containing two right angles and no pairs of parallel sides?

E) $(-4, 0), (0, 4), (4, 0), (0, -4)$
F) $(0, 0), (0, 2), (4, 4), (6, 0)$
G) $(0, 0), (0, 3), (7, 7), (7, 0)$
H) $(-4, 0), (0, 4), (3, 0), (0, -4)$

13.

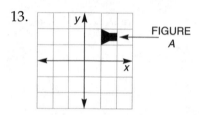

Which of the following represents the result of reflecting figure *A* in the *y*-axis and then reflecting that image in the *x*-axis?

A)

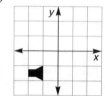

B)

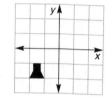

C)

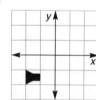

D)

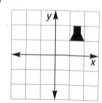

14. The baselines of a baseball diamond form a square with side lengths of 90 feet.

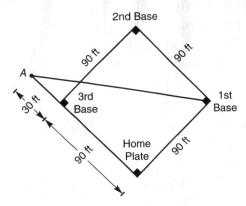

A player catches a ball at point *A*, which is on the foul line 30 feet beyond 3rd base. How far from 1st base is the player when he catches the ball?

E) 120 ft
F) 150 ft
G) 180 ft
H) 210 ft

15. The table below indicates a relationship between *a* and *b*.

a	b
0	−2
1	1
2	4
.	.
.	.
5	13
.	.
.	.
8	22

Which of the equations below expresses the relationship between *a* and *b* that is indicated in the table?

A) $b = a^2$
B) $b = 2a + 3$
C) $b = 3a - 2$
D) $b = a + 3$

16. Each month, a high school does a feature newspaper article on one of its students, who is picked at random. The numbers of male and female students in each grade in that high school are shown in the table below.

NUMBER OF STUDENTS							
Grade 9		Grade 10		Grade 11		Grade 12	
M	F	M	F	M	F	M	F
28	22	31	20	25	26	25	23

Based on this table, what is the probability the student chosen will be a female student in grade 9?

E) .11
F) .22
G) .24
H) .44

17. For a sale, a shopkeeper lowers the original price of an item by 20 percent. After the sale, the shopkeeper raises the price of that item by 20 percent of its sale price. The price of the item then is:

A) More than the original price
B) Less than the original price
C) The same as the original price
D) There is not enough information to compare the two prices.

18. Which of the following graphs most likely shows an automobile's resale value plotted against its age?

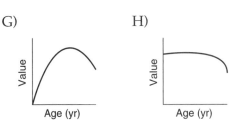

19. Which of the following sets of lengths does NOT represent a triangle?

A) 1, 1, 1
B) 6, 8, 10
C) 2, 3, 5
D) 9, 12, 15

20. The angles of a triangle are in the ratio of $1:2:7$. What kind of triangle results?

E) Isosceles
F) Right
G) Acute
H) Obtuse

21. A right triangle has legs of 7 inches and 24 inches. Find the cosine of the smaller of the two acute angles of the triangle.

A) $\dfrac{7}{25}$
B) $\dfrac{24}{25}$
C) $\dfrac{7}{24}$
D) $\dfrac{25}{24}$

22. A dart is thrown at the circular region below. If the dart is equally likely to hit any point inside the circle, what is the probability that it hits the region outside of the inscribed square?

E) .68
F) .36
G) .25
H) .18

23. Which of these statements is TRUE?

A) All squares are similar.
B) All triangles are similar.
C) All rectangles are similar.
D) All parallelograms are similar.

24. Suppose that each time a ball bounces, it goes up $\dfrac{1}{2}$ the distance it fell. If that ball is dropped from a height of x feet, which of these expressions represents the total distance it has traveled when it hits the floor for the fifth time?

E) $x + \dfrac{1}{2} + \dfrac{1}{4} + \dfrac{1}{8} + \dfrac{1}{16}$

F) $x + \dfrac{1}{2} + \dfrac{1}{2} + \dfrac{1}{4} + \dfrac{1}{4} + \dfrac{1}{8} + \dfrac{1}{8} + \dfrac{1}{16} + \dfrac{1}{16}$

G) $x + \dfrac{x}{2} + \dfrac{x}{2} + \dfrac{x}{4} + \dfrac{x}{4} + \dfrac{x}{8} + \dfrac{x}{8} + \dfrac{x}{16} + \dfrac{x}{16}$

H) $(x)\left(\dfrac{1}{2}\right)\left(\dfrac{1}{4}\right)\left(\dfrac{1}{8}\right)\left(\dfrac{1}{16}\right)$

Directions: Show all your work and provide an explanation as directed in the question. Your score for the following question will be based on accuracy and the completeness of your process or explanation.

25. The math exam scores for 21 students in Mr. Walker's homeroom were:

65 90 82 78 94 92 88 86 70 68 75
88 90 85 61 81 79 82 84 83 90

A. The mean of the above scores is 81. What are the median and the mode?
B. Construct a bar graph showing the frequency or number of scores in each of the score ranges.
C. What is the best general indicator of this class's performance on the exam—the mean, median, or mode? Explain your answer.

26. All 1,376 students attending Cary High School voted for president of the Student Council. With approximately one-fifth of the votes counted, the leading candidate had 185 votes. Assuming that candidate obtained the same proportion of the total number of votes, the total number of votes she received would be between:

    A) 250 and 300   B) 450 and 500
    C) 600 and 700   D) 900 and 950

27. Based on the graph below, which car takes less time to go from 0 to 60 mph, and about how much less time does it take?

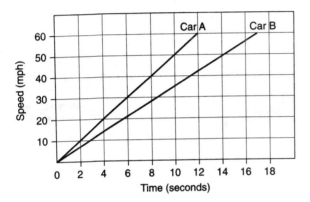

    E) Car A by about 5 seconds
    F) Car B by about 5 seconds
    G) Car A by about $2\frac{1}{2}$ seconds
    H) Car B by about $2\frac{1}{2}$ seconds

28. Sal's Drugstore is having a sale of photographic film.

Film Sale
a roll of ALPHA film: 20-exposure film for $2.30
a roll of BETA film: 12-exposure film for $1.50
a roll of GAMMA film: 30-exposure film for $3.15

    Place the brands of film in order from least cost per exposure to greatest cost per exposure.

    A) Alpha, Beta, Gamma
    B) Beta, Alpha, Gamma
    C) Gamma, Alpha, Beta
    D) Gamma, Beta, Alpha

29. The cost of first-class postage recently changed from 34¢ to 37¢. This change translates to what percent increase?

    E) 3%   F) 4%   G) 6.5%   H) 8.8%

30. The whole numbers from 1 to 36 are each written on a small slip of paper and placed in a box. If one slip of paper is selected at random from the box, what is the probability that the number selected is a factor of 36 and also a multiple of 8?

    A) $\frac{13}{36}$ B) $\frac{1}{36}$ C) $\frac{1}{4}$ D) 0

31. If $f(x) = 2^x + 3^x + 6^x$, what is $f(1) - f(-1)$?

    E) 0   F) 10   G) 11   H) 22

32. Suppose you construct a series of trapezoid trains using the following isosceles trapezoid block:

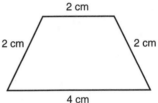

    A 2-trapezoid train looks like:

    A 3-trapezoid train looks like:

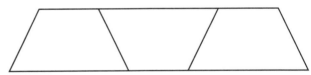

    Which of the following statements is NOT going to be true?

    A) An 8-trapezoid train would be a parallelogram.
    B) A 9-trapezoid train would be an isosceles trapezoid.
    C) The perimeter of a 9-trapezoid train would be 64 cm.
    D) The perimeter of a trapezoid train would always equal an even number of centimeters.

33. If $2^x = 4^y = k$ where $1{,}000 < k < 2{,}000$ and x and y are integers, what is the value of $x - y$?

E) -5 F) 0 G) 5 H) 10

34. While interviewing students at Washington High School, Paul asked 20 students (picked at random) what their favorite fall sport is. Maria asked 50 different students (picked at random) the same question. George combined Paul's data and Maria's data. All three graphed their results:

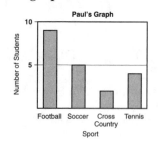

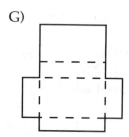

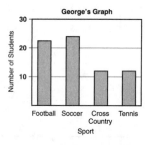

Which of these graphs could be used to give the most reliable estimate of the percentage of the Washington High School student population whose favorite fall sport is soccer?

A) Paul's
B) Maria's
C) George's
D) There is no reason to use one graph rather than another.

35. Which of these pieces of cardboard cannot be folded along the dotted lines to make a closed box?

E)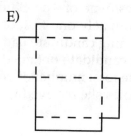

F)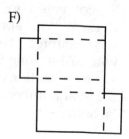

G)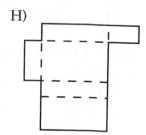

H) (image to the right)

36. What is the weight of one of the cubes if each pyramid weighs 2 pounds?

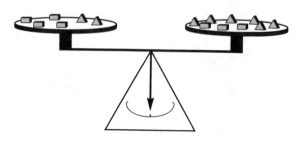

A) $\frac{1}{4}$ pound
B) 4 pounds
C) 6 pounds
D) 8 pounds

37. At what point does the graph of $3x - 2y = 6$ cross the x-axis?

E) $(0, -3)$ F) $(-3, 0)$
G) $(0, 2)$ H) $(2, 0)$

38. The graph shows a relationship between distance and time. Which statement is FALSE?

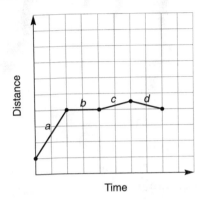

A) Segment *a* shows a sharp increase in distance.

B) Segment *b* shows distance remaining constant.

C) Segment *c* shows a gradual increase in distance.

D) Segment *d* shows a sharp decrease in distance.

39. Which graph below shows points that satisfy the equation $y = -\frac{2}{3}x + 2$?

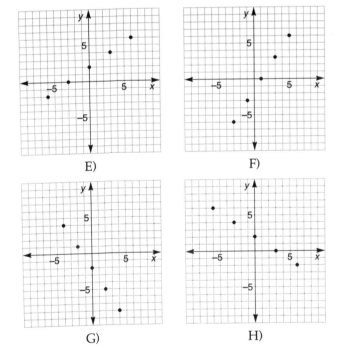

40. There are three extracurricular activity groups in a school—band, glee club, and science club. There are some students in each of those groups. Every student belongs to at least one of them, but some belong to more than one. Which of the following diagrams would best represent this situation?

A)    B)

C)   D)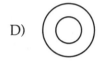

41. The length of the diagonal on a square is 6 units. What is the area of the square?

E) 12 units²
F) 18 units²
G) 12√2 units²
H) 18√2 units²

42. What is the maximum value of the function $f(x) = -x^2 + 8x + 6$?

A) 54   B) 22
C) −10   D) −42

43. Which of the following represents an exponential decay function?

E) $y = 4x$ F) $y = 4^x$
G) $y = 4^{-x}$ H) $y = x^2$

44. A jar contains 7 white marbles and 11 red marbles. A white marble is removed from the jar and set aside. What is the probability that the next marble that is removed is white?

A) $\frac{6}{17}$ B) $\frac{7}{17}$

C) $\frac{11}{17}$ D) $\frac{6}{7}$

45. What is the amplitude of the graph of $y = 6 \cos 2x$?

E) 2   F) 4

G) 6   H) 10

46. A random sample of 10,000 people was taken to determine the number of hours spent on the Internet per week. The results of the survey showed a normal distribution with a mean of 4.5 hours and a standard deviation of 0.5 hour. What is the median number of hours spent on the internet?

A) 0.5 hour

B) 4.0 hours

C) 4.5 hours

D) 5.0 hours

47. Which of the following scatter plots represents a strong positive correlation?

E)
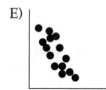

F)
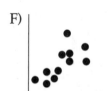

G)
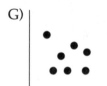

H)
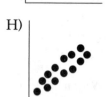

48. What is the solution of $\frac{1}{64} = 2^{2-4n}$?

A) $n = -2$ B) $n = 0$

C) $n = 1$ D) $n = 2$

49. What happens to the value of y as x becomes larger in the following equation?

$$y = \frac{1}{x}$$

E) y becomes larger.

F) y stays the same.

G) y becomes smaller.

H) y changes from positive to negative.

Directions: Show all your work and provide an explanation as directed in the question. Your score for the following question will be based on accuracy and the completeness of your process or explanation.

50. You are forming three-digit numbers from the six digits listed below. Repetition of digits is not allowed.

$$\boxed{3 \quad 4 \quad 5 \quad 6 \quad 7 \quad 8}$$

A. How many three-digit numbers can be formed?

B. How many three-digit numbers can be formed if you are allowed to repeat digits? Explain your process.

C. If repetition of digits is not allowed, how many three-digit numbers will be multiples of 5 greater than 500?

51. Which system of inequality is represented by the graph shown below?

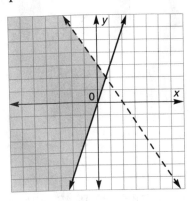

A) $y < 3x$ and $y \geq -2x + 3$

B) $y = \frac{1}{3}x$ and $y \geq -2x - 3$

C) $y \leq 3x$ and $y < -2x + 3$

D) $y \geq 3x$ and $y < -2x + 3$

52. The numbers of hours worked varies inversely as the number of people working on the job. It takes 12 hours for 4 people to finish the job. How many people are needed to finish the job in 8 hours?

E) 2 people

F) 4 people

G) 6 people

H) 8 people

53. The mean of a set of test scores is 83. If a score of 85 is added to the set and a new mean is calculated,

A) the new mean is greater than 83

B) the new mean is less than 83

C) the new mean is 83

D) the effect on the new mean cannot be determined

54. Mr. and Mrs. Baldwin and their 4 children went to the museum. The table below shows the ticket prices. If the Baldwins paid a total of $31, which of these could be the ages of their four children?

MUSEUM TICKETS	
Adults	$9.00
Seniors	$5.00
Students (13–18)	$5.00
Children (4–12)	$3.00
Children under 4	FREE

E) 14, 12, 8, and 6 years old

F) 15, 4, 3, and 2 years old

G) 16, 14, 10, and 2 years old

H) 18, 16, 14, and 13 years old

55. What is the circumference of a circle whose area is 121π square units?

A) 11 units   B) 22 units

C) 11π units   D) 22π units

56. In the isosceles triangle shown below, what is the altitude, h?

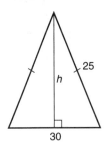

E) 25 units   F) 23 units

G) 22 units   H) 20 units

57. What are the coordinates of the center and the length of the radius of the circle whose equation is $(x + 1)^2 + y^2 = 9$?

A) center at $(1, 0)$; $r = 9$

B) center at $(1, 0)$; $r = 3$

C) center at $(0, 1)$; $r = 9$

D) center at $(-1, 0)$; $r = 3$

58. What is an accurate estimation of the area under the curve $y = x^2$ for the interval 0 to 1 and with 4 subintervals?

E) 0.50   F) 0.47

G) 0.34   H) 0.22

59. What is the sum of the infinite series shown below?

$$\frac{3}{10} + \frac{3}{100} + \frac{3}{1,000} + \frac{3}{10,000} + \cdots$$

A) $\frac{1}{10}$ B) $\frac{3}{11}$

C) $\frac{1}{3}$ D) 1

60. If $A = \begin{bmatrix} 4 & -1 \\ 0 & 1 \end{bmatrix}$ and $B = \begin{bmatrix} 1 & 2 \\ 0 & 3 \end{bmatrix}$, then $AB =$

E) $\begin{bmatrix} 5 & 4 \\ 3 & 0 \end{bmatrix}$

F) $\begin{bmatrix} 4 & 5 \\ 0 & 3 \end{bmatrix}$

G) $\begin{bmatrix} 1 & 0 \\ 0 & 1 \end{bmatrix}$

H) $\begin{bmatrix} 4 & 1 \\ 0 & 3 \end{bmatrix}$

61. The histogram shows final averages of the students enrolled in Algebra 1 at the North End High School. What percent of the students scored B or better in the course?

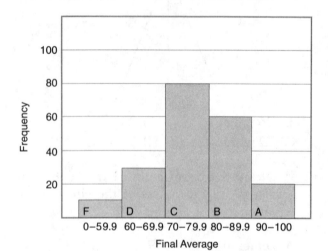

A) 20%   B) 40%

C) 60%   D) 80%

62. Find x to the nearest tenth of an inch.

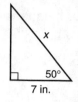

E) 4.5   F) 8.3   G) 9.1   H) 10.9

63. Simplify: $\frac{6x^2 + 12x^3}{-6x^2}$

A) $1 - 2x$ B) $-1 - 2x$
C) $-x + 2x^2$ D) $2x - 1$

64. What is the equation of the line that passes through $(-1, 5)$ and has a slope of 4?

E) $-4x + y = 9$
F) $4x + y = 9$
G) $-x + y = 5$
H) $x + y = 5$

65. A sphere has a radius of 6 cm. What happens to its surface area when the radius is doubled?

A) It is doubled.
B) It is multiplied by 4.
C) It is multiplied by 6.
D) It is multiplied by 24.

66. The area of $\triangle ABC$ which has a height of 18 units and a base of 16 units is equal to the area of a square. What is the length of a side of the square?

E) 12 units
F) $12\sqrt{2}$ units
G) 24 units
H) $24\sqrt{2}$ units

67. Which of the numbers below has all the following characteristics?
• It is a multiple of 9.
• It is a factor of 144.
• It is a perfect square.

A) 18   B) 36   C) 49   D) 72

68. During a winter storm in northern Maine, the temperature dropped from 20°F at 5 p.m. to −10°F at 3 a.m. What was the average rate of change in the temperature?

E) −7.5°F per hour
F) −3.75°F per hour
G) −3°F per hour
H) −1°F per hour

69. For which of the following situations would you use the mean to analyze the data?

A) The preferred color marker students buy
B) The day of the week on which most students are born
C) The grades a class received on a test
D) The difference between the age of the oldest and youngest students in the class

70. The mean is 82.75 and the standard deviation is 2.25. If the scores were normally distributed, which of the following scores would be most likely to occur?

E) 90   F) 87.25   G) 80.5   H) 77

71. The formula $S = 3F - 24$ can be used to find a man's shoe size, S, for a given foot length measured in inches F. What is the foot length of a man whose shoe size is 9?

A) 3 inches   B) 5 inches
C) 9 inches   D) 11 inches

72. In parallelogram $ABCD$, $m\angle A = 14x + 2$ and $m\angle B = 16x - 2$. Find $m\angle D$.

E) 6   F) 30   G) 86   H) 94

Directions: Show all your work and provide an explanation as directed in the question. Your score for the following question will be based on accuracy and the completeness of your process or explanation.

73. A. A rectangular solid has the dimensions $4 \times 6 \times 5$. A cylinder has equal volume. What is one set of values for the height and the radius of the cylinder?

  B. Is it possible for a cube to have the same volume if the lengths of the edges of the cube must be whole numbers. If yes, indicate the length of an edge. If no, between what two whole numbers is the exact answer?

74. Two angles of a triangle measure 68° and 52°. Which is the measure of an exterior angle of the triangle?

A) 28°

B) 60°

C) 120°

D) 138°

75. Which of the following is the most accurate estimation of the area under the curve $y = -x^2 + 2x + 15$?

E) *y*

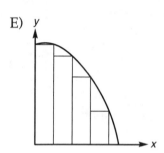

F) *y*

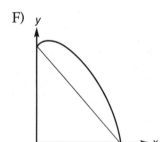

G) *y*

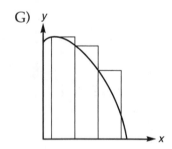

H) *y*

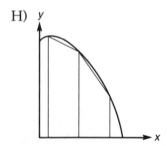

76. Melissa saved money by working over the summer. Before school started, she spent 25% of the money on jewelry and then spend $\frac{2}{3}$ of the remaining money on a digital camera. She still had $213 left. How much money did Melissa have before she started shopping?

A) $568

B) $639

C) $852

D) $2,556

77. A rectangle has vertices $P(3, 10)$, $Q(8, 10)$, $R(8, -2)$, and $S(3, -2)$. How long is the diagonal of this rectangle?

E) 12

F) $\sqrt{150}$

G) 12.5

H) 13

78. The statement "If x is divisible by 3, then it is divisible by 6" is false if x equals

A) 12

B) 15

C) 25

D) 30

79. A maximum of 400 feet of fencing is available to enclose a rectangular garden. Which inequality, where l is the length and w is the width of the garden, must be true?

E) $lw \leq 400$

F) $2l + w \leq 400$

G) $l + w \leq 200$

H) $2(l + w) \leq 200$

80. To choose a student in the class to go up to the board, your teacher puts the names of all the students on colored chips. He uses 10 blue chips, 4 white chips, 3 yellow chips, and 3 orange chips. What is the probability that your name is on a white chip?

A) 15%

B) 20%

C) 30%

D) 50%

81. In the accompanying diagram of triangle ABC, $\overline{DE} \parallel \overline{AB}$, $DE = 2x$, $AB = 5x - 1$, $CE = 3x$, and $BE = 1$. What is the length of $\overline{AB}$?

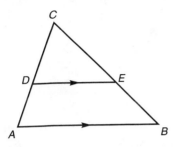

E) $\dfrac{5}{9}$

F) $\dfrac{10}{9}$

G) $\dfrac{15}{9}$

H) $\dfrac{16}{9}$

82. What is the distance between points $(-3, 2)$ and $(-2, 3)$?

A) 1
B) $\sqrt{2}$
C) $\sqrt{5}$
D) $\sqrt{10}$

83. What is the vertex of the equation $y = \dfrac{1}{2}x^2 + 2x + 3$?

E) $(-6, 9)$
F) $(-2, 1)$
G) $(0, 3)$
H) $(4, 19)$

84. What is the image of point $(-3, 6)$ under a reflection in the x-axis?

A) $(3, 6)$
B) $(3, -6)$
C) $(-3, -6)$
D) $(6, -3)$

85. The nth term in the sequence is given by the expression $3n - 1$. The first three terms in the sequence are:

E) 0, 3, 6
F) 1, 2, 3
G) 2, 5, 8
H) 3, 5, 7

86. A package being shipped must have a combined length, width, and height that is less than or equal to 20 inches. Josh has a box that is 8 in. wide and 6 in. long. What is the maximum height it can have?

A) 2 in.   B) 4 in.
C) 6 in.   D) 8 in.

87. The diameter of a bacterium in a culture dish, in inches is 5×10^{-4}. This expression is equivalent to:

E) 0.00005
F) 0.0005
G) 0.005
H) 0.05

88. If $f(x) = 5x - 2$ and $g(x) = 2x - 5$, then $f(g(2)) =$

A) 43   B) 7
C) -7 D) -43

Directions: Show all your work and provide an explanation as directed in the question. Your score for the following question will be based on accuracy and the completeness of your process or explanation.

89. The cost (C) of selling x electronic games in a store is modeled by the equation $C = \dfrac{3,200,000}{x} + 60,000$. The store profit ($P$) for these sales is modeled by the equation $P = 500x$. What is the minimum number of the electronic games that have to be sold for the profit to be greater than cost?

SAMPLE PSSA TEST #2

Section 1

Directions: You are **not** allowed to use a calculator for questions 1 through 5.

1. What must be added to $(-3)^3$ to produce a sum of 0?

   A) −27   B) 0   C) 9   D) 27

2. About 15 percent of the students are absent from school today. If 595 students are in the school today, how many students are enrolled in the school?

   E) 89   F) 506   G) 700   H) 3,967

3. $\dfrac{0.5010}{0.05} =$

   A) 0.102   B) 1.02   C) 10.02   D) 102

4. Light travels at a speed of about 186,781.7 miles per second. How far would light travel in 365 days?

   E) 5.87×10^{12} miles
   F) 6.79×10^{7} miles
   G) 7.05×10^{13} miles
   H) 9.7×10^{10} miles

5. On some days, a bakery packages cupcakes 2 to a box. On other days, cupcakes are packaged in boxes of 4 or 6. On a given day all of the cupcakes baked were packaged and there was one cupcake left over. Which of the following could **not** be the number of cupcakes baked on that day?

   A) 22   B) 25   C) 49   D) 97

Directions: You may use a calculate for the remainder of the questions on this test.

6. Which of the following is **not** a property of all parallelograms?

   E) The diagonals bisect each other.
   F) Both pairs of opposite sides are parallel.
   G) The figure has one right angle.
   H) Both pairs of opposite sides are congruent.

7. Three students started at the same flagpole in the middle of a large, flat, grassy area and chose three different directions in which to walk. Each walked for 10 yards in a straight line away from that pole. Suppose many more students did this, each walking in a direction different from the directions chosen by all the others. If you think of the final positions of the students as being points, which of the following figures would contain all of those points?

   A) Circle
   B) Square
   C) Rhombus
   D) Triangle

8. If $3y - 5 = 2 + 14y$, then $y =$

E) $-\dfrac{7}{11}$ 　　　F) $-\dfrac{3}{17}$

G) $\dfrac{3}{17}$ 　　　H) $\dfrac{7}{11}$

9. On some days, a history teacher has the students in a particular class work in groups of 4, on other days in groups of 6 or 8. However, when all students are present, there is always one student left over after the groups are formed. Which of the following could be the number of students in that class?

A) 37 　　　B) 33

C) 29 　　　D) 25

10. The general partners in a small company, Miranda, Cohen, and Brown, share its profits in the ratio of $3 : 2 : 5$, respectively. If that company's profits amount to $24,300 this year, what is Mr. Miranda's share?

E) $2,430 　　　F) $7,290

G) $8,100 　　　H) $14,580

11. Performing which set of transformations on the white figure below will NOT result in the white figure covering the black figure completely?

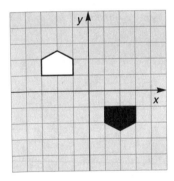

A) Reflection in the y-axis followed by reflection in the x-axis

B) Translation 4 units to the right followed by reflection in the x-axis

C) Reflection in the y-axis followed by translation 4 units down

D) Rotation of $180°$ about the origin

12. You are to form four-digit numbers using the digits below. If $a =$ the number of four-digit numbers if repetition is allowed and $b =$ the number if repetition of digits is not allowed, what is the value of $a - b$?

1, 2, 4, 6, 8, 9

E) 232 　　F) 696 　　G) 936 　　H) 1,040

13. Four friends are planning to eat at a restaurant where complete dinners cost between $12.00 and $17.00 per person. They want to leave the waiter a tip amounting to 15% of their total bill. Which of the following is the closest to what the four friends will need to leave for their combined TOTAL tip?

A) $2.00 　B) $4.00 　　C) $9.00 　　D) $15.00

14. Fifteen students' scores on their last math test are represented in the bar graph below.

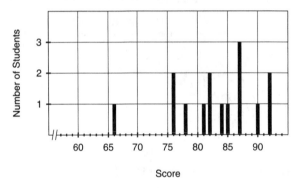

What are the mean, median, and mode for the set of scores represented in the graph above?

E) Mean = 83, median = 84, mode = 87

F) Mean = 84, median = 83, mode = 87

G) Mean = 83, median = 87, mode = 84

H) Mean = 84, median = 87, mode = 83

15. Consider the number 36; some pairs of matching positive integer factors of 36 are (2, 18), (3, 12), (4, 9), (6, 6), . . . (12, 3), (18, 2). Suppose someone graphs all possible pairs of matching positive integer factors of a given positive integer. Which of the following most likely represents such a graph?

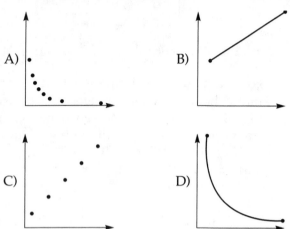

A)

B)

C)

D)

16. Which point on the number line below could represent the product of U and X?

E) Point T
F) Point V
G) Point W
H) Point Y

17. A diagram of a rectangle with dimensions 6 inches by 8 inches is placed in a copy machine that is set to enlarge all dimensions by 10 percent. Will the resulting figure fit on an $8\frac{1}{2}" \times 11"$ sheet of paper?

A) Yes; it will fit with room to spare.
B) Yes; it will just fit with no room to spare.
C) No; one dimension will fit, but not the other.
D) No; both dimensions will be too large.

18. For 45 cents, a snack-foot vending machine dispenses a small bag of chips that weighs one and one-eighth ounces. At this rate, the cost of one pound of these chips would be between:

E) $2.30 and $2.75
F) $4.30 and $4.75
G) $6.30 and $6.75
H) $8.30 and $8.75

19. The graph of function $f(x)$ is given below.

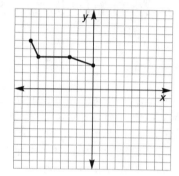

Which graph would represent $f(x) - 2$?

A)

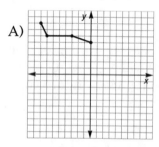

B)

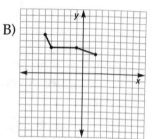

C)

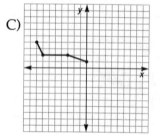

D)

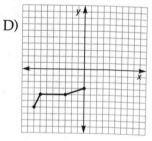

20. A right triangle has two sides of length 2 cm and 5 cm. Which of the following could be the length of the third side?

I. 3 cm   II. $\sqrt{21}$ cm   III. $\sqrt{29}$ cm

E) I only
F) III only
G) I and III
H) II and III

21. For the given right triangle, the ratio $\dfrac{9}{41}$ defines

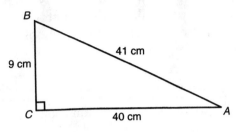

A) sin A   B) cos A   C) tan A   D) sin B

22. Triangle *MNP* is an isosceles triangle with a vertex angle of 40°. If $\overline{AB} \parallel \overline{DC} \parallel \overline{NP}$, what is the measure of $\angle ABC$?

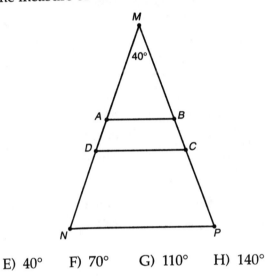

E) 40°   F) 70°   G) 110°   H) 140°

23. The tenth term of the geometric sequence $\dfrac{1}{3}, 1, 3, 9, 27, \ldots$ is:

A) 2,187   B) 6,561   C) 19,683   D) 59,049

24. Which one of the following points is included in the region defined by $-2 \le x < 8$ and $4 < y < 12$?

E) $(-2, 7)$ F) $(-2, 4)$
G) $(-2, -2)$ H) $(8, 12)$

Directions: Show all your work and provide an explanation as directed in the question. Your score for the following question will be based on accuracy and the completeness of your process or explanation.

25. The annual salaries of all employees of a small company are listed below.

President:	$110,000
Vice President:	$60,000
Senior Professional:	$50,000; $48,000; $48,000; $44,000
Junior Professional:	$36,000; $36,000; $36,000; $32,000
Clerical Staff:	$22,000; $18,000; $14,000

What are the mean, the median, and the mode of the salaries of the employees of this company? How is each of these statistics affected if one excludes the president's salary? What do your findings tell you about the statistic that should probably be used in discussions of the salary of a typical professional football player? Explain.

26. What is the height of an equilateral triangle whose perimeter is 18?

    A) 3
    B) $3\sqrt{2}$
    C) $3\sqrt{3}$
    D) 4

27. Matrix A represents the enrollment of Memorial High School. Matrix B represents the enrollment of North High School. The columns represent the grades 9–12, respectively. The rows represent male and female, respectively.

$$A = \begin{bmatrix} 143 & 163 & 158 & 162 \\ 152 & 160 & 165 & 168 \end{bmatrix}$$

$$B = \begin{bmatrix} 167 & 143 & 173 & 151 \\ 158 & 152 & 168 & 147 \end{bmatrix}$$

What is the total number of twelfth-grade girls at the two high schools combined?

    E) 290   F) 313   G) 315   H) 333

28. Suppose the U.S. Post Office has proposed increasing the cost of first-class postage to 40¢ for the first ounce or fraction thereof and 25¢ for each additional ounce or fraction thereof. Which of the graphs below best represents the cost of mailing a first-class item depending on the weight of that item in ounces?

A)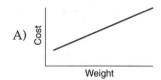

B)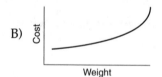

C)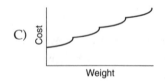

D)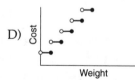

29. The students who took the written driver's test at a particular testing center one day were from three different high schools. Their test scores are given below.

Name	School	Score
Adams, J.	Gunnison	62
Baker, P.	Taylor	76
Chin, H.	Gunnison	87
Drabowski, C.	Braddock	79
Elmore, J.	Taylor	64
Ferris, W.	Braddock	83
Garver, G.	Gunnison	81
Greer, P.	Braddock	84
Harris, R.	Gunnison	92
Jacoby, P.	Taylor	92
Kelly, M.	Braddock	88
Lassiter, L.	Braddock	94
Martin, S.	Gunnison	82
Petrocelli, R.	Gunnison	74
Ramirez, R.	Taylor	84
Saunders, M.	Taylor	80
Thompson, L.	Braddock	89
Wilson, P.	Gunnison	90

All these students participated in the driver's education program offered in their own high school. Based on the students' test scores, which school's driver's education program appears to prepare its students best for the written driver's test?

    E) Braddock
    F) Gunnison
    G) Taylor
    H) Two schools appear to prepare their students equally well.

30. John has a 10-question quiz on Friday. His father agrees to give him on Saturday his regular $5 allowance plus 75 cents for each question he answered correctly on Friday's quiz. However, he will not give John any more than twice his weekly allowance. Which inequality below accurately represents the situation described above?

A) $0.75n \leq 10$
B) $5 - 0.75n \leq 10$
C) $0.75n + 5 \leq 10$
D) $(0.75 + 5)n \leq 10$

31. A plane passing through a solid gives you a cross section of the solid. For example, the cross section of a solid pyramid shown below is a triangular region. (See shaded figure.)

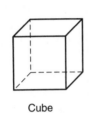

Pyramid   Cube

Which of the following plane figures cannot be a cross section of a solid cube?

E)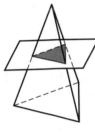

F)

G)

H)

32.

Each of the students in a class rolled a number cube one hundred times and graphed how many times each number came up. (Each face of the cube is labeled with just one of the digits 1, 2, 3, 4, 5, 6.) Which graph below most likely represents the one the students made of the results of their whole class?

A)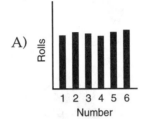

B)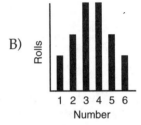

C)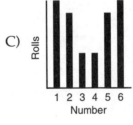

D)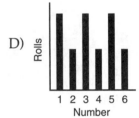

33. You are playing a game in which you move a chip on a number line. Where you move the chip is determined by the cards you draw from a pack. Each card has an integer printed on it. Your chip is now at the position shown below.

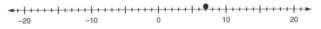

On each turn, you move your chip to the location with the coordinate equal to the sum of the coordinate of your current location and the number on the card you draw. Suppose you draw cards with the following sequence of numbers: $-2, 6, -7, -12, -4$. What is the coordinate of the location of your chip after you complete this sequence of moves?

E) 12   F) 11
G) -12 H) -19

34. The Burger Baron Restaurant is open from 6 a.m. until midnight and serves all meals. Every half hour during an 8-hour period last Tuesday, Ronald counted the number of customers in that restaurant. He graphed his data but forgot to label the time-of-day axis.

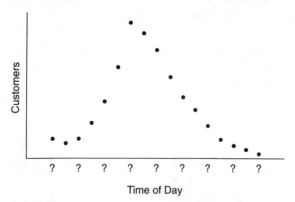

Time of Day

Which of the following time-of-day axis is most likely labeled the way it should have been in Ronald's graph?

A)

3 p.m.	4	5	6	7	8	9	10	11

B)

10 a.m.	11	12 p.m.	1	2	3	4	5	6

C)

12 p.m.	1	2	3	4	5	6	7	8

D)

6 a.m.	7	8	9	10	11	12 p.m.	1	2

35. Keisha works for a florist making bouquets. On a given day the florist has daisies, carnations, roses, lilies, and poppies in stock. How many combinations of flowers can she have for bouquets if she wants to include at least three different types of flowers?

E) 10   F) 15   G) 16   H) 60

36. What is the pattern of the units digit in the sequence $8^1, 8^2, 8^3, 8^4, \ldots, 8^n$?

A) 8, 4, 6, 2   B) 8, 6, 4, 2
C) 8, 2, 4, 6   D) 8, 4, 2, 6

37. A card is drawn at random from a standard deck of 52 playing cards. The card is put back in the deck, and a card is again drawn at random. Find the probability that the first card is a diamond and the second card is also a diamond.

E) $\frac{1}{2}$ F) $\frac{1}{4}$ G) $\frac{3}{13}$ H) $\frac{1}{16}$

38. Which of the following figures does NOT have both line symmetry and rotational symmetry?

A)    B)

C)   D)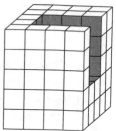

39. A solid box-shaped structure is made of layers of unit cubes stacked one above the other. A $2 \times 3 \times 3$ block of unit cubes has been removed from this structure. Assume that no cubes other than the ones in the region indicated by shading have been removed. How many unit cubes are contained in the structure pictured above?

E) 73   F) 82   G) 94   H) 100

40. Jane threw a dart that landed in the 3-point area of the target pictured below. Bill threw a dart that landed in its 1-point area.

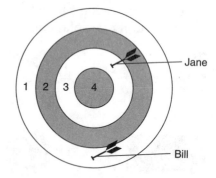

Each of them has just one more dart to throw. It is now Jane's turn. In what area(s) of the target could Jane throw her dart so that she is sure to win, that is, so that Bill's total points cannot tie or exceed her total points?

A) In the 4-point area only
B) In the 4-point or in the 3-point area only
C) In the 4-point, in the 3-point, or in the 2-point area
D) Jane cannot be sure she will win until after she and Bill both throw their darts.

41. Which of the following functions has a minimum value of 5?

E)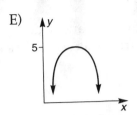

F)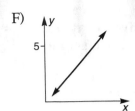

G)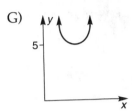

H)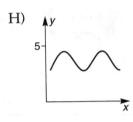

42. Which of the following is the range of this relation?

$$\{(-4, 0), (2, 4), (-1, 0), (-3, 5)\}$$

A) $\{-4, 2, -1, 3\}$
B) $\{0, 4, 5\}$
C) $\{-4, -3, -1, 5\}$
D) $\{0\}$

43. The dimensions of a rectangular park are 66 yards by 88 yards. Juanita needs to walk from the southeast corner of the park to the northwest corner. How many yards longer is it to walk along the edges than to walk along the diagonal?

E) 4   F) 44   G) 54   H) 110

44. If $x = -4$, what is the value of the expression $x^2 + x^3$?

A) 80   B) 48   C) −48   D) −80

45. The diagonal of a square is 12 units. What is the area of the square?

E) 24 units^2
F) 72 units^2
G) $24\sqrt{2}$ units^2
H) $72\sqrt{2}$ units^2

46. The median height of the players on a basketball team is 6 ft 4 in. This means:

A) the tallest player is 6 ft 4 in.
B) no player is shorter than 6 ft 4 in.
C) an equal number of players are taller than 6 ft 4 in. and shorter than 6 ft 4 in.
D) most of the players are 6 ft 4 in.

47. The difference between the sum of the interior angles of a triangle and the sum of its exterior angles is

E) −180°
F) 0°
G) 180°
H) 360°

48. $A = \begin{bmatrix} 4 & -1 \\ 2 & 3 \end{bmatrix}$, $B = \begin{bmatrix} -1 & -3 \\ 0 & 6 \end{bmatrix}$, and $C = \begin{bmatrix} 2 & 3 \\ 5 & 8 \end{bmatrix}$

What is $AC - B$?

A) $\begin{bmatrix} 3 & 4 \\ 14 & 30 \end{bmatrix}$

B) $\begin{bmatrix} 2 & 1 \\ 14 & 36 \end{bmatrix}$

C) $\begin{bmatrix} 4 & 7 \\ 19 & 24 \end{bmatrix}$

D) $\begin{bmatrix} 2 & -4 \\ -3 & -5 \end{bmatrix}$

49. Which regression equation best fits the data shown below?

E) $y = 2x + 5$
F) $y = 2x - 5$
G) $y = -2x + 5$
H) $y = -2x - 5$

Directions: Show all your work and provide an explanation as directed in the question. Your score for the following question will be based on accuracy and the completeness of your process or explanation.

50. Every Wednesday at the Pizza Express, the manager gives away free slices of pizza and soda. Every eighth customer gets a free slice of pizza and every twelfth customer gets a free soda. The Pizza Express served 87 customers last Wednesday.

    A. How many free sodas were given away last Wednesday?

    B How many free slices of pizza were given away?

    C Did any customer receive both a free slice of pizza and a free soda? If so how many customers?

    D. If soda sells for $1.00 and a slice of pizza sells for $1.25, how much did the Pizza Express lose in income by giving away these items? Justify your answer.

Section 3

51. How many cubes with a side of length 2 inches can be packed into a box with the dimensions of 12 inches by 6 inches by 3 inches?

    A) 216   B) 27   C) 18   D) 3

52. Which of the following represents an exponential growth function?

    E) $P(t) = 5t^2$
    F) $P(t) = -5t^2$
    G) $P(t) = 5^t$
    H) $P(t) = 5^{-t}$

53. What is the equation of the line that passes through the points (4, 6) and (0, −2)?

    A) $y = 2x - 2$
    B) $y = -2x + 2$
    C) $y = x + 2$
    D) $y = -x + 2$

54. In parallelogram $QRST$, $QR = 3x + 5$; $RT = 2x + 7$; $ST = 6x + 14$. What is RT?

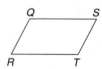

    E) −3   F) −1   G) 1   H) 3

55. On a standardized test with a normal distribution, the mean was 42 and the standard deviation was 2.6. Which score could be expected to occur less than 5 percent of the time?

    A) 50   B) 45   C) 39   D) 37

56. The shaded half plane in the accompanying figure is a graph of which inequality?

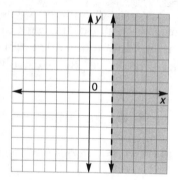

    E) $x > 2$
    F) $y > 2$
    G) $x < 2$
    H) $y \geq 1$

57. A ladder 39 feet long leans against a building and reaches the bottom ledge of a window. If the foot of the ladder is 15 feet from the foot of the building, how high is the window ledge above the ground?

    A) 24 feet
    B) 24.2 feet
    C) 36 feet
    D) 41.8 feet

58. The volume of a gas, V, is inversely proportional to its pressure, P. Write an equation of the variation when the volume of gas is 343 cubic units at a pressure of 200.

   E) $VP = 6{,}860$
   F) $V = 6{,}860P$
   G) $VP = 68{,}600$
   H) $P = 6.8V$

59. What are the coordinates of the center and the length of the radius of the circle whose equation is $(x + 2)^2 + y^2 = 25$?

   A) center at $(2, 0)$; $r = 5$
   B) center at $(-2, 0)$; $r = 5$
   C) center at $(0, 2)$; $r = 5$
   D) center at $(0, -2)$; $r = 5$

60. The regression equation that models the number of chocolate candies (C) a machine makes per minute is based on the temperature T, in degrees Fahrenheit, has been found to be $C = 7T - 59$. How many pieces of chocolate candy are expected if the temperature is $32°$ Fahrenheit?

   E) 7   F) 165   G) 284   H) 869

61. Pairs of interior and exterior angles in a polygon are:

   A) always equal
   B) never equal
   C) complementary
   D) supplementary

62. If 1 ounce of silver costs \$5.50, what will $2\frac{1}{2}$ pounds of silver cost?

   E) \$88   F) \$176   G) \$200   H) \$220

63. If the surface area of a cube is 96 cm^2, what is the length of a side?

   A) 3 cm
   B) 4 cm
   C) 5 cm
   D) 6 cm

64. There are 20 students in a club. In how many different ways can a president, vice president, treasurer, and secretary be elected from the club members?

   E) 20
   F) 40
   G) 11,880
   H) 116,280

65. If $a = A + bt$, what is the value of t when $a = 116$, $A = 20$, and $b = 32$?

   A) 3,732
   B) 96
   C) 64
   D) 3

66. Simplify: $\dfrac{a^4 b^3 c^7}{a^{-2} b^2 c^{-1}}$

   E) $a^{-1} b c^{-8}$
   F) $a^6 b c^8$
   G) $a^2 b^5 c^6$
   H) $a^{-2} b^{-1} c^{-6}$

67. What is the minimum value of the function $y = x^2 - 8x + 5$?

   A) -11
   B) -7
   C) 5
   D) 11

68. What is the amplitude of the function $y = \dfrac{1}{2} \cos 3x$?

   E) $\dfrac{1}{2}$
   F) 1
   G) 2
   H) 3

69. If $4.5^x = 97$, an approximate value of x is:

   A) 2.15
   B) 3.04
   C) 3.16
   D) 3.47

70. Which of the following numbers is between $\frac{1}{10,000}$ and $\frac{1}{100,000}$, and is correctly expressed in scientific notation?

    E) 4.5×10^{-3}
    F) 4.5×10^{3}
    G) 4.5×10^{-4}
    H) 4.5×10^{-5}

71. A picture has a ratio of length to width of 8 to 5. If the width is 35 cm, how many centimeters is the length of the picture?

    A) 22
    B) 35
    C) 48
    D) 56

72. The toll on a bridge is $2 for a car and driver and $0.75 for each additional passenger. If the toll for Marigold's car was $4.25, how many people were riding in it?

    E) 2
    F) 3
    G) 4
    H) 5

Directions: Show all your work and provide an explanation as directed in the question. Your score for the following question will be based on accuracy and the completeness of your process or explanation.

73. The table gives the average weight for men of different heights. The data is for men with medium frames, ages 30 to 39 years old.

MEN	
Height (in.)	Weight (lb)
64	145
66	153
68	161
70	170
72	179
74	188
76	199

    A. Make a scatter plot of the given data. Put height on the horizontal axis and weight on the vertical axis.

    B. Draw a line of best fit and determine an regression equation that can be used to describe the data.

    C. Predict the average weight of a man 84 inches tall.

74. $\sqrt{8} \times \sqrt{30} =$

   A) $4\sqrt{15}$
   B) $15\sqrt{4}$
   C) $12\sqrt{20}$
   D) $10\sqrt{24}$

75. Three numbers are consecutive integers. The square of the second number is 8 more than the sum of the other two numbers. Which of the following is a solution?

   E) 0, 1, 2
   F) 1, 2, 3
   G) 2, 3, 4
   H) 3, 4, 5

76. If x varies directly as y and $x = 2.4$ when $y = 6$, which is a possible ordered pair for (x, y)?

   A) (24, 6)
   B) (0.4, 1)
   C) (0.4, 2.5)
   D) (1, 2.4)

77. Wire braces are needed for the 80-foot ridgepole of a circus tent. Each brace is supposed to make a 60° angle with the ground. Find, to the nearest foot, how long each brace should be.

   E) 46 feet
   F) 69 feet
   G) 92 feet
   H) 139 feet

78. The midpoint of a line segment AB is $(-1, 5)$. If the coordinates of A are $(-3, 2)$, what are the coordinates of B?

   A) (1, 10)
   B) (1, 8)
   C) (0, 7)
   D) (-5, 8)

79. Which word has vertical line symmetry?

   E) WOW   F) EVE
   G) DAD   H) BOB

80. Which must be a value in the data set?

   A) mean
   B) median
   C) mode
   D) none of the above

81. Meg buys 2 kinds of lettuce, 2 kinds of tomatoes, and 3 kinds of dressing. To make a salad, she will use 1 kind of lettuce, 1 kind of tomato, and 1 kind of dressing. How many salads can she make?

   E) 3   F) 6   G) 7   H) 12

82. If a football team played 40 games in a season and won 24 of them, what percent of the games did the team win?

   A) 16%
   B) 24%
   C) 40%
   D) 60%

83. If the temperature was −39.5° yesterday and +6.7° today, by how much did the temperature rise?

   E) 3.28°
   F) 4.62°
   G) 32.8°
   H) 46.2°

84. The ratio of the surface areas of two cubes is 3 to 4. What is the ratio of the volume of the smaller cube to the volume of the larger cube?

   A) 3 to 8
   B) $\sqrt{3}$ to 2
   C) 3 to 4
   D) $3\sqrt{3}$ to 8

85. What is the minimum value of the equation $(2x + 1)(2x - 3) = 0$?

   E) 5   F) 4   G) −4   H) −5

86. If this pattern is continued, how many dots will be needed to represent the ninth term?

A) 81
B) 90
C) 110
D) 132

87. A circle is inscribed in a 2-by-2 square. A grain of rice is dropped onto the square. What is the probability that the rice lands on part of the square but not the circle?

E) 4
F) π
G) $4 - \pi$
H) $\dfrac{(4 - \pi)}{4}$

88. In the accompanying diagram of triangle ABC, segment BC is extended through C to D. If $m\angle ABC = 4x - 6$, $m\angle BAC = 8x$, and $m\angle ACD = 10x + 10$, find $m\angle ACB$.

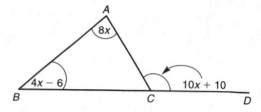

A) 26
B) 60
C) 90
D) 120

Directions: Show all your work and provide an explanation as directed in the question. Your score for the following question will be based on accuracy and the completeness of your process or explanation.

89. A rocket carrying fireworks is launched from a hill 80 feet above a lake. The rocket will fall into the lake after exploding at its maximum height. The rocket's height, h, above the surface of the lake is given by $h = -16t^2 + 64t + 80$, where t is time in seconds.

A. At what time, t, does the rocket reach the maximum height?
B. What is the maximum height of the rocket?
C. How long will it take for the rocket to hit the lake?

Section 1

Directions: You are **not** allowed to use a calculator for questions 1 through 5.

1. Plastic spoons come in packages of 20, plastic forks in packages of 15, and plastic knives in packages of 12. A place setting requires a knife, a spoon, and a fork. What is the least number of packages of spoons, forks, and knives you can buy in order to get an equal number of each?

   A) 3 spoons, 4 forks, 5 knives
   B) 4 spoons, 3 forks, 5 knives
   C) 3 spoons, 5 forks, 4 knives
   D) 5 spoons, 4 forks, 3 knives

2. The cost of a blank tape went from $3.50 to $3.85. Find the percent of increase.

   E) 0.01%
   F) 0.10%
   G) 1%
   H) 10%

3. $\dfrac{0.0248}{0.008} =$

   A) 0.031
   B) 0.310
   C) 3.10
   D) 31.0

4. Between what two integers does 4.23×10^{-5} lie?

   E) 1 and 2
   F) 0 and 1
   G) -4 and -5
   H) -5 and -6

5. Patrick is paid at a rate of $9.50 an hour for the first 40 hours of a week that he works. He is paid time and a half for any hours over 40. How much more will Patrick make working 50 hours compared with working 46 hours?

   A) $57.00
   B) $85.00
   C) $142.50
   D) $522.50

Directions: You may use a calculator for the remainder of the questions on this test.

6. An ordering code at a manufacturing company is issued in the following pattern.

digit	letter	letter	digit	digit

Every digit or letter can be used. How many different ordering codes can be produced by the manufacturing company?

E) 676,000

F) 325,000

G) 105,000

H) 67,000

7. The graph of $y = 3x$ is shown below. Which statement below is true about the graph of $y = 3x + 2$?

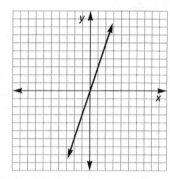

A) It is perpendicular to the graph of $y = 3x$.

B) It is a translation (slide) of the graph of $y = 3x$ two units up.

C) It intersects the graph of $y = 3x$ at the origin.

D) It is a translation (slide) of the graph of $y = 3x$ two units to the right.

8. Weatherpersons predict tomorrow's weather based on what has happened in the past on the days following days just like today. During the past 50 years, there have been 380 December days that have been just like today, and of those, 200 have been followed by a clear day. Which of the following is the approximate probability of a clear day tomorrow that would be given by a weatherperson using the prediction rule described in this problem?

E) 13 percent

F) 34 percent

G) 53 percent

H) 66 percent

9. Which of these inequalities would be most helpful in solving the problem stated below?

> Bart spent an evening playing video games and drinking sodas. Each video game cost 25 cents to play, and sodas cost 60 cents each. Bart had $8 to spend only on video games and sodas. If he had only 3 sodas and played as many video games as he could, how many video games did he play?

A) $0.25x + 1.80 \leq 8$

B) $x + 1.80 \leq 8$

C) $0.60x + 0.75 \leq 8$

D) $3x + 0.25 \leq 8$

10. Which statements are equivalent to one another?

   I. Every year, Americans spend $2 million on exercise equipment and $10 million on potato chips.

   II. Every year, Americans spend 5 times as much on potato chips as they do on exercise equipment.

   III. Every year, Americans spend 20% as much on exercise equipment as they do on potato chips.

E) I and II only

F) I and III only

G) II and III only

H) I, II, and III

11. The squares pictured below are all congruent to the one shown at the right. Each of the squares has part of its interior shaded. Which of the squares appears to have the same fraction of its interior shaded as the given one has?

I.   II.   III.   IV.

A) All of them

B) I and II only

C) I, III, and IV only

D) None of them

12. Twin primes are primes that are two consecutive odd integers, such as 3, 5; 11, 13; 17, 19. How many twin primes (pairs) are there between 10 and 100?

E) 5   F) 6   G) 7   H) 8

13. If the product of 7 integers is positive, then, at most, how many of the integers could be negative?

A) 2   B) 4   C) 6   D) 7

14. Six slips of paper with the letters A through F written on them are placed into a shoe box. The six slips are drawn one by one from the box. What is the probability that the first three to be drawn are A, D, F in any order?

E) $\frac{1}{20}$ F) $\frac{1}{6}$ G) $\frac{1}{3}$ H) $\frac{1}{2}$

15. Given: Circle A represents even numbers.
    Circle B represents perfect squares.
    Circle C represents powers of 10.

Which of the following would be included in the shaded region?

A) {100, 200, 300}
B) {64, 100, 144}
C) {10, 100, 1,000}
D) {100, 10,000, 1,000,000}

16. A printing company makes bumper stickers that cost $0.75 per copy plus a $5.00 set-up fee. If you spend $80 to purchase a supply of bumper stickers, how many do you get?

E) 50   F) 75   G) 100   H) 150

17. The Mustangs and the Bruins play in a basketball tournament. The team that first wins three games wins the tournament. Assuming ties are not possible, find the number of possible ways in which the tournament can occur.

A) 6   B) 9   C) 20   D) 24

18. During a baseball season, 70 percent of the major league outfielders had at least 20 home runs. Knowing this, which of the following must be greater than or equal to 20?

 I. The mean number of home runs
 II. The mode of the number of home runs
 III. The median number of home runs

E) I only   F) II only
G) III only   H) I and II

19. Malcolm graphed all possible combinations of the numbers of correct and incorrect responses students could obtain on a 20-question true-false test. Which graph below MOST LIKELY resembles Malcolm's graph?

A) 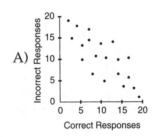   B)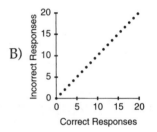

C) 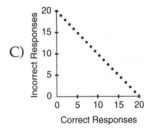   D)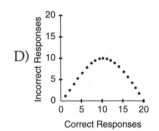

20. The graph of $x + y = 8$ crosses the x-axis at point A. The graph of $2x - y = 8$ crosses the line $y = 6$ at point B. What is the distance from point A to point B?

E) 6   F) $\sqrt{37}$ G) 7   H) $\sqrt{53}$

21. The given figure consists of 9 congruent squares. Which of the following is a square you could remove and not change the perimeter of the entire figure?

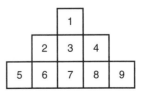

A) Square 1   B) Square 2
C) Square 7   D) Square 9

22. How many degrees are in the angle between the hands of a clock at 9:30?

E) 90°   F) 95°   G) 105°   H) 120°

23. A special operation is defined by the rule (for real numbers):

$$a * b = \frac{a + b}{2}$$

For example, $6 * 10 = \frac{1}{2}(6 + 10) = \frac{1}{2}(16) = 8$.

Which of the following is NOT a valid property concerning this special operation?

A) $a * a = a$
B) $a * b = b * a$
C) $a * (-a) = 0$
D) $a * (b + c) = (a * b) + (a * c)$

24. A linear function is displayed in the given table. When graphed, where would the line cross the x-axis?

x	y
4	3
6	1
10	-3

E) $(0, 7)$ F) $(7, -1)$
G) $(7, 0)$ H) $(8, 0)$

Directions: Show all your work and provide an explanation as directed in the question. Your score for the following question will be based on accuracy and the completeness of your process or explanation.

25. A cylindrical jar with height 8 inches and diameter 6 inches is filled to 75% of its capacity with juice. The juice is then poured into another cylindrical container with a 10-inch diameter and height of 4 inches.

   A. To what percent of its capacity is the second container filled with juice? Show your procedure.

   B. The juice is poured into a third container such that the entire amount of juice only takes up 27% of the capacity of the container. As a result, what would one pair of possible dimensions be for the diameter and height of this third container? Show your approach.

Section 2

26. Which of the following is the graph of $y = 2^{-0.45x}$?

A)
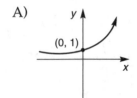

B)
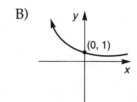

C)
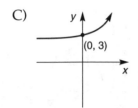

D)
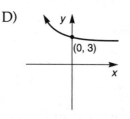

27. Three vertices of an isosceles trapezoid are at $(-4, 0)$, $(4, 0)$, and $(-1, 6)$. The bases of the figure are horizontal. Find the number of square units in the area of the isosceles trapezoid.

E) 27   F) 30   G) 54   H) 60

28. Which of the following equations has two real solutions?

A) $2^x = 32$ B) $x^2 + 16 = 0$
C) $\frac{1}{x} = \frac{7}{11}$ D) $|x - 6| = 9$

29. Parallelogram *ABCD* is not a rectangle. Which of these statements is NOT always true?

    E) The diagonals are equal in length.
    F) The diagonals bisect each other.
    G) There is no line of symmetry.
    H) All are true.

30. The whole numbers from 1 to 40 are each written on a small slip of paper and placed in a box. One slip of paper is selected at random from the box. What is the probability that the number selected is prime if you are given that it is a factor of 36?

    A) 0   B) $\dfrac{1}{20}$ C) $\dfrac{1}{18}$ D) $\dfrac{2}{9}$

31. Which of the following would NOT change the mean for these five scores?

    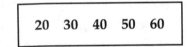

    I. Add two scores: a 10 and a 70.
    II. Add three more scores of 40.
    III. Add 5 to each score.

    E) I only   F) II only
    G) I and II   H) I, II, and III

32. The Straight as an Arrow Company paints lines on the streets of different towns. The company charges $100 plus $0.25 per foot. Which of the following is a reasonable graph for length vs. total charge?

    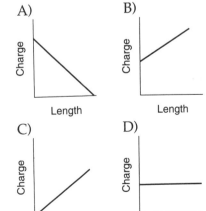

33. What is the value of $a + b + c$ if $(12)(18)(750) = (2^a)(3^b)(5^c)$?

    E) 9   F) 10   G) 11   H) 12

34. The numbers -3, -4, and 6 are each used once and substituted at random for a, b, and c in the equation $ax + b = c$. What is the probability that x turns out to be negative?

    A) 0   B) $\dfrac{1}{3}$ C) $\dfrac{1}{2}$ D) 1

35. What is the simplified expression for the shaded area of the given rectangle?

    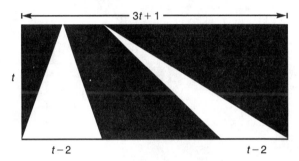

    E) $2t^2 + 3t$ F) $2t^2 - t$
    G) $2t^2$ H) $3t^2 - t$

36.

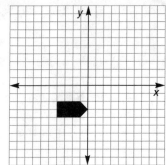

If the figure on the grid above were translated 3 units to the right and then reflected in the *x*-axis, which picture below would show the result?

A)

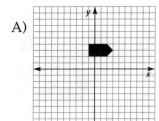

B)

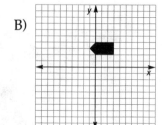

C)

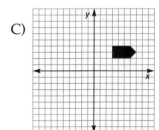

D)

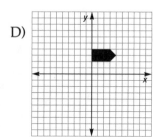

37. The graph at the right corresponds to Mrs. Johnson's auto trip from one town to another.

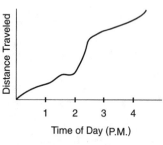

What was most likely happening between 2:00 and 2:30 p.m.?

E) Mrs. Johnson was in heavy traffic.

F) Mrs. Johnson had stopped for lunch.

G) Mrs. Johnson was looking for a parking place downtown.

H) Mrs. Johnson was traveling on a highway.

38. The congruent triangular regions pictured below could be glued together along entire matching sides to form different quadrilateral regions, depending on which pairs of sides are glued together. Which two sides should be glued together to form the region with the smallest perimeter?

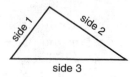 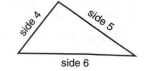

A) Sides 1 and 4

B) Sides 2 and 5

C) Sides 3 and 6

D) The perimeters of all the quadrilateral regions formed in that way would be the same.

39. Four friends share an amount of money. The shares are in the ratio $1 : 2 : 3 : 6$. If the difference between the largest share and the smallest share is $200, what was the original amount to be shared?

E) $400   F) $480   G) $1,200   H) $4,800

40. Which of the following expressions has a maximum value of 7?

A) $x^2 + 2x + 6$

B) $2x^2 + 6x + 7$

C) $-x^2 + 2x + 6$

D) $-2x^2 + 6x + 7$

41. Which of the following relations is **not** a function?

E) $\{(-1, 0), (2, 1), (-3, 4), (5, -1)\}$

F) $\{(1, 1), (-1, 2), (3, 6), (7, 8)\}$

G) $\{(1, 1), (3, 1), (1, 8), (2, -3)\}$

H) $\{(-4, 4), (2, 5), (3, 1), (7, -8)\}$

42. The radius of a cone is doubled and the height remains the same. The volume is multiplied by $\left(V = \dfrac{1}{3}\pi r^2 h \right)$:

A) 2   B) 4   C) 6   D) 8

43. For every cup of sugar in a recipe, 5 cups of flour are needed. If 3 cups of sugar are used, how many cups of flour are needed?

E) 3 cups   F) 5 cups
G) 10 cups   H) 15 cups

44. If $a = 2$, what is the value of the expression $a^4 - a^2 + 1$?

A) 21   B) 13   C) 12   D) 1

45. The area of a square is 64 in.². What is the length of the diagonal?

E) 8 in.   F) 16 in.
G) $8\sqrt{2}$ in.   H) $16\sqrt{2}$ in.

46. For a set of data showing the number of books read by Ms. Corson's AP English class, the median was 8 and the average was 12. Which statement must be true?

A) Fifty percent of the students read 8 books.
B) Fifty percent of the students read 12 books.
C) At least one student read more than 12 books.
D) Most students read 8 books.

47. A road sign is shaped like a regular hexagon. If the length of one side is represented by $k + 8$, its perimeter would be represented by

E) $6k + 8$ F) $8k + 8$
G) $6k + 48$ H) $8k + 64$

48. $A = \begin{bmatrix} 3 & -1 & 0 \\ 4 & 1 & 2 \end{bmatrix}$ and $B = \begin{bmatrix} 1 & 0 \\ 2 & 1 \\ 3 & 3 \end{bmatrix}$.

What is AB?

A) $\begin{bmatrix} 1 & -1 \\ 12 & 7 \end{bmatrix}$

B) $\begin{bmatrix} 12 & 7 \\ 1 & -1 \end{bmatrix}$

C) $\begin{bmatrix} 3 & -1 & 0 \\ 10 & -1 & 2 \\ 21 & 0 & 6 \end{bmatrix}$

D) $\begin{bmatrix} 0 & -1 & 3 \\ 2 & -1 & 10 \\ 6 & 0 & 21 \end{bmatrix}$

49. Which regression equation best fits the data shown below?

E) $y = 2x^2 - 7x + 3$
F) $y = -2x^2 + 7x - 3$
G) $y = x$
H) $y = x + 2$

Directions: Show all your work and provide an explanation as directed in the question. Your score for the following question will be based on accuracy and the completeness of your process or explanation.

50. An auditorium has 40 rows of seats. There are 10 seats in the first row, 12 seats in the second row, and so on, with 2 more seats in each row than in the previous row.

A. How many seats are in the auditorium? Explain how you arrived at your answer.
B. Two students, Tom and Brandon, were looking at the seating arrangement in the auditorium. Tom came to the conclusion that 50% of the seats must be in the first 20 rows, since there are 40 rows in the auditorium. Brandon had a feeling that this couldn't possibly be so. Who is correct? Explain your thinking.
C. If 50% is not correct, give the correct percent for the fraction of the seats in the first 20 rows and show how you arrived at the value.

51. Amanda needs to pack square boxes, with a length of 3 cm on each side, into a larger box with the dimensions shown below. How many boxes can she pack?

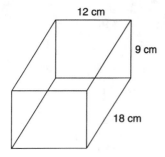

12 cm

9 cm

18 cm

A) 1,944 B) 108
C) 72 D) 27

52. What is the diameter of a circle whose area is 225π units^2?

E) 15 F) 30
G) 15π H) 30π

53. When a baseball is hit into the air, its height in feet during the flight is given by the function $h(t) = 140 + 420t - 14t^2$ where $h(t)$ is the height in t seconds. What is the maximum height of the baseball?

A) 15 feet B) 140 feet
C) 3,290 feet D) 3,300 feet

54. A store has 3 entrances. Shoppers can go between the first floor and the second floor by a stairway, an elevator, and an escalator. How many ways can a shopper enter from outside, go to the second floor, return to the first floor, and leave the building?

E) 12 F) 27
G) 81 H) 243

55. If tan $\angle A = 0.75$ and the side adjacent to $\angle A$ is 12 units long, how long is the side opposite $\angle A$?

A) 85 units B) 37 units
C) 16 units D) 9 units

56. The vertices of a rectangle are $(-2, 3)$, $(4, 3)$, $(4, 7)$, and $(-2, 7)$. If the midpoints of the four sides are joined, what kind of quadrilateral is formed?

E) Rectangle
F) Rhombus
G) Square
H) Trapezoid

57. Express $\dfrac{(2a^2b^4)^2}{2a^3b^{-5}}$ without using negative exponents.

A) $1ab^3$ B) $2ab^{13}$
C) $\dfrac{2a}{b}$ D) $\dfrac{2b^3}{a}$

58. The test scores in Mrs. Kate's statistics class are normally distributed with a mean of 85 and a standard deviation of 5. Between what two scores would 95.4 percent of the scores fall?

E) 70–100 F) 75–95
G) 80–90 H) 85–90

59. The profits of an Internet auction company can be represented by the function $P = -t^2 + 8t + 12$, where P represents profits in hundreds of thousands of dollars and t represents the years since the company started in the year 2000. According to the model, in what year will the company have maximum profits?

A) 1996 B) 2000
C) 2004 D) 2008

60. What is the equation of the line that passes through the point $(-2, -1)$ and has a slope of $-\dfrac{3}{7}$?

E) $3x + 7y = -13$
F) $3x + y = 13$
G) $7y - 3x = -13$
H) $x + y = 13$

61. Which set of inequalities describes the shaded area of the graph?

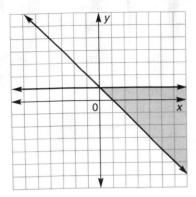

A) $y < 1$ and $x + y > 2$
B) $y \leq 1$ and $x + y \geq 2$
C) $y < 3x$ and $y \geq -2x + 3$
D) $y > 3x$ and $y < -2x + 3$

62. The amount of tip each waiter receives after a wedding is inversely proportional to the number of waiters serving the event. If the total amount for tips at the Klaiwith-Sims wedding was $1,200 and n represents the number waiters and t represents the tip received, which of these represents the relationship between n and t?

E) $n = \dfrac{t}{1,200}$

F) $1,200 = \dfrac{n}{t}$

G) $1,200 = \dfrac{t}{n}$

H) $n = \dfrac{1,200}{t}$

63. Ms. Christie, a salesperson, is paid $300 a week plus commission. Her commission is 5% of her weekly sales. In the month of January, her weekly sales totals were:

Week 1	Week 2	Week 3	Week 4
$8,576	$9,500	$7,362	$10,567

What is her average weekly commission?

A) $429   B) $450
C) $528   D) $1,800

64. If the altitude of an equilateral triangle is $21\sqrt{3}$ inches, what is the perimeter of the triangle?

E) 63 inches
F) 99.4 inches
G) 109.1 inches
H) 126 inches

65. Jessica is planting a quarter-circle garden in her square yard. As shown below, one side of the yard is 30 feet long. To the nearest tenth of a square yard, what part of her yard will not be included in the garden?

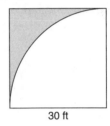

30 ft

A) 900.0   B) 706.9
C) 193.1   D) 192.1

66. Johnny has taken four math tests and has a mean score of 89 points. What does he need to earn on his fifth test to make the mean score exactly 90 points?

E) 90   F) 92
G) 94   H) 95

67. If $\angle A$ and $\angle B$ are complementary angles, which of the following is not correct?

A) $(\sin A)(\sin B) = \cos B$
B) $(\tan A)(\tan B) = 1$
C) $\sin(A + B) = 1$
D) $\sin B = \sin A$

68. A building casts a shadow 24 feet long. At the same time, Andy, who is 5 feet tall, casts a 3-foot shadow. What is the height of the building?

E) 14.4 ft   F) 30 ft
G) 40 ft   H) 60.5 ft

69. The volume of a cylinder is 216 in.³. What is the volume of a cone with the same radius and height as the cylinder? ($V = \pi r^2 h$)

A) 54 in.³   B) 72 in.³
C) 108 in.³   D) 648 in.³

70. A scale model of a house is $\frac{1}{48}$ the actual size of the house. If the actual house is 30 ft wide, how wide is the scale model?

E) 625 in.   F) 7.5 in.
G) 10 in.   H) 1.6 ft.

71. The scatter plot shown below could represent two sets of data with what kind of relationship?

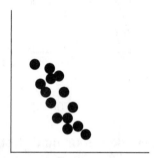

A) Strong negative correlation
B) Strong positive correlation
C) Negative correlation
D) Positive correlation

72. Mr. Johnson records the number of miles traveled each time he fills up his gas tank and has recently noticed that his car has been getting lower gas mileage. He has calculated that the mileage he gets per gallon is changing according to the function $y = 28 - 0.65x$. On his twelfth fill-up, how many miles per gallon did he get?

E) 27.35
F) 20.20
G) 16.00
H) 7.80

Directions: Show all your work and provide an explanation as directed in the question. Your score for the following question will be based on accuracy and the completeness of your process or explanation.

73. Figure *ABCD* is a square.

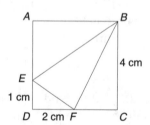

A. To the nearest tenth of a centimeter, find the perimeter of triangle *EFB*.
B. Vanessa was able to show that triangle *EFB* is a right triangle. Explain a method to show this.
C. As a result, Vanessa found the area of triangle *EFB* by using the formula for the area of a triangle. Her friend Matt was able to find the area of triangle *EFB* by using the area of other figures. What did Matt do? How many square centimeters are in the area of triangle *EFB*?

74. The table below is the data from a survey of eight female high school juniors comparing right foot size and height.

Right foot (cm)	Height (cm)
22.1	157.1
22.9	160.8
23.1	161.4
23.4	161
24.1	162.8
24.6	164
25.4	164.7
26.1	164

The linear regression equation for these data is approximately:

A) $y = 2.06x - 113$
B) $y = 2.06x + 113$
C) $y = 1.65x + 122.4$
D) $y = 1.65x - 122.4$

75. How many solutions are there to this system of equations?

$y = 6x$
$3x + 2y = 5$

E) One
F) Two
G) Infinitely many
H) None

76. Which of the following is an equation for a circle?

A) $(x - 1)^2 = 16 + y^2$
B) $(x - 1)^2 = 16 - y^2$
C) $(x - 1)^2 = 16 - y$
D) $(x - 1)^2 = 16 + y$

77. If $f(x) = 3x - 1$, what is the number missing from the table?

x	$f(x)$
0	−1
2	5
5	14
?	17
11	32

E) 9 F) 8 G) 7 H) 6

78. A concert promoter is offering 2 free tickets for every 15 tickets bought. A school music club buys 115 tickets. How many free tickets does the club receive?

A) 2 tickets
B) 7 tickets
C) 10 tickets
D) 14 tickets

79. The drawing shows a cube with an edge of 6 inches. The shaded region is a rectangle. What is the perimeter of the shaded region?

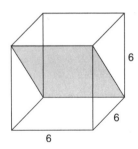

E) 24 inches
F) $12 + 12\sqrt{2}$ inches
G) $12 + 12\sqrt{3}$ inches
H) 36 inches

80. Examine the pattern:

MONDAYMONDAYMONDAY . . .

If this pattern is continued, what letter will be in the 121st position?

A) M B) N C) D D) Y

81. In rolling two dice, the probability of obtaining a sum of 12 (the largest possible sum) is $\frac{1}{36}$. What is the probability of obtaining the largest possible sum when you roll five dice?

   E) $\frac{5}{36}$

   F) $\frac{1}{216}$

   G) $\frac{1}{296}$

   H) $\frac{1}{7,776}$

82. Rectangle $ABCD$ is similar to rectangle $WXYZ$, with $\overline{AB}$ corresponding to $\overline{WX}$. If $AB = 24$, $BC = 30$, and $WX = 16$, what is the area of rectangle $WXYZ$?

   A) 20
   B) 204.8
   C) 320
   D) 720

83. What is the area of a square whose perimeter is represented by $12x^2$?

   E) $6x\sqrt{2}$
   F) $9x^4$
   G) $12x^2$
   H) $144x^2$

84. When Kimberly bought her new car, she found that there were 72 different ways her car could be equipped. Her choices included four choices of engine and three choices of transmission. If her only other choice was color, how many choices of color did she have?

   A) 6
   B) 12
   C) 60
   D) 65

85. Frank, George, and Hernando are a plumber, a cabinet maker, and an electrician, though not necessarily in that order. Each can do all work appropriate to his own field but no work in other fields. Frank was not able to install a new electric line in his home. Hernando was not able to make cabinets. George is also a building contractor who hired one of the other people to do his electrical work. Which statement must be true?

   E) Hernando is an electrician.
   F) George is a cabinet maker.
   G) Frank is a plumber.
   H) Frank is an electrician.

86. The perimeter of an equilateral triangle varies directly as the length of a side. When the length of a side is doubled, the perimeter of the triangle is:

   A) halved
   B) doubled
   C) multiplied by 3
   D) divided by 3

87. A woman has a ladder that is 13 feet long. If she sets the base of the ladder on level ground 5 feet from the side of a house, how many feet above the ground will the top of the ladder be when it rests against the house?

   E) 8
   F) 9
   G) 11
   H) 12

88. Which of the following methods would provide the most accurate estimation of the area under the curve $y = x^2 - 15x + 54$ from -6 to -1 with 14 subintervals?

   A) trapezoid method
   B) rectangle method with rectangles formed by the left endpoint of the subinterval
   C) rectangle method with rectangles formed by the right endpoint of the subinterval
   D) finding the area of the triangle inscribed under the curve

Directions: Show all your work and provide an explanation as directed in the question. Your score for the following question will be based on accuracy and the completeness of your process or explanation.

89. A rock is thrown vertically from the ground with a speed of 24 meters per second, and it reaches a height of $2 + 24t - 4.9t^2$ after t seconds.

   A. How many seconds after the rock is thrown will it reach maximum height? Give your answer to the nearest hundredth of a second.

   B. To the nearest hundredth of a meter, what is the maximum height the rock will reach?

   C. How many seconds after the rock is thrown will it hit the ground? Give your answer to the nearest hundredth of a second.

INDEX